Portrait of a Kaleidoscope Life

Copyright © 2025 by Douglas W. Johnson.
All rights reserved.

No part of this book may be reproduced in any form or by any electronic or mechanical means, including information storage and retrieval systems, without written permission from the author, except for the use of brief quotations in a book review.

Ten Hut Media, A Subsidiary of Severn River Publishing
tenhutmedia.com

ISBN: 978-1-96400-719-9 (Paperback)
ISBN: 978-1-96400-721-2 (Hardcover)

Praise for *Portrait of a Kaleidoscope Life*

"A delightful inspiring read that is rich in humor, insight, and life lessons…"
—Harvey B. Wolkov, MD, MSc, FACR, FASTRO, FACRO

"This book is a powerful reminder that even amidst chaos, a life of purpose and reinvention is possible."
—William E. Todd, former US Ambassador

"…a biographical masterpiece!"
—Mike Kingery, retired F-14, B-737 and RV-7 aviator and U.S. Navy Commander

"What a remarkable life…A must read!!!"
—Ed McIlhenny, Brig Gen (Ret) USAF

"…much more than a memoir…"
—Paul E. Ladnier, Professor Emeritus, University of North Florida

"A worthy read!"
—Col (USAF Rft) David G. Schall, MD, MPH, FACS

"…brilliant, inspiring memoir…reads like a thriller…"
—Chris Davey, author of the Will Turner series of historical novels

"…Doug Johnson is a true 'Renaissance man.'"
—Sonja Schoeppel, MD, Radiation Oncologist and Florida Radiation Oncology Group Partner, Retired

"…a brilliant and colorful collage of medicine, aviation, art, travel, and investigative curiosity."
—Richard W. Sloan, MD, Physician/Master Pilot/Colonel, USAF/Ret

Portrait of a Kaleidoscope Life

Chasing Clouds, Cancer, Culture and Creativity

Douglas W. Johnson M.D.

*Dedicated to Evelyn, William, Miles, and
Desmond, our hope for the future…*

Sue, my wife, partner, and co-pilot for the last 50 years…

And to all the leaders and professors who ignited the spark…

TABLE OF CONTENTS

Preface: Melding Passions of Aviation, Medicine, Travel and Art 1
Introduction. 5
Chapter 1: Pre-Me 7
Chapter 2: On being a Military Brat 12
Chapter 3: The early years 15
Chapter 4: Zaragoza, Spain 19
Chapter 5: New Hampshire 25
Chapter 6: Nebraska. 29
Chapter 7: Alabama 34
Chapter 8: Texas. 37
Chapter 9: New York 44
Chapter 10: California 53
Chapter 11: Virginia Tech 60
Chapter 12: Medical College of Virginia 76
Chapter 13: Internship. 84
Chapter 14: Stanford 97
Chapter 15: Travis AFB 112
Chapter 16: FROG 124
Figures. 141
Chapter 17: USAF Reserves 173
Chapter 18: Flying higher 186
Chapter 19: Adventure down under. 192
Chapter 20: Rekindled hope 202
Chapter 21: Cancer strikes 208
Chapter 22: Expansion. 211
Chapter 23: Going National. 214

Chapter 24: ICON 217
Chapter 25: Paths diverge. 221
Chapter 26: One cheer for HIPAA. 229
Chapter 27: Sniffing out cancer 234
Chapter 28: Taking wing 240
Chapter 29: The Flying Physicians Association. 247
Chapter 30: Nests afar 256
Chapter 31: Flying misadventures 262
Chapter 32: Globetrotting 272
Chapter 33: My cancer. 281
Chapter 34: An artistic journey 284
Chapter 35: A painting is life 292
Chapter 36: Comments on Leadership. 294
Chapter 37: Pearls 297
Chapter 38: My kaleidoscope life 300
Bibliography. 303
Acronyms. 305
Name Index 309

PREFACE

Melding passions of aviation, medicine, travel and art

*"Drive toward your goals, get there, and
then enjoy the fruits of your labors."*

Andrew L. Johnson

"Pull off and stop here." My flight instructor released his harness and exited the Cessna, calling over his shoulder. "Take it around three times, then come back and get me." With a hint of a smile and a slight nod, he slammed the door and walked away from the idling plane.

Sitting alone in the cockpit, comprehension dawned: he was clearing me for my first solo flight. Recently acquired muscle memory kicked in, and after checking instruments, obtaining tower clearance, and double-checking the controls, I smoothly advanced the throttle. Speed gathered as the runway flashed by. I rose into the calm, cool air over the San Jose Airport runway that fateful afternoon in late1980. Once safely on downwind, I briefly exulted in the feeling of independence, confidence, and joy of finally realizing a long-standing dream. An arduous and tortuous path had led to this pivotal moment…

Later, in the Naval Air Station (NAS) Moffett Flying Club ready room, time-honored tradition was upheld as the instructor cut my shirt back away, marked it up, and hung the tattered cloth on a wall beside those of prior solo students, adding to the gallery of rags testifying to the accomplishment and dedication of student pilots first spreading their wings. (Figure 1)

Pondering the event later that night while celebrating with my wife and fellow aviation student Sue, I realized that my life was studded with serial solos: first setting seemingly insurmountable goals, doggedly working towards them, and ultimately either celebrating their joyous fulfillment or learning from their tragic failures, before adding yet more challenges. This pattern was to be repeated for the rest of my life. But why?

I was raised in the era of Sputnik, Telstar, Mercury, Gemini, and Apollo. I loved everything related to aviation but was laser-focused on the dream of entering the astronaut corps, rising above the atmosphere one day.

Over ensuing decades, I strove to reach that goal one way or the other. Rebuffed time and time again, my world expanded to eventually become a mixed and colorful quilt of endeavors, career paths, and accomplishments. Those seemingly disjointed images reflected different journeys over time, sometimes diverging and later converging, sometimes as bright as the sun and other times as dark as a deep well, all weaving an intricate pattern that became my life story. Over time I met with, learned from, and blended into amazing cultures throughout the USA and across the world. I changed career paths and specialties, and I overcame seemingly insurmountable obstacles to accomplish my dream of flying. Through it all, I attempted to artistically capture my journeys, thoughts, and moods.

It would seem as though my life changed and evolved through the years just as the view through the lens of a kaleidoscope changes with every twist and motion, revealing forever new and fascinating patterns of interest and beauty. That idea applies to all of us. Early in life, our paths are determined by kaleidoscope view changes made by movements mostly initiated by others; but as we grow and learn, we have the opportunity to take greater control of the kaleidoscope with our own hands and minds. With that freedom, we create our own constantly changing patterns to ultimately weave our distinct life quilt.

Spoiler alert: I never became an astronaut, but that kaleidoscopic life led me down many avenues of mystery and fulfillment I hadn't foreseen. The view through that lens can point to a unique path forward for every one of us. It pointed me toward the military—my career in the United State Air Force (USAF) opened countless doors and provided magical opportunities far beyond what I envisioned.

Several years ago I sat in my clinic with a former cancer patient and now friend. After finishing my exam and reviewing his test results, we caught up on our families, travels, and current exploits. Near the end of our visit, he stopped, chuckled, and said, "Wow, doc, what a crazy journey you've had. You should write a book!" Hours later, I pondered those comments; now, years later, I've decided to follow his advice.

Why write a book? Perhaps to encourage younger generations to pursue passions and reassure them that they don't need to lock themselves into any single rutted road in life. There will be ample opportunity to branch out and explore other paths, with many vehicles to carry them along.

Why now? As I reflect on the concept of "growing up" in America over the last fifty years, I see a recent disturbing trend that needs to be addressed. Whereas young adults in my generation quietly chose a career path based largely on family precedent or what they had gleaned from a book or two at the local library, today's youth seem to be paralyzed by the sheer volume of possibilities assailing them daily via social media, television, and the internet.

It was common for my peers to pick a career field based upon limited knowledge and later switch to another arena if it didn't suit us, without stigma or judgement. Today, however, many young people are afraid to leap into anything, petrified that they might make the wrong initial choice.

I would hope by example to reassure them. My kaleidoscopic life journey, replete with its unexpected twists, turns, rocky roads, and initial setbacks ultimately afforded me tremendous satisfaction—a unique but similar journey awaits today's young adults. Paraphrasing the Nike athletic-wear's recent logo "Just Do It," an educated early leap into the river of life should be embraced, not shunned. The sooner a person grabs the kaleidoscope, the sooner he will take the reins to change his view, reveal new and exciting patterns, and mold his or her journey.

For me, the focus on becoming an astronaut bounced me jarringly around the side tunnels of general and military aviation, medicine, adventure travel, and art; I wouldn't trade a minute of that time. My advice to young people is to pick a focus—any focus—and strive with all your being toward it. Then, hang on for the ride…

You will surely be amazed at where you end up, and how you got there.

INTRODUCTION

"Your most valuable asset is your integrity."
—Andrew L. Johnson

I was one of millions born of the "Greatest Generation" of Americans, to hard-working and patriotic middle-class parents. Without much money but surrounded by a loving and supportive family, I was encouraged to become self-reliant, set lofty goals, and strive for my dreams. My parents strongly believed in the American Dream—that of life, liberty, and the pursuit of happiness—and instilled those convictions in me at an early age: lofty goals required relentless work, but success could be realized more often than not.

Americans of the 1950's were imbued with a sense of great promise and hope in our United States of America (USA), with the country having survived two World Wars and a Great Depression all within the prior thirty-five years. Their hopes for greater prosperity for all Americans were based upon a strong work ethic, religious tolerance, and a melting pot of immigrants from all corners of the world bringing unique skill sets and viewpoints to help forge an even stronger nation. Prosperity was not something doled out—it was earned. It was expected that if you worked hard, you would improve the lot of yourself, your family, and your community. Our parents had been products of dark times in America but also times of great technological progress, and in the 1950's they were intent on realizing a brighter future.

Patriotism and the idea of serving were not just espoused in my family, they were lived daily. My paternal grandfather, Arthur C. Johnson, "Served and Protected" the inhabitants of New York City as a policeman and detective from just after the turn of the Twentieth Century until 1944, and his father-in-law served as a City Architect designing and building the community of West Hartford, Connecticut. My father, Andrew L. Johnson, served our country via twenty-eight years of active duty in the USAF, during which he served in three wars. The Johnson family was expected to serve, and I knew from early on that I would be expected to contribute to that tradition. One of my father's earliest pieces of advice to me was, "Try to leave the world just a bit better than you found it." Despite that, he never pushed me in one direction or another, stating, "I don't care what you want to be. If you want to be a ditch-digger, that's fine, but strive to be the best ditch-digger out there." Those sage words left me a broad leeway to forge my own path in life and discover my own best way to serve.

Looking back, four life passions have molded me: *aviation, travel, medicine*, and *art*. From early childhood, aviation has represented a sense of freedom and a release from daily tensions and worries. Flying drew my world closer through speedy travel and the ability to see the "grand picture" in daily life. Caring for and interacting with cancer patients and their families and being their knight and champion in their fight for life for forty years has been the most rewarding service of my life. Throughout the decades, an appreciation for viewing and creating art has helped me through rough times, provided a relief from daily stresses, and helped me remember and document good times with good people, as well as emotionally document tough times.

My journey to discover and act on these passions is deeply rooted in my origin story. That story is a complex weave combining family, circumstance, timing, and opportunity: a weave illuminated by life's spinning kaleidoscope. Pondering how and what I have become has been a joyful journey down memory lane and has provided insights I hadn't previously recognized.

CHAPTER 1

PRE-ME

"Everyone matters, no matter their rank, status, appearance, or creed."

—ANDREW L. JOHNSON

My father, Andrew "Andy" Larson Johnson, was born in 1930, of hardy Swedish stock in Manhattan, New York. Both his paternal and maternal grandparents had emigrated from Sweden in the mid-1860s.

Andy's father, Arthur C. Johnson, born in 1886, was a New York City policeman and detective on the International Squad from 1910-1944 and was involved in several high-profile cases including the Lindbergh baby kidnapping, bringing down the Tammany Hall and Cry Baby gangs, and reporting the Hindenburg disaster from Lakehurst, New Jersey, on the scene in 1937 (Ref1). After Arthur retired from the police force, Andy along with his mother and three siblings all moved to the hamlet of Wellfleet on Cape Cod, Massachusetts, while his father moved to Saudi Arabia for several years to work security for the Aramco company to boost his meager police pension. Andrew's mother, Lillian I. (Larson) Johnson, was a stoic woman with a stern disposition who took a job in the Wellfleet Town Clerk's office. Andy and his siblings were largely on their own and learned to be self-reliant at an early age.

Though not a great student, Andy was curious and resourceful in high school, trying to solve problems creatively both at home and school. At one point he promised his school principal that he could fix the miss-timed school bells; unfortunately, he fell through the ceiling of a main classroom while climbing around the school attic. (He had no experience with electrical systems, but thought he could reason the problem out, if only he could find the darned bells!) His standard quote throughout his life was "Trust me." Discouraged and impatient with school, Andy ran away from home at the age of sixteen, hitchhiking to Miami. Once there, he and a friend bought a used Harley motorcycle and created a package delivery service for a short time. Realizing it was a dead-end job, however, he sold the bike, returned to Cape Cod, and with hard work ultimately graduated fourth in his high school class. Decades later he would chuckle and confess that there were only four people in that class! Despite those rough beginnings, my father was one of the wisest men I ever knew.

Lacking job prospects in tiny Wellfleet after graduation in 1949, Andy elected to follow his older brother Art to Logan, Utah, where Art was an aviation cadet with the newly formed USAF. Andy drove a cab there to earn money for rent and meals at a favorite haunt—the Blue Bird Café. (In an odd twist of fate, the Blue Bird Cafe, a Logan staple since 1924, was owned by the father of my future brother-in-law, Joel Cardon.) Although Art washed out of flight training (later to become a successful Presbyterian Minister), he convinced Andy to sign up for the USAF to "do something with his life." The Berlin Airlift's relief of besieged German citizens during the early Cold War intrigued Andy. With a signature and successful recruiting office physical, Andy's twenty-eight-year career in the USAF began.

Andy thrived in the regimented life of the USAF, graduating at the top of his basic training class at Lackland Air Force Base (AFB), Texas. He was extremely proud of the fact that he was in the first truly integrated squadron in the USAF, whose picture was featured in the June 1950 edition of *"Our World"* magazine. (Figure 2) (Ref2)

Andy rose through enlisted and officer ranks over the ensuing twenty-eight years, tackling assignments around the world and ultimately retiring as a Lieutenant Colonel in 1978. He served in the Korean and Vietnam wars, receiving the Bronze Star and several other commendations. Always proud of his enlisted roots, he was honored at one point to command the worldwide Senior NCO Assignments Division of the Military Personnel Center in San Antonio. Throughout his career, he held numerous national security assignments and helped keep the USA safe during the Cold War era. After retiring from the National Security Agency, he served with Bendix Field Engineering, the Allied Signal Corporation, and later created and led Sentinel Resources, Inc., a security-related firm in Northern Virginia. Concurrently, Andy made time for artistic pursuits outside the office, including furniture making, decoupage, and singing. He was a member of the Masonic Order, a lifelong Rotarian, and a volunteer Hearing Officer at the State Attorney's Office in Jacksonville, FL, helping troubled youth.

In 1951, as a Staff Sergeant assigned to Stewart AFB near Newburgh, New York, Andy was introduced by telephone to a young high school student, Barbara Joan Rosborough, daughter of William (Bill) and Amy Rosborough, as a potential blind date. Barbara asked him over the phone if he was a Catholic. Not wanting to miss the opportunity to meet, Andy (raised a Lutheran) hesitated, and then replied, "Sure I am!" She replied, "That's too bad because my parents said I can't date a Catholic." "Wait, wait" was his hurried response. Once the air was cleared, they arranged for Barbara's mother to drive her to the base as a chaperone on that first date. The day of the meeting arrived, and Andy had hiked down to the gate, where a friend of his was on guard duty. Andy hid below the counter in the guard shack. By prior arrangement, the guard would scope out Barbara upon her arrival at the gate. He would signal a surreptitious thumbs up to Andy if she was a "looker" or a thumbs down if not. Fortunately, Andy received a solid thumbs up, so up he popped to introduce himself! They were both smitten, and a few short weeks later were engaged.

Plans for marriage had to be moved up unexpectedly, as Andy received overseas orders to serve in the Korean War, stationed with Flight D, 3rd Air Rescue Squadron at Ashiya AFB in Japan: a three-year unaccompanied tour of duty. Thus, only six weeks after their October 1951 marriage, Andy headed off to war, and Barbara returned to her parents' house. Only eighteen years old, Barbara found a teller's job at the Columbus Trust Bank in Newburgh for a year, when Andy surprised her with news that they were now allowing dependents to join their spouses in Japan.

Thus, in 1952, my mother for the first time left not only her hometown, but also her state and her country, bound for Japan. She journeyed alone by train across the USA and spent a few days visiting distant relatives near Seattle, Washington, after which she boarded a troop ship bound for Japan. It was a rough journey as the ship weathered a typhoon enroute, which was especially harrowing after a disastrous lifeboat drill at the beginning of the trip. The drill involved casting several rafts into the water, upon which most of the aged cork rafts promptly sank.

Eventually debarking in Japan, my mother secretly wondered if she would even recognize Andy: after all, she had only known him for a few months before he left and hadn't seen him in over a year. The reunion went well, fortunately, although Andy informed her that they would need to live off base (indeed on another island entirely), as there were no family quarters at Ashiya. Putting on a brave game face, Barbara proceeded to set up their apartment in a foreign land, surrounded by a foreign culture and language in a recently conquered and currently occupied country. Their residence was less than one hundred miles from Hiroshima, a city decimated by the first atomic bomb dropped a mere seven years before. The local women were not very open or inviting to her, and she spent her days anxiously awaiting Andy's return from the base in the late evenings. Her unease during the time in Japan lasted a lifetime: she never had a desire to return there and shunned all Japanese products for decades. She confided late in life the best thing that came from the Japanese assignment was her pregnancy with me, discovered just before she left.

Barbara's family was not surprised that she managed to almost single-handedly set up a household in a foreign land, as she too was raised from hardy stock. Her father's side was Scotch-Irish, having immigrated to the USA during the potato famines of the 1800s. After only a fourth-grade education, William J. "Bill" Rosborough left school to take odd jobs to help support his family. He continued to do so for the remainder of his life: from driving delivery trucks to working as a "repo man" for the Columbus Trust Bank. Despite his limited formal education, Bill was highly intelligent and was a voracious reader with a quick wit. Her mother, Amy Florence Henderson, came from an even longer heritage—her eleventh great-grandfather Henry Fowler had reportedly arrived in Massachusetts in the 1500s. The ensuing Fowler's, Dusenbury's, and Henderson's all settled in the Hudson River valley north of New York City. To make ends meet, Amy took a job at the Columbus Trust Bank as well, eventually serving as an executive secretary there. Indeed, we had so many relatives working at the Columbus Trust on and off during the Twentieth century that we jokingly renamed it from its formal moniker "The Friendly Bank" to a more apt "The Family Bank."

After Andy was reassigned to Stewart AFB in late 1953, my parents returned from Japan to an apartment near Newburgh. One early night in June, my mother went into labor. The closest military hospital was at the nearby West Point United States Military Academy (USMA). A few hours after entering the Academy grounds, a young lad first showed his face in the wee hours of June 6, 1954: Douglas William Johnson. In homage to his former "boss" in Japan, Dad named me after Gen. Douglas MacArthur, Supreme Commander for the Allied Powers during the Japanese occupation.

So began my journey as an Air Force "Brat," moving with my military family across the world every six-twelve months and attending eleven different schools during my twelve grade-school years. With each twist of my life's kaleidoscope, a new view of the world opened and a new adventure unfolded.

CHAPTER 2

ON BEING A MILITARY BRAT

The term "Military Brat" is used affectionately in reference to children of military personnel from all service branches—Army, Navy, Air Force, Marines, Coast Guard, and now Space Force—through the decades. Brats have a unique and special kinship worthy of a brief aside here for the uninitiated. Studies of the group have revealed many characteristics that might not be as common in non-military families.

As a group, Brats are *patriotic*: they are raised in an environment that fosters the concept of "duty to God and Country, before duty to self." They have lived in remote corners of the world without the advantages US citizens take for granted. They appreciate our nation's prosperity and the sacrifices it took to win them, as well as those needed to keep them. At US bases around the world, *"Taps"* is played every afternoon over loudspeakers. Cars come to a stop as their occupants exit the vehicles and stand at attention with hands over hearts until the music is finished and the US flag is lowered before proceeding on their way. Before every movie shown in the base theater, the entire audience stands for the National Anthem. Almost every Brat family has known someone personally that died for his country.

Brats learn to be *responsible* at an early age: a dependent's bad behavior can derail the career of his military parent, and he knows it. Good behavior, respect for authority and elders, courtesy to others, social manners, and even proper telephone answering technique are drilled into Brats at an early age. (When answering our home phone at age five, I was taught to say, "*Johnson residence, Douglas speaking, how may I help you?*") Brats learn to be comfortable around adults, as they are often taken along to adult functions—frequent moves and few nearby friends make babysitters a rare commodity. They are taught to introduce themselves to adults with a confident handshake and strong clear voice, while looking directly into the eyes of the adult they are addressing.

Brats are *independent*, as well. Military life is a serious one, and there is little room for coddling. Brats learn to play well alone or with just siblings, as after early summer transfers it might be two or three months until they meet a fresh set of friends at their new school. Self-reliance, whether it is to arrange one's possessions in a new space efficiently, walk to the commissary to purchase food for the family, or to find constructive ways to while away the hours, is not just a good trait, it is a critical one. For me, the library at each new station became my haven and opened doors to new worlds through literature no matter where in the world I was reading it. A life-long passion for science fiction kept me scouring the library racks over those long summers and helped foster my fascination with aeronautical and space subjects.

Brats are *creative*: the times they are alone are often protracted, and creativity becomes an outlet unhindered by place, language, or income. Often left to their own devices, they learn to problem-solve and resolve issues or create solutions without requiring much input from others. Indeed, they mostly create for themselves, not for the adulation of others.

Brats are *tolerant* of foreign customs and peoples. They learn to observe people in different locations and different cultures as they move around: they know that THEY are the foreigners, not the local population, and they need to learn how to adapt to fit in. Along with this period of observation usually comes an appreciation for others and their different ways. They learn to listen more than talk.

Brats *can be intolerant* of fellow citizens: their instilled senses of responsibility, independence, and creativity lead them to expect the same of their peers and countrymen. They are frustrated when others don't live up to the same expectations. Put bluntly, they *don't suffer fools well.*

Brats tend to be *loners*: with the constant moves, Brats learn to build a defensive shell around their feelings, as they realize that new friendships they make growing up will largely be transient. The rare people they do let "behind the curtain" form a small nucleus of deep friendships for life; these relationships they will defend fiercely. This social isolation can be maladaptive as well: depression and substance abuse are not uncommon in the group.

Brats are often *high achievers*: their determination, creativity, and self-reliance often allow them to rise to the top of any profession they follow. Notable examples of successful Brats include Kris Kristofferson, John Denver, Christina Aguilera, Bruce Willis, Jessica Alba, Reese Witherspoon, Tiger Woods, Newt Gingrich, Michael J. Fox, Jim Morrison, Elton John, Gore Vidal, Bob Marley, Robert Duvall, Shaquille O'Neal, Mark Hamill, L. Ron Hubbard, John McCain, Lionel Richie, Stephen Stills, Emmylou Harris, Sharon Tate, Priscilla Presley, and Natalie Morales.

Understanding this foundation of a Brat's life can provide insight into his future personality and aspirations. My wife, after watching a documentary describing the Brat personality a few years back, remarked, "Now I finally know why you are the way you are…"

CHAPTER 3

THE EARLY YEARS

"Never try to con a con artist."
—Andrew L. Johnson

In 1954, changes were afoot in the USA. The Supreme Court ruled in the Brown vs. Board of Education case, finally leading to the integration of public schools. Elvis Presley released his first single, *"That's all right."* The USA and USSR were locked in a Cold War, and that War was slowly heating up. On my birthday, June 6, the USA tested a hydrogen bomb on Bikini Atoll in the south Pacific...

Shortly after birth, I was whisked up into the whirlwind of military dependent life as a Military Brat. For a year, the three of us moved to West Lafayette, Indiana, where my father was assigned to a recruiting station at Purdue University. My mother ran the family financial numbers and told my dad that Staff Sergeant pay wasn't going to keep them afloat. They had already sold a bunch of possessions and were down to eating meat once a week (usually a hot dog), but that still wasn't enough if my mother was going to be a stay-at-home mom. She encouraged him to apply for Officer Candidate School (OCS), knowing that Andy wanted to make a career in the USAF and that officers were entitled to higher pay. Much to her delight and his relief, he was accepted into the OCS school at Lackland AFB in San Antonio, Texas. Nine months after their move to San Antonio, Andy graduated from OCS as a freshly minted 2nd Lieutenant.

With new gold bars on my father's collar, we moved next to Salina, Kansas, home to two Air Force installations: Smokey Hill AFB and Schilling AFB, both in the Strategic Air Command. The nuclear deterrent fleet based there was a national asset and closely guarded.

An interesting anecdote from his arrival in Kansas highlights my dad's intellect, resourcefulness, and can-do attitude. Andy had gone ahead of us to get things set up there before we moved. It was customary in 1956 for any newly arriving officer to report to the Schilling AFB base commander, which Andy did on a Friday afternoon.

The base commander closed the door, and said something to the effect, "Lt. Johnson, nobody knows you here yet and you don't usually need to report back until Monday morning. However, I have a special assignment for you, and you are to report only to me. The wing commander up the road at Smokey Hill has just installed extensive multi-layer security perimeters there to guard the nuclear-capable B-47 Stratojet fleet. Your job on Saturday night is to take this sack of fake wooden bombs, pretend to be a saboteur, and see how many layers of security you can penetrate before they catch you. Once you're caught, tell them to call me immediately so that I can get you debriefed, released, and back to my base." My father grabbed the bag, saluted, about-faced, and departed the commander's office.

The commander never heard a word from Smokey Hill the next night or Sunday morning from either the base authorities or from my father. He sent the Military Police (MP) to the Visiting Officers Quarters (VOQ) on Sunday morning and sure enough they found my father soundly asleep. The MPs dragged him before the commander, who read him the riot act for disobeying orders and clearly not executing the mission. When finally asked if he had anything to say, Andy merely said, "Sir, I completed the mission as requested and returned to my quarters early this morning." "Bullshit, I don't believe you," replied the commander. That commander, my father, and the MPs rode in a command car back over to Smokey Hill to check out his story. After passing multiple armed guards and security checks, their vehicle was allowed onto the ramp and approached the B-47's. To the commander's utter surprise, there was an orange wooden "explosive" tied neatly to each of the jets' nose gear all up and down the line for over a half mile. And not just a few: EVERY bomber on the ramp! Flabbergasted, the commander demanded to know how Andy had evaded all the security measures. My father replied, "It was simple: I waited until 0200 in the morning, parked my car outside the base on the opposite side of the runway from all the facilities, hopped the fence with my bombs, snuck across the quiet dark runway, and attached one to each bomber. Afterwards I headed back out into the darkness away from the flight line and made my way back to the VOQ." The commander's face reddened with indignation and his temper blew. Fortunately, his anger was directed not at my father, but rather at those in charge at Smokey Hill. Before the end of the day, the wing commander had been sacked along with security leadership at Smokey Hill. The base commander returned with my father to Schilling AFB down the road, instructed him to keep quiet about the matter, and not show his face at Smokey Hill ever again, for fear of reprisals… It wasn't until decades later that the story emerged.

Personally, my memories are dim from our three-year stay in Salina as I wasn't quite two when we arrived and left before turning five. Nevertheless, some flashes of memory include watching tornados from the living room window of our tiny rental home (Figure 3), sitting in the shade of a telephone pole when sent to play outside as there were no trees, and locking my mother in the bathroom. My father had cleverly reversed the lock on the bathroom door so that I couldn't lock myself in there and never imagined that for fun I would lock my mother in the bathroom from the hallway the very next day. Mom eventually called out to a next-door neighbor through the small bathroom window; that kind lady, in turn, came over and released my prisoner. I also remember my father building model airplanes with me, which we hung from my bedroom ceiling. My favorite model was the Grumman HU-16 Albatross that had been used during his assignment in Japan with the Air Sea Rescue squadron during the Korean War. On the small black and white television in the living room of that small home, I also remember the first cartoons I ever saw, starring a couple of crazy (and by today's standards culturally inappropriate) crows: *Heckle and Jekyll*. We had a collie in Salina as well, of course named Lassie. Lassie was my constant companion.

One point of contention between my parents and me involves another very early memory—that of a hospital room adorned with Disney characters and pink walls. My mother remembered that room as well, but she swore there was no way I could've remembered it, as that was when I had my tonsils removed in Indiana. I was barely one year old at the time. Although it is but a dreamlike flash, I still swear I remember that room…

In late 1958, my father received his next set of orders, this time to Spain. The good news was that we could go, too, but only after he had been there for a few months arranging off-base housing. My mother, father, Lassie, and I all piled onto a train for the pre-Christmas ride from Kansas to New York, where we spent the holiday with Barbara's family before following my father to Zaragoza in the spring.

CHAPTER 4

ZARAGOZA, SPAIN

Gypsies, bullfights, and life passions ignite

1959 saw the rise of Fidel Castro and his communist government in Cuba, only ninety miles from USA soil. Alaska and Hawaii became the forty-ninth and fiftieth US States. The first plain-paper copier, the Xerox 914, came to market, and Able and Baker became the first two primates launched into space.

In the spring of 1959, it was finally time for my mother and me to trek across the Atlantic to join my father. Just before leaving we arranged for Lassie to be taken care of by my paternal grandmother on Cape Cod, as it was difficult to take pets overseas. I never saw Lassie again, and I was told years later that my grandmother had given the dog to a neighbor "on a farm so he'd have more room to run." In retrospect, I think something untoward had happened to Lassie, as I never recalled seeing any farms on the Cape, but I'll never know for sure.

Memories are a bit hazy about that trip, as I was still not quite five years old. I do distinctly remember my mother wearing a pretty dress and hat, with me in a suit and tie, as we climbed the air stairs up to a chartered red and white Lockheed Constellation airliner (perhaps a Trans World Airways ship) bound for Madrid. I also remember the plush red velour airline seats that seemed massive. The flight further inspired my interest in aviation: it was a step up from building model airplanes back in Kansas.

Landing to refuel midway across the Atlantic, the "Connie" alit at Lajes AFB in the Azores. As the stopover was to take a few hours, we were all bussed up the hill to the Officer's Club to get some refreshments. My mother ordered me a Coke, which I quickly drank. It was delicious, and I asked for another. After ordering, a young Lieutenant leaned across from another table and said to my mother, "Ma'am, are you aware that when you order a Coke here, it is really a Coke-High?" After seeing her blank stare, he chuckled and continued, "That's a mix of Coke and rum." No wonder I loved it. Mortified, my mother canceled the refill. A few hours later, we boarded the military bus and were whisked back down to the airstrip for the final flight leg to Torrejon AFB in Madrid.

I never would have predicted that I would once again sit on that same tarmac in the Azores almost fifty years later. In 2009, Sue and I were completing a National Geographic trip around the world when our jet stopped briefly in the Azores. We had departed from Marrakesh, but as current US sanctions precluded direct flights between Morocco and the States, we were required to make an intermediate stop at a neutral airport. As we deplaned briefly to stretch our legs on the ramp, I had the eerie feeling I had been on that spot before. I asked one of the locals if there had ever been a USAF Base there, he replied that indeed I was standing on that base, which had been ceded back to Portugal years previously. Looking up the hillside, I wondered if they were still serving Coke-Highs in the Club. Sixty years after my initial visit, Sue and I yet again returned to the Azores for a more extended stay. With friends from the USA, we embarked on a hiking tour of several beautiful islands in that gorgeous province of Portugal. No one we met there in 2019 had ever heard of a Coke-High. It must have been a local concoction known only to the Lajes Air Base personnel of the 1950's.

But I digress… Upon landing in Madrid in 1959, we cleared customs and reunited with my father, who drove us the final three hours to his duty station in Zaragoza. As on-base housing was very limited for junior officers, he had rented a flat in the countryside miles away in a new development built for military families amid open sheep grazing pastures. We climbed the steps to our second-story flat, and my three-year adventure in Spain began.

Situated atop the high plains of central Spain, athwart the River Ebro, Zaragoza was founded over 2000 years previously as a major trading port connecting the hill country of northwest Spain to the Mediterranean Sea. The city had a rich cultural heritage dating from the pre-Roman era, through the Visigoths and Moors, and was eventually the Capitol of Aragon. Its university is one of the oldest in Europe, founded in 1542, and is home to a rich passion for the arts; indeed, famed artist Francisco Goya spent much of his life there.

Of course, as a young child, a four-year-old, I knew none of that. I remember the independence of roaming those open plains and pastures, meeting the local children who taught me Spanish, collecting clean drinking water from mules (large mobile water tanks towed to our neighborhood twice weekly from the base), letting turbid bath tap water sit for ten minutes so the silt would settle first before squatting to bathe, buying homemade rolls from a child's bicycle basket in the morning for a couple of pesetas, and visiting the gypsy kids and their parents as they moved their flocks of sheep back and forth across Iberia following the seasonal rains. When camping around Zaragoza, the Gypsy families lived in crude huts built in caves along the bluffs. As it happened, those bluffs were within walking distance from our flat.

I still chuckle at memories of that bread bought from the bicycle kid. An enterprising Spanish family near the American compound made and sold bread rolls throughout the week. They would load the bread in their young son's bicycle basket and send him off into the compound to sell it. Business was slow at the beginning, so he would often stop and chat with me. I would regularly buy one or two rolls. They were delicious. My mother found out, however, and was mortified. For some reason, she had it in her head that the Spaniards urinated on the dough before baking the bread to poison the Americans! Even as a small boy, I thought that was ridiculous. I eventually convinced her to try one, and she was an immediate convert: we were one of that family's best customers from then on…

While my mother was away during the days volunteering at the Base Hospital as a Red Cross "Gray Lady," I would sneak off to visit my Gypsy kid friends at their camps; they and their elders would regale me with stories of their life as we sat around roaring campfires. American parents always worried about their kids being stolen by the "dirty thieving untrustworthy" Gypsies, but I found them to be very family-oriented, gregarious, and friendly toward me and my fellow truants. One of many life lessons I picked up in Spain is that one should judge others on their behavior rather than preconceptions. I also began to realize that parents everywhere want essentially the same things for their children: a roof over their heads, food in their bellies, and the opportunity for a better life than they had. Later, in adulthood, these realizations were tempered with the sad fact that those ideals are too frequently sidelined by the radicalism of a few that can ruin life for the many.

As a grown up five-year-old that summer of 1959, I had learned enough basic Castilian Spanish that my parents would take me downtown to the markets or even the auto mechanic to serve as their translator. I felt like a valued integral part of my little family. One fine Saturday my mom and dad decided to reward me for my help by taking me to a true Spanish cultural experience: a bullfight.

The custom back then was to take young children to "gentle" junior bullfights at first until their sensitivities were dulled, whereafter they could witness the larger spectacle of the grand arenas. These junior venues featured smaller bulls and new young matadors. Off we went to my first, and only, junior bullfight. It was a bloody disaster, at least in my parents' eyes. One small bull managed to sequentially gore three young matadors, all of whom had to be carried away on stretchers, bleeding and screaming. I was impressed. The rule was that if a bull managed to defeat three matadors in one fight, he was allowed to retire and live a long and peaceful life. My parents and I both learned valuable lessons that day: my parents learned never to take a young kid to a bullfight, and I learned that the best way to succeed in life is to never give up. Bravo to that young bull, who from then forward was my childhood hero!

My first year of school began in the fall of 1959 at a joint Spanish/American kindergarten in downtown Zaragoza. A US school had not yet been completed on the Air Base, so we attended classes that contained both American kids and locals. My only memento of that year is a scrapbook picture of all of us on the stage in an old building, standing proudly in our caps and flowing white gowns on the day of kindergarten graduation. Sometime during the following year, the base school was completed. (The Department of Defense was building up a large network of overseas schools for American dependents worldwide.) I finished up the last part of first grade and first half of second grade in that DOD school on the base. On weekends we would dine at the Zaragoza Officer's Club after church. During one Sunday brunch, my father pointed out a young Spanish officer seated two tables away from us. That officer was Juan Carlos I, future king of Spain (1975-2014), who was training with the USAF at that time.

Though I wouldn't realize it until decades later, another passion was born in Spain: a passion to create art. During our time in Spain, we periodically loaded up our sedan and headed out to explore surrounding areas. On one weekend journey, we stopped at a roadside stand, where my folks purchased a local artist's oil painting depicting a shepherd tending his flock in the foothills of the Pyrenees Mountains. Looking back, that one painting encapsulated three years of memories and experiences of the countryside, people, and architecture that I'd acquired in Spain. The painting became a fixture in every home at every base we were assigned to thereafter, and now, over sixty years later, it still hangs on my wall. (Figure 4) That an oil painting could spark such emotions affected me deeply, and spurred me to start my own drawing, as I reflected on the places and times we later experienced.

My fondest memory from the time in Spain, however, had nothing to do with Spain itself, but rather with further stoking the fire of my aviation passion. In that era, USAF bases were made up of composite squadrons: bombers, fighters, and tankers all co-existed on the same base. A young pilot friend of my father invited me to the flight line one evening, where he let me sit in the cockpit of his sleek Convair F-102 Delta Dagger interceptor (known by its pilots as "The Deuce"). A product of the Cold War, the Deuce was a sleek space-aged design built to intercept and defeat invading Soviet Union bombers. I was speechless as I sat in that ejection seat surrounded by levers, knobs, dials, gauges, and those unique triangular canopy windows: I felt at home. I knew then that I was destined to become a pilot, and I was hooked for life. Indeed, it was the first time I recall having thought about my future goals and desires. Decades later I tried to document that feeling with an oil painting of that memory sitting deep in the cockpit of the Deuce. (Figure 5)

In January 1962, my kaleidoscopic view of life shifted as my father received transfer orders to Pease AFB, New Hampshire, just a bit north of Boston. Movers packed us up, and once again our life was in boxes. There was no luxurious "Connie" for us this time, however, but rather a long noisy trip home in the bowels of a USAF C-124 Globemaster cargo plane, known affectionately by its crews as "Old Shaky." We made numerous refueling stops on the way back across the Atlantic, including foggy and rainy Prestwick, Scotland, frozen and snow-packed Iceland, and equally cold and blustery Goose Bay, Labrador, before finally alighting in the USA. The highlight of that trip was an invitation from the pilots to climb the two-story ladder from the cargo deck to join them briefly in the cockpit. I was once again dazzled by the banks of lights, switches, and levers surrounding the pilots and engineers. What magic was this?

In what was to become a regular pattern with reassignments, my mother and I flew on to New York to stay with my grandparents in Newburgh while my father proceeded directly to Pease AFB to settle into his new duties and find us a place to live.

CHAPTER 5

New Hampshire

Duck and cover, and goodbye, Mr. President

While Andy was off to Pease AFB, my mother and I settled into snowy Newburgh, where I finished the latter half of second grade at Union Grove Elementary School—the same school attended by mother and her siblings a generation before. My grandparents' home in Newburgh was often filled with laughter, and always with love. While watching my stout grandmother cook up her delicious spaghetti sauce shortly after our arrival, she leaned over and asked me to say something in Spanish to her. Without hesitation, I quipped, "Tu es un elefante" (you are an elephant)! Ouch—my first of many foot-in-mouth moments. Fortunately, she heartily laughed and kept on stirring. Even my grandfather, who was supposedly the authoritarian taskmaster of the family, had a forgiving and mischievous twinkle in his eye when dealing with me and his other grandkids.

Two embarrassments at school that winter in New York are etched in my memory, both related to the freezing February cold: the first when I lost my snow boot two feet deep in a snowbank at school recess, requiring a custodian with a snow shovel to dig out my footwear, and the second when I stupidly licked my tongue on the frozen flagpole on a dare from other students. Much to their delight, and my chagrin, I was solidly stuck to the pole until a teacher came out with a warm wet washcloth to unfasten my tongue. Live and learn…

Our extended family in Newburgh provided a built-in social network. I became close to many cousins, including David, Nancy, and Debbie Roberts, as well as Dan, Dean, Dale and later Dwight Ludwig (the latter four were Army Brats). Our adventures and misadventures together on and off over the years would forever bond us.

That summer, after a brief visit with my paternal grandparents on Cape Cod, we settled into our house in North Hampton, New Hampshire. Our modest ranch home on Woodland Road was big enough for my dad to erect the HO-scale train set he had bought for me in Spain. The train setup became an attraction for other boys in the area, and I befriended another third grader across the street, Joel Buffington. The Buffington's lived on a small farm replete with a huge old barn, apple orchards, and hay fields. My new buddies and I spent day after day over the summers and weekends on the farm. We swung on ropes from the barn rafters, created an awesome two-story tree fort in a withered apple tree, and baled and stacked hay in the fall.

I also learned a lesson in responsibility from my father on that farm: one day while hurling apples near the barn in a mock "war" between kids, I sent one right through a glass window on an old decrepit wing of the barn. I was mortified, but thought "what the heck," as many other windows in the unused building were already broken. When relating the day's events at dinner that night, however, my father was not amused. He told me that it was irrelevant that other damage to the barn already existed, and that I needed to make amends for the damage I had caused. He marched me across the street, where I apologized to Mr. Buffington. Although Mr. Buffington didn't really seem to care about the window anyway, my father certainly did. He took me to a hardware store the next day, where we bought a pane of glass, a scraper, and caulk glazing. He and I went to the barn, and over an hour, he taught me how to remove the broken pane, clean the frame, and reinstall the new glass. It was now the finest piece of glass in the entire barn. We then had a long chat about how important it was to own up to one's mistakes and make amends, even if it was "no big deal" to others. "You should be your own moral compass," he opined. This occasion was also the first time I heard his credo to always leave something a little better than you found it. That sage advice has followed me ever since: to this day, if someone loans me a car or a tool, I always fill the fuel tank or clean and polish the item before I return it. Oh, and I don't throw apples anymore…

1962-1964 were serious years for other reasons, too. The Cold War between the USA and the USSR was in full swing, and the possibility of nuclear Armageddon was a daily reality. I remember the box of "survival supplies" that my parents kept in our closet and the weekly "duck and cover" drills we practiced in school to supposedly protect us if an atomic bomb went off nearby. The gallows humor amongst older students in the know, however, suggested that putting your head between your knees while sitting against a wall was merely to allow you time to kiss your rear end goodbye.

There was no humor, however, when the principal announced over the school public address system one morning that President Kennedy had been shot in Dallas. School was adjourned early, and it was at home that we learned that John Kennedy had died. Not only was he gone, but some of my youthful innocence was as well.

Our stay in North Hampton was also marred by an idiotic antic I acted out one morning at the school bus stop. Having been an avid fan of the Three Stooges comedy show, I decided to try out one of their "moves" on another kid waiting for the bus. Suffice it to say, I knocked him out after hitting the top of his head with a rock. He fell in a ditch, the bus arrived, I hopped on and went to school. A while later I was called to the principal's office, where my parents sat, horrified by my actions. The kid was going to be okay, fortunately, and no charges were pressed. Not my finest moment… Oh, and I was banned from watching the Three Stooges for five years.

Not all was grim in New Hampshire, however. The smells of fall, the harvests, and Halloween forays were highlights. We got another collie, of course named Lassie, who was my new best friend. Most importantly, our family grew with the addition of my little sister, Susan Lynn. Unbeknownst to me at the time, my parents had been trying for years to conceive again, but after three miscarriages, they elected to adopt. Susan came to us only a few weeks old and I had an immediate new family role: that of Susan's big brother! It was an adjustment not being the center of attention any longer, but I was anxious for her to "grow up" so that I could show her things and chat with her.

Time passed, and in December 1963 my dad got new transfer orders, this time to the Headquarters of the Strategic Air Command at Offutt AFB, Nebraska. Once again the packers came. While Andy went to Nebraska to get things set up for us, my mom, sister, and I headed back to the Rosborough homestead on Wintergreen Avenue in Newburgh. There, I finished fourth grade back at Union Grove Elementary School. As an older, wiser kid, I knew to keep my tongue in my mouth this time.

More fond family memories were made in those next few months. My Uncle Ed Henderson unexpectedly buying me ice skates at Christmas for use on nearby Winona Lake, riding along with Grandpa Rosborough in his truck to deliver FRAM auto parts all over Newburgh, and accompanying my grandmother to fetch homemade crumb cakes from a private bakery. (Yes, the elefante still loved me!)

In early summer, we completed our move to Nebraska, settling into a new home in Bellevue, just outside the Offutt AFB gates.

CHAPTER 6

NEBRASKA

Walkie-talkies, snow forts, and the Vulcan bomber

In 1964, the Civil Rights act was signed by President Lyndon Johnson, the Beatles visited America to appear on the Ed Sullivan show, and boxer Cassius Clay reinvented himself as Muhammad Ali.

From 1964-1966 we lived in a newer home at 1505 Freeman Drive in Belleview: an attractive little ranch style house with three bedrooms and a basement big enough to set up the trains again. Situated on a long rising hillside with a high school at the top of the street and my elementary school at the bottom, we had lots of children in the neighborhood and a huge cornfield and creek bed to play in behind us. Nearby Omaha was home to huge cattle slaughterhouses, and when an ill wind was blowing, the stench of blood and death descended on our neighborhood. On the bright side, Omaha steaks were outstanding, and you would order them by the inch (thickness) at local restaurants. My mouth still waters today with the memory.

In those days, the heavy winter snowstorms provided many days off school, during which we often built multi-room snow forts in the six-foot deep drifts and had vigorous fun-filled snowball fights with all the neighborhood children. In the spring and fall, I rolled up and down the sidewalks with a newly introduced toy called a skateboard (that original design was simply a set of metal roller skate wheels screwed onto a flat oak plank). In the summers, we got into all kinds of mischief including pea-shooter wars and creating aerial incendiaries out of lighter fluid, household cleaning supplies, and old model airplanes.

I became an avid airplane model builder during this time, with dozens of completed kits hanging by strings thumbtacked to my bedroom ceiling. One defective kit stands out in my memory; however, due to a packaging error, one section of the kit had been omitted from the box. Now, most parents today would have simply returned the kit for a replacement, but not my dad. He always believed that to get better service, one should "inform power", i.e., go straight to the top with a problem. To that end, he tracked down the contact information for the president of Revell Models (keep in mind that this was before the internet). He crafted a missive to the president describing the packaging defect and sent it off. Weeks later, a large box arrived in the mail, addressed to me. Inside was a personal letter of apology from the Revell president's office. Not only had he sent a replacement kit but also included ten other models for me to build. I've never forgotten my father's advice to "speak to power" to get things accomplished, or the spirit of atonement from the leader of that company. I was a confirmed Revell model advocate from that day forward.

Money was tight, but my father found creative ways for us to save. He negotiated a deal with our landlord to forgive a couple months' rent if we would paint the house exterior (a frequent necessity with the harsh Nebraska climate). While he and my mother climbed ladders to reach the wooden siding and my sister was parked in a playpen in the front yard, I was assigned the task of painting all the cinderblock around the base of the house with a small paintbrush. If you ever want an exercise requiring patience and determination, try painting cinderblock with a brush: painting all the holes, creases, and cavities in that material is akin to planting grass in a yard one blade at a time. Endless weeks later, my portion of the task was complete. That experience taught me the concept of "time is money" and I was convinced dad should have negotiated a better deal on that rent break.

I also learned a sobering lesson in Nebraska about preparedness. During my sixth-grade year, an opportunity arose to participate in a track and field competition at the high school. For some reason, I thought it would be fun to participate. I looked through the brochure and selected a walking race to participate in just a week before the event, thinking, "How hard can that be?" Well, the fateful race day soon came, the starting gun sounded, and—totally unprepared—off I walked. A few years—or was it just minutes—later, I limped across the finish line, in last place by a long shot. My poor parents could only come up with, "Well, we are proud of you for trying."

Though I felt like crawling under a rock that day, I did carry away a few life lessons. First, *if you are going to tackle something, go all in. Do the preparation and know your subject thoroughly.* Second, once prepared, locked, and loaded for a task, *never give up: compensate, create, and overcome.* No one has truly failed in a task unless and until he has given up. Third, *don't stress over not coming out on top; if you've done your best, you have nothing to be ashamed of.* I incorporated these tenets in my life ever since.

A brighter highlight in Nebraska related to technology. For Christmas in 1965 my dad presented me with a shiny pair of expensive Sears walkie-talkies. For hours in the spring, I would walk around the neighborhood, transmitting and asking if anyone could hear me. On one clear day, out of the blue I got a response to my query from a fellow with a clipped British accent. Asking who he was, he informed me that he was a radio operator just arriving from England in an RAF aircraft. We chatted for a minute or so. I presumed he was just someone pulling my young leg when at that moment a gorgeous, huge bat-winged Vulcan bomber roared overhead on its way to land at nearby Offutt AFB. I was ecstatic and couldn't wait to relate my experience that evening over dinner. Apparently, the USAF and our British allies traded visits on a regular basis back then. Once again, I felt the tug of aviation.

Chapter 6

In the spring of 1966, my dad received orders to attend Air Command and Staff College at Maxwell AFB, Alabama. Before our move there, however, my mother became extremely ill and was hospitalized in Nebraska. My grandparents flew in from New York and whisked sister Susan and I back to the Hudson Valley. Once there, we lived with my Aunt Donna and Uncle Dan Ludwig at West Point, where Dan was an engineering professor at the US Military Academy (USMA).

It was an eventful summer. My cousin Danny and I found an old basketball-sized cannonball while hiking in the hills above and behind the USMA and spent an hour kicking it downhill, trying to roll it home, as neither of us could lift it. That plan worked until the cannonball lodged against a fallen tree. Dejected, we returned to Danny's quarters on base and filled in his parents about our lost treasure. They were more alarmed than excited about our discovery: we had failed to appreciate the fact that it might explode! An Army ordnance disposal team (or, as we called it at the time, the "bomb squad") was called out, and they removed our find from the woods. The USMA History Department theorized that it might have been a dud fired from a British warship during the War of 1812, missing West Point but lodging in the hillside above and behind the military stockade.

Uncle Dan "taught" me to swim that summer at a pond near the USMA. His teaching method was fairly draconian: he pointed to a raft fifty yards away in the middle of the pond, said he'd meet me there, and threw me into deep water off the shore-side pier, embodying the true spirit of "sink or swim." My strokes weren't pretty, but I didn't drown and eventually made it to the raft. The stark memory of that traumatic ordeal subliminally planted a seed, as seven years later I became a Red Cross Water Safety Instructor and taught swimming lessons throughout my college years.

We later learned that my mother had been air-evacuated back to the East Coast for emergency surgery to remove extensive intraabdominal scar tissue related to a medication she had been taking for migraine headaches. The scar tissue was crimping off her kidney function and she was in bad shape. The surgery was a success, fortunately, and she mended well. She was one of two documented sentinel patients who developed retroperitoneal fibrosis after using Sansert (methylsergide maleate). Sansert was later pulled from the USA market due to that risk of potentially lethal fibrosis. By late summer she was better, we were reunited, and off we moved to the heart of Dixie.

CHAPTER 7

ALABAMA

Model rockets and NASA

Montgomery, Alabama, was still suffused with racial tension in 1966, one year after the famous Selma to Montgomery march led by Martin Luther King, Jr. Living in a quiet suburb just outside the back gate of Gunter AFB, however, I saw none of that tension for the year we lived there.

Instead, more mundane memories include having home air conditioning for the first time, provided by a huge "swamp cooler" about the size of a restaurant walk-in freezer, getting a brief chance to drive a used Ford Fairlane with a manual three-speed column shifter up and down the terrain in our neighborhood, and building a go-cart from 2x4's and lawnmower wheels. My father opted to take the first run downhill in the cart on our street, and as he attempted to turn the corner at the bottom of the hill was summarily ejected from the contraption. I ran down to inspect what I was sure to be his dead body. Bruised, with a torn shirt, ripped trousers and bleeding kneecaps, his only comment when he sat up was, "Notice how I rolled after falling off to protect myself?" He didn't look too protected to me, but I thought it probably wasn't the best time to comment. He didn't look too amused, either, when I glibly responded, "Guess we should have installed brakes."

My go-cart days were over, so I thought I'd try learning the guitar. Though I imagined I could sing like Caruso in the shower, those talents didn't translate to guitar skills whatsoever: I'm pretty sure my guitar instructor breathed a sigh of relief when I moved away a year later.

Redemption for my lack of musical talent came at Goodwyn Junior High School as I found less dangerous but more stimulating activities to conquer at my new school. Goodwyn had a Model Rocket Club, where club members perused lengthy rocketry technical reports published by Estes Industries in Colorado. Once mastering the basics of aerodynamics, dynamic balance and pressure, etc., we built model rocket kits and launched them from the school football field. What fun! I was hooked and subsequently read even more about rocketry and NASA. These were heady times for the space program, as the USA was in a heated "moon race" with the USSR and a crash development program was underway. The NASA Mercury program (single-seat) was followed by the then ongoing Gemini program (two-seat), and the three seat Apollo program was soon to begin. Apollo would eventually carry Americans to the moon in 1968 and land there in 1969, but that was still a dream.

In early 1967, NASA and the nation were rocked by the deadly Apollo 1 fire at Cape Canaveral that claimed the lives of three pioneering astronauts. In the midst of this despair, our class took a field trip up the road to the Huntsville Redstone Arsenal, where they were building the mighty F-1 engines that would propel Apollo to the moon. I witnessed the determination and grit of that team and yearned to join the effort someday as an astronaut or engineer. My career aspirations pivoted on the spot from being simply a pilot to becoming a part of our nation's space program.

One of the qualifications for astronauts was physical fitness, so I looked around to see what sport I might master. With my gangly frog legs, I could jump well, so the track and field coach made me a standing broad jumper and hurdler for the school. I never excelled at the latter but was able to jump just over nine feet forward from a standing position.

Chapter 7

In military households, there was an often quoted saying: "Spring has sprung, the grass has ris', I wonder where my transfer is." Sure enough, just about the time I was getting good at the broad jump, the kaleidoscope spun once again and Andy got new orders: this time to Randolph AFB, Texas. After the movers cleared out our house in June 1967 and my seventh-grade year wound to a close, we were in the car again and headed west to San Antonio.

CHAPTER 8

TEXAS

Rockets, success, and dashed dreams

The civil unrest during the summer of 1967 was marked by 150 race riots in major US cities. Earlier in the year, the Apollo 1 fire at Cape Canaveral claimed the lives of astronauts Gus Grissom, Roger Chafee, and Ed White—not only a national human tragedy but also a severe setback to NASA's ambitious space race to the moon.

My eighth-tenth grade years on Randolph AFB (1967-70) in San Antonio were special: It was the first time that we lived on an Air Force Base rather than in a surrounding civilian community.

Randolph was a hub of activity. The base was home of the Military Personnel Center where Andy was in charge of senior NCO worldwide assignments for the USAF and home of jet pilot training activity in raucous T-37 "Tweetie Bird" Cessna jets (so loud that pilots jokingly claimed they "converted Jet-A fuel directly to noise," and so slow that they had to "watch for bird strikes from the rear") and sleek supersonic T-38 "Talon" jets. We did everything on base: lived in base housing, shopped in the Base Exchange and Commissary, attended Sunday school and church, used the medical facilities when needed, bowled on dependents' bowling leagues, and lounged around the Officer's Club swimming pool. I also spent countless hours scouring the ample base library to locate and

Chapter 8

read almost their entire science fiction collection. When not reading or studying, I was mesmerized by the constant stream of aircraft taking off or landing at the base.

The Randolph High School was located on the far side of a runway and catered to dependents from seventh-twelfth grades. The school featured excellent teaching staff as well as extensive labs and workshops for technical training and even a state-champion football team. One of the best courses I ever took was Basic Shop at Randolph High. Over a year we learned to operate a forge and craft metal tools, run an entire woodshop including band saws, lathes, joiners, and planers (all used to make furniture and trinkets to take home), navigate electrical theory and systems to create circuits and build amateur radios, and take and process photographs in the extensive darkroom. I have used the skills learned in that class in my daily life ever since and lament that most shop programs across the country are now long-gone, victims of concerns over liability.

My new photography skills prompted me to volunteer as a school photographer along with another classmate. As budding photojournalists, we attended all official school functions and sports events to capture images for our school newspaper. Little did I realize that photography could be a contact sport: one Friday night during a home football game, I was on the sidelines focusing on the action to capture the perfect shot. The only "shot" I got, though, was squarely to my torso when a herd of players ran over me as they fell out of bounds. Once the scrum was cleared away, I was dragged up with a bloody nose and a bent camera. On the bright side, I racked up some serious sympathy points with nearby cute cheerleaders…

And speaking of cute females, I fell in love with my chemistry teacher in tenth grade at Randolph. Not only was she a great instructor who let us play with all the chemicals before and after class, but she was also the spitting image of Dianna Rigg, a British hottie often dressed in formfitting leathers on a British television spy series called "*The Avengers.*" I spent hours of extra time pushing around globs of liquid mercury with my hands on her lab desktop just for the opportunity to talk to her.

You'd probably need to be in a hazmat suit today to handle that stuff legally. Ah, the things we do for love…

I met many interesting folks at school, one of whom unintentionally sparked my interest in paleoanthropology. While sitting in Biology class one day, I perused a chapter on ancient hominids that included an artist's rendering of what a Neanderthal male might have looked like. Just then, I happened to glance to my left. Two rows away I saw the profile of one student silhouetted in the classroom window that looked exactly like the rendering in my book. "Holy moly," I thought, "They still exist!" Decades later found me travelling via Land Rover across vast dusty African plains in Tanzania while discussing this very "cross-pollinating" subject with another passenger who happened to be a National Geographic author. Scientific evidence had just revealed that Neanderthals and Homo sapiens had indeed intermingled long ago (another case of "any port in a storm" on a dark and stormy night in some cave, I suppose) and that we ALL have two to four percent of our makeup composed of Neanderthal genes. I suspect my classmate back at Randolph had received more than his share, though…

While at Randolph, I also developed a flair for research and writing. Long before Ancestry.com or the internet, I managed to interview family members from around the country, and through their input fleshed out our family tree with over one hundred members as a biology class project. I collected information about hair and eye color, height, physique, known diseases, occupations, and dates of birth and death; all that data was then plotted out on two poster-boards.

Having read scores of science fiction novels by then, I decided to try my hand at writing a short story in that genre. The plot featured a hidden space station parked in an orbit opposite the sun from earth by an alien race eons before, meant to welcome humanity only when our species had acquired the ability to traverse space to discover it. Pretty clever, I thought—and my English professor agreed, giving me top marks for the project. Unfortunately, both my family tree and short story end products fell victim to the moving process as we left Texas in

1970. The box containing these packed items went into storage, never to reappear again.

As opposed to my successful sci-fi short story effort, however, another literary "masterpiece" landed me in hot water. Ironically, that piece wasn't made up—it depicted an actual borderline psychotic mathematics teacher at the school. In math class, he would become hysterical when students missed a point he was trying to get across, jumping up and down on the top of his desk and slamming yardsticks so hard on students' desks that the rulers splintered and went flying off in all directions. I don't remember what he was teaching but clearly remember those weekly tantrums and the scores of wooden yardsticks he destroyed. The whole story was so bizarre that I thought it would make a great essay for English class. In glorious and descriptive detail, I crafted the essay and turned it in to my English teacher. Shortly thereafter that essay somehow got posted to the bulletin board in the teachers' lounge. A day later I was summoned to the principal's office, and my father was likewise summoned from work to join me. It was pointed out in no uncertain terms that what I had written was inappropriate and libelous (per the offended math teacher). Averring that my comments reflected the absolute truth didn't help my case, much to my dismay. After a prolonged silence, the principal told me that if I were to ever write such a treatise again, to be sure to change the names in the paper. We were then dismissed. My father just shook his head and went back to work. I went back to English class, where the teacher happened to be handing back those graded assignments. She gave me a wink and an A+ on the paper.

I learned two lessons that day: First, unvarnished truth should be leavened with a tad of discretion for a literary device to be effective and well received. Second, I was reminded that in the military world, the transgressions of a child can derail a parent's entire career in a heartbeat. Luckily, my father and I both survived this episode, but I was much more careful about my actions thereafter. My grades continued to improve throughout my tenure at Randolph High—I did well in most subjects with the exceptions of physical education (earning the sad but accurate moniker of "4-eyes" in softball practice) and typing class, where my ineptitude at the keyboard resulted in frequent scathing derision by my teacher.

My interests in aviation, model airplane building, and rocket construction continued unabated. In those days, the Estes Model Rocket company would hold monthly national rocket design contests, awarding honors for unique and practical rocket designs. I won that contest in November 1969 and received a nice certificate and letter from Vernon Estes, the company president. The story of my rocket design award was written up in both the local base and San Antonio newspapers and even landed me an interview on a local radio station. I was most excited and honored, however, to be asked to display my rockets along with the technical publications I had used to build them at my beloved base library. (Figure 6) Despite the good press, however, our launch site on base was permanently closed soon thereafter following an incident in which a fellow rocketeer (who shall remain nameless) managed to ignite a grass fire around the launch pad while attempting to launch on a breezy day. After several fire engines extinguished the rapidly spreading blaze, he and his father were escorted by the Military Police to the base commander's office. The commander was not amused: before being extinguished, the flames had come within fifty yards of the base's Jet-A fuel storage depot.

As I matured, my love of aviation and desire for a military or NASA career blossomed, but two medical sticking points arose that seemingly curtailed those plans.

The first issue was my eyes: I was extremely nearsighted (about 20/250). I had hoped my vision would improve with age, but it didn't. The military services were fickle on pilot training for myopes: if short of pilots, vision waivers were easy to get. If flush with applicants, though, waivers were rarely issued. As I was growing up in the baby boom population bulge, there were a lot of applicants, so my chances were not looking good.

The second issue involved my heart: Our base family doctor had given me a preliminary screening physical required to apply to the USAF

Academy. Unfortunately, he detected a heart murmur. The murmur had been noted previously in my early childhood and had been asymptomatic. In that pre-ultrasound era in the 1960's, the cause of the murmur was a mystery. The only thing my mother had been told is that I should refrain from heavy exertion—a recommendation I had studiously ignored all my life.

Now, with the chance that the murmur would torpedo any possibility of attending the USAF Academy, I was desperate to find some way to clarify what was going on in my ticker, as I was convinced it was a non-issue. The ultimate USAF referral institution, Wilford Hall USAF Medical Center, was located at nearby Lackland AFB. Our doctor at Randolph made a referral for cardiac evaluation at Wilford Hall, where those same staff cardiologists were making cardiac go/no-go decisions for all Air Force aviators. The cardiologists said that if I was really committed to finding out if there was some critical valve problem or a hole between two heart chambers, the only way to check was with a relatively new experimental procedure called a cardiac catheterization. Though my parents tried to talk me out of it (they had to sign a waiver describing a one percent risk of death from the procedure), I was adamant that we proceed, as failure to do so would merit an automatic disqualification from ever becoming a military pilot.

Soon thereafter, a catheter was placed in my heart via my right arm, and the evaluation was completed. When I awoke some time later, the cardiologist came in to give us the results: after all the procedure hype and consternation we had gone through, the results were inconclusive. The cardiologists couldn't detect any cause for the murmur: no obvious valve problem and no inter-chamber hole. Even more bleakly, they stated that even an equivocal cardiac catheterization like mine would disqualify me from applying to the Air Force Academy. I was crushed and even suffered a few minutes of hysterical blindness after the news. My vision came back, but my dreams were dashed.

Could I ever surmount these obstacles? I was frustrated not only by the murmur itself, but that even after aggressive testing the doctors still were unable to pin down its cause or potential impact on my life. These clinicians were in essence telling me to forget my dreams. I refused to accept that fate and grew determined that I would somehow and someday overcome my cardiac obstacle. Years later my murmur was found to be a benign common condition called asymptomatic mitral valve prolapse, something affecting about ten percent of the US population. I was right all along—it was not a significant issue—but couldn't prove that during my teenage years.

Before the cardiac catheterization fiasco, I had rarely thought about training to become a physician, but this interaction started wheels turning in my head. As a doctor, I could explore and help solve these medical mysteries. I could be the kind of doctor who works around people's problems, enabling me to tell them an emphatic "Yes" to their dreams, rather than "No, No, No." When I mentioned this notion to my parents, my mother confided that when I was only six weeks old, my Aunt Donna had taken me on a whim to a New York fortune teller who had predicted that I would become a physician one day. A bit of foreshadowing, to be sure… Another option I considered was to become an aeronautical engineer—at least I would be close to the action, if not directly in the cockpit. I was torn between those two career paths until fate made the decision easier just over two years later.

I had little time to ponder, though, as another disruption to our family equilibrium arose in the spring of 1970 when Andy received orders for his second wartime posting: this time to Vietnam. He would be away for an entire year, so once our household goods were packed and sent to storage, and my mother, sister, and I headed back to Newburgh, where I spent an eventful eleventh grade year junior high school year while living with my grandparents and an uncle all under one cozy roof.

CHAPTER 9

NEW YORK

Family, physics, and Vietnam

Newburgh was historically a sleepy hamlet surrounded by small farmsteads and home of the Strooks textile factory, located on the pastoral western banks of the Hudson River. The region was rife with local lore ranging from tales of Rip Van Winkle to the Headless Horseman. By the 1960's it had become a remote bedroom community for New York City, a ninety-minute train ride south. Generations of family from my mother's Scottish, English, Irish, and Dutch roots including the Henderson's, Cornish's, Rosborough's and the Dusenbury's still lived in the area, affording us a rich and wonderful support system upon our arrival in the summer of 1970.

For the ensuing year, our home was with my grandparents Amy and Bill Rosborough and my uncle Jon Rosborough on Wintergreen Avenue just west of Newburgh. Though technically my uncle, Jon was closer to me in age than he was to his own sisters, so he felt more like an elder brother. Upon graduating from Wake Forest University, Jon had served two years with the US Army manning a missile battery in Korea. Upon completing his ROTC commitment, he had recently returned to Newburgh to assume a hospital administration position locally. Newly repatriated to the USA, Jon lived with his parents (and us) until he got his own apartment many months later. He was quite a prankster and passed on much of his humorous take on daily life to me. Jon taught me to not take myself too seriously, to appreciate the small things in life, and to try to look for positivity even in dire circumstances—an attitude that had served him well in Korea.

Relatives or close family friends permeated Newburgh: My Uncle Ed Henderson, himself a retired USAF Reserve Colonel, was president of the Columbus Trust Bank, and my grandmother Amy Rosborough (Ed's sister) was his executive secretary. Through the years before and since, at least five other family members, including my mother Barbara, worked at that bank at one time or another. Other relatives were deacons at our Moulton Memorial Baptist Church (I was conscripted into being an altar boy during the year), store owners, factory workers, farmers, and turnpike policemen, as well as teachers and administrators in the public high school I was to attend: the Newburgh Free Academy (NFA).

Large family gatherings were the norm for all birthdays and holidays. Christmas was always a special event, when the entire family room of my grandparents' home was filled with presents by Christmas Eve, and thirty or more relatives would show up on Christmas Day to open gifts over many hours. The day would culminate with a huge potluck feast. My grandmother Amy's' sister, Hazel Roe, lived next door, and the common backyard area between their homes was host to festivities in the warmer months as well: Easter brunches, Fourth of July celebrations, weddings, and even post-funeral wakes.

My great-grandmother Elsie Henderson lived just down the street and would walk up to these celebrations with her husband. Elsie was an adamant teetotaler and would swell with righteous indignation should she ever spy alcohol at a party. As the teenaged newbie to the crew, I was assigned a perch near a front living room window as the lookout. At first sight of her walking up the street, I was to raise the alarm with the men in our house, whereupon in a grand flurry of activity, all the open booze was capped, corked, and hidden in various cabinets, closets, and even the ironing board nook. After she passed through the house on the way to the rear yard, the alcohol would slowly reappear in a remote part of the kitchen or the laundry room for the remainder of the night.

Uncle Ed, the bank president, didn't have any children of his own, but he and his wife Esther loved and doted on all their nephews and nieces. Ed was a wonderful organ player and before his banking career had earned money playing in movie houses during films from the silent era. He and Esther hosted the annual Thanksgiving feast at their home where he would regale us with stories from those earlier times. Ed and Esther's "baby" was their fifty-one-foot Chris Craft yacht that he kept in the Newburgh marina. Every summer weekend the couple could be found sanding and re-varnishing the teak or polishing the extensive brass that covered the beautiful boat. They would invite small groups of family members to take day cruises with them down the Hudson River past West Point. An especially coveted invitation was the Fourth of July evening cruise, when firework displays could be visible from Newburgh, Beacon, Poughkeepsie, and other towns along the water. Several years later, my new bride Sue and I were honored to share one of these July cruise spectacles.

The town had five claims to fame, three of them related to the military. Newburgh was situated near two military bases: Stewart AFB and West Point's United States Military Academy. It was also where General George Washington based his headquarters during a bleak winter early in the Revolutionary War. In the 1930's, Newburgh was rated the most beautiful small town in America. Finally, Newburgh was one of two towns whose water supply naturally contained fluoride. It was based on the low frequency of dental cavities in the populations of these two towns that fluoride was later added to city water supplies throughout the nation.

By the late 1960's, however, the town was having issues. Like many smaller communities in which small farming was falling out of favor, the community was losing many of its youth to New York City where they had better prospects for higher-paying jobs. Many local stores closed, and the beautiful brownstone townhouses in the urban core were falling into disrepair. Furthermore, a flight of indigent minorities was migrating to Newburgh from New York City, where rising housing costs had forced them out. The net effect was a racial tension that wracked the town, the appearance of drug dens, brothels, rundown streets, and rising crime in the urban core. Downtown Newburgh was becoming too dangerous for the average person to reside, so the middle class fled to the outskirts of town where my family lived.

The only place I had direct exposure to racial strife in 1970-71 was at NFA, where all social groups intermingled. During my high school junior year, we had frequent riots on the campus and at least two stabbings (one of which was five feet from me as I waited to board the school bus one afternoon). By the second semester, we had uniformed police officers with guard dogs stationed in every major hallway inside the school. Racial tension was new to me, as it was not nearly as common in military communities. (The USAF had been completely integrated since 1950, by command of President Truman.)

Despite the strife, NFA was an outstanding large public school that had served the entire community for generations: my mother and all her siblings and cousins had attended NFA, Aunt Hazel worked in the front office, and Aunt Esther taught speech and elocution. The school boasted not only excellent science classes and laboratories, but also a planetarium, auto workshop, and cosmetology school.

My love of all sciences was bolstered by myriad opportunities offered at NFA that year. I completed a year of chemistry via a concentrated summer program before the start of the regular school year which allowed me to take a physics course during the regular session. An outstanding, enthusiastic young physics professor led us through instruction and experimentation to understand the nuances of this sophisticated science. His upbeat effective teaching methods changed my life. He loved to teach by example, using games and riddles that really made the lessons memorable.

On the first day of physics class, for instance, he inscribed the letters "C-G-X-U-V-I-R" across the top of the blackboard. He never said a word about those letters, and when queried about them weeks later stated the inscription was a puzzle for us to figure out. Several days later I decoded his riddle: the letters stood for the orderly progression of frequencies of the electromagnetic spectrum: Cosmic, Gamma, X-ray, Ultraviolet, Visible, Infrared, and Radio waves. Over fifty years later, that blackboard inscription is still clearly etched in my memory.

On another day we had been addressing the concepts of work (energy expended over time), geometry, and gravity. To tie these items together, he proposed we figure out the distance an arrow shot from a bow would travel if we knew the tension on the string in pounds, the acceleration distance before the arrow left the bow once released, and the angle up from the horizon from which it was shot. We calculated tables of prediction with all these factors and then hiked out on the football field where we all took turns shooting arrows while other students measured angles, force, distance, etc. To our amazement, the actual distance the arrows traveled matched within a few percentage points the theoretical predictions. The physics professor had demonstrated that theory had real world applications.

By chance, four of us from that class also ended up in his study hall. Our physics guru asked if we'd rather do something more interesting than just sitting quietly during that period. Receiving a rousing "Yes," he proceeded to explain and derive Einstein's equations with the four of us over the next few months! To do so, he first had to teach us calculus, which we all took in stride. His enthusiasm was infectious. I was enthralled with physics thereafter; indeed, physics came to play a major role in my professional life.

In 1969, the USA successfully landed on the moon during the Apollo 11 mission and by 1970, NASA had created a travelling interactive educational program targeting selected high schools to enlighten students and the local public about ongoing NASA projects. NASA solicited local student educators to participate. Selectees would study assigned NASA subjects and then teach those topics to the local populace during the event. Props would be brought in and set up, and the highlight of the week would be a visit by a current astronaut. When NFA was selected as a program site, I signed up for several teaching opportunities well in advance, and NASA, in turn, sent me stacks of materials to study and memorize.

At the NASA event at NFA, I lectured on orbital mechanics, the Lunar Excursion Module (LEM) moon lander, and the lunar space suit. I walked the hallways for hours in one of those suits, and only wished they had attached a working cooling unit to it—I was drenched in sweat by the end of each shift. A visit by astronaut Stewart "Stew" Roosa was the highlight of the event. I wanted more than ever to fly, not just in the atmosphere, but out into space. Stew Roosa had emphasized the importance of strong academics as a requirement to work for NASA, so I continued to put my nose to the grindstone, and my grades soared along with my ambitions. With a solid and expanding science and math knowledge base, perhaps NASA could use me as an aerospace engineer someday? Relating these aspirations to my mother, she quietly replied that engineering would be nice, but not to forget the fortune teller's prediction that medicine was in my future! Although she twisted that burr under my saddle innocently, her words later proved prophetic.

While my father served in Vietnam, Jon took it upon himself to play surrogate father by educating me about some non-nerdy topics like dating, cars, and "cool" attire. The latter was a stretch, as my usual wardrobe included white socks, too-short pants, nerd coke-bottle thick glasses, and a pocket protector filled with multicolored pens, all complementing my gleaming full-mouth silver braces. By the time my father returned from Vietnam a year later, Jon proudly showed off his efforts, as I now wore "cool" striped bellbottom jeans, two-tone platform shoes and sported a long "hippie" haircut. My father shook his head and wandered off, mumbling something about the fact that Jon had ruined me! An hour later, we were off to the barber shop to tune me up…

Dating girls was a foreign concept as well: I had never even been on a date with a girl, much less kissed one. I could have used a gradual introduction to the topic, but that idea apparently slipped Jon's mind. Imagine my confusion when Jon's opening foray into the subject of dating was a lecture about the necessity of using rubbers. His comment I have never forgotten. "Doug, sleeping with a girl while wearing a rubber is like going to bed with your socks on, but in the morning at least your feet come out clean!" I had no earthly idea what he was talking about… Nevertheless, once we got past that awkward beginning, he did call in some favors of friends with daughters, and I took a couple of young ladies to dinner and a movie. And I finally got a first kiss…

Jon and I connected much better with the car arena: mechanical things I could understand. He taught me to drive his beautiful stick-shift Buick GS400 convertible around the neighborhood and after days of coaching got me prepared to successfully earn my New York State driver's license in 1971. His coaching munificence only went so far; when he traded up to a beautiful new forest-green Datsun 240Z shortly thereafter, he wouldn't let me near it.

Throughout that year in Newburgh, my mother made a valiant effort to keep in touch with Andy, who was based at Tan Son Nhut Air Base in Saigon. Reel-to-reel tape recorders and cassette decks were all the rage at the time, so rather than letter writing we would gather around the tape deck each night to recount our days. The following day the tape would be mailed to an APO address (mail to/from Vietnam was free for the troops) and a week or so later my father would listen to what we were doing in New York. Of course, he was doing the same thing on his end, so once the system got going, we were each receiving a tape every day or two, albeit with news that was a week or more old. I still remember hearing a thunderous explosion in the background on one of his tapes, followed by a lot of yelling, commotion, and doors slamming. He came back about ten minutes later and resumed his remarks. Apparently, someone had tossed a grenade over the fence into his compound (a regular occurrence). He had run out to the bomb shelter so fast that he'd forgotten to stop the tape. Midway through his tour overseas, he and my mother were able to meet in Hawaii for a week of Rest and Relaxation (R&R), while my sister Susan and I were left in our grandparents' capable hands.

Upon completing a wartime tour in Vietnam, a supposed perk for returnees was preference given to any requested subsequent duty assignment in the USA. My dad put in a simple request: an assignment anywhere on the East Coast (and therefore close to both his and my mother's families). Of course, the USAF Personnel Center in its "infinite wisdom" assigned him instead to George AFB, a remote base on the high desert of southern California.

Andy's happy return to the USA from Vietnam was marred by one unfortunate incident. Returning from the war, veterans were required to wear uniforms when transiting civilian airports. My father landed in San Francisco enroute to New York in his formal Class A uniform. Years later, he confessed that while walking through the terminal, he was spit upon by anti-war protesters, and totally humiliated. That event angers me to this day. Sure, the war was unpopular by that time, but he and his compatriots were merely carrying out the duties assigned them by the President of the United States to the best of their ability. The idiocy of anti-war and anti-government fanatics sticks in my craw even now, and probably is one reason I later jumped at the chance to join the USAF myself. I was proud of the service my father and his contemporaries paid to the USA then and remain so now.

Following our joyful reunion in Newburgh, we spent a few weeks visiting both families in New York and Cape Cod and getting our Chevy station wagon ready for the long trip west. In late June 1971 my parents, Susan, Lassie, and I piled into the packed car and set off. As a newly licensed New York driver, I was excited to share the driving on this great cross-country adventure. All went well until we reached western Arizona days later when the Chevy's air conditioning died, and the car began to overheat. The car's black vinyl interior absorbed the desert heat, and the cabin temperature rose precipitously as we traversed the summertime inferno that was Needles, California. To make matters worse, to cool the engine we had to put the cabin interior heat full ON to wick away as much engine heat as possible from under the hood. Five miserable hours later we rolled into Victorville, California, home of George AFB and a training center for F-4 Phantom pilots. This proved to be my last move with parents before high school graduation.

CHAPTER 10

California

A new me, high marks, and a future vision

For the second time in my life, we were living on a military base. George AFB was situated several miles north of Victorville, in the high desert of California, halfway between Los Angeles and Barstow and only about fifteen miles from the famous Joshua Tree National Forest. An hour or two north was the site of a more famous base, Edwards AFB, where just twenty-five years earlier Chuck Yeager had broken the sound barrier in the Bell X-1 rocket-powered ship named "Glamorous Glennis." Little did I know that twenty years later, Chuck, Glennis, and I would cross paths professionally.

South of George AFB lived another noteworthy celebrity couple of cowboy and television fame: Roy and Ginger Rogers lived in nearby Apple Valley. The Roy Rogers Museum was located there and was a popular attraction for Los Angeles gamblers heading northeast on I-15 to play the Las Vegas gaming tables. Roy was still occasionally seen dropping by a local shopping mart or gas station on his motorcycle, and his famous television horse Trigger was stuffed and available for viewing in the museum.

At over 4000 feet elevation, the Mohave Desert was cold at night and boiling during the day for much of the year. On base, we were assigned a modest home on Alaska Circle, a humorous street name considering the waves of heat routinely melting its asphalt. Poisonous critters abounded on the base including dens of rattlesnakes and scorpions. Standard practice included tapping out your shoes every morning before donning them to dislodge any scorpions bedding down inside them overnight, and otherwise watching where you stepped constantly. I began my senior year at Victor Valley High School (VVHS) in the fall of 1971, traveling to and from VVHS by school bus for my first semester. Mornings required wrapping snugly in a Pendleton sweater-shirt and heading across the frozen fields to my bus stop: one could only do this because the snakes were too cold to move that early. Returning from school in the afternoon was a different matter, however, with temperatures routinely soaring above one hundred degrees Fahrenheit. On those afternoons all the rattlers were squirming, testy, and hungry. I avoided the fields altogether and walked the long way home on paved streets to judiciously avoid them.

Of course, we had arrived at George AFB a few months before school started, so I knew no one. Once again, the library was my haven and I spent hours there daily reading not just science fiction, but also checking out some aeronautical engineering books.

What was it like as a child attending eleven schools over my twelve grade-school years? It had its pros and cons. To back up a bit, with all the moves, relatives used to ask whether or not I was sad about leaving all my friends every year or so. In truth, the constant moves did affect my psyche a bit, as it did the psyches of thousands of other military brats of the era. Profiles analyzing the brat population years later found that they tended to gird and isolate themselves emotionally by not allowing many people to get close, as they realized that in most cases new acquaintances would disappear into the fabric of time with the next set of transfer orders. As adults, most brats reported fewer long term intimate friendships than the general population. The few close friendships they did develop, they cherished.

My standard response at the time to that question about leaving my friends was a bit more flippant; however, I would answer that, "Yes, I'm leaving all my friends but am also leaving all my enemies." To some degree, one could reinvent oneself with every move, and hopefully for the better. California in the early 1970s was a place of change and upheaval, both musically and socially. Having been the ultimate Poindexter nerd in New York, I was ready to blossom into the "hip new Doug, Mark XII."

That first summer in Victorville was indeed a time of metamorphosis for me. Gone were my straight pants, pocket protectors, and platform shoes. I traded glasses for contact lenses and my braces came off. I made an overt decision to shed my shyness around girls in my senior high school year—I was ready to start some serious dating and socializing. I went to the pool daily after the library, got a tan, and built up some muscles with all the swimming. The last item on my list to complete my makeover was to visit the California Department of Motor Vehicles (DMV) and trade out my fresh New York license for a newly minted California one.

Big mistake… I was only seventeen years old and had not taken a driver's education class in Newburgh, as it wasn't required in New York. Upon showing the California DMV clerk my New York license, he stated that he could not issue a California driver license to a seventeen-year-old without him having passed a school driver's education course. Adding insult to injury, he also confiscated my New York license! So much for driving to school: my "California surfer-dude makeover" was delayed another several months…

Academics that year were pretty much a breeze. California public school curricula were way behind those of New York, academically: my senior year was essentially a repeat of everything I had just done in Newburgh. I spent many free hours volunteering as a photographer for the school newspaper and launching mice in model rockets in high-G science experiments. All the mice survived the launches (sustaining over 17G's for a few seconds) and continued to successfully run post-flight mazes I had set up, but two died in a "ground accident." While driving the mice home for the Christmas break, I stopped abruptly to avoid a dog crossing the road. The dog was fine, but the mouse cage in the rear of the hatchback went flying forward, crashing into seats and other boxes. I had mice on my steering wheel and running across my dashboard. Two unfortunately got squished between boxes in the back and were dead on arrival. On a brighter biological note that year, I was finally talking to girls and becoming an extrovert in general.

My "coolness" was complete when my father bought us a second car: a 6-month-old stick-shift 1971 Ford Pinto, replete with an 8-track tape player, a hound's-tooth checkered vinyl top and lots of chrome trim. After a few weeks, I was able to "confiscate" the Pinto for my use travelling to/from school and on dates. Of course, in true California fashion, I had to dress it up by installing chrome mud flaps, an oak stick shift knob, and wide Firestone 500 tires, as well as painting the gas tank a light powder blue! Tacky? Yes indeed, but it all made great sense to a teenager in 1971. In a valiant effort to keep my focus away from skirts and on academics, my dad glued on a metal plaque between the two front seats stating, *"Drive toward your goals, get there, and THEN enjoy the fruits of your labors."* That plaque survived another eight years, many girlfriends, and three more moves.

I enjoyed getting to know the fairer sex that year, and as an innocent "nice boy" I was accepted by the young ladies' parents as a model gentleman. Well, mostly.

While cruising through the year (both literally and academically), I put more serious thought into my future, assuming that a military life was impossible because of my heart murmur. Aerospace engineering was my prime choice and entre to NASA work, but I didn't want to completely shut the door on medicine yet. I joined the Health Careers Club at VVHS, and to hone my slide rule skills, was a competitive "Mathlete" in the school Math Club. I also found time to compete in some statewide Science and Debate competitions.

It was standard practice in those days to administer Stanford-Binet IQ tests to seniors. Although the results were supposedly confidential,

I managed to get a peek at my file in the school office one day and was pleasantly surprised to see that I had scored in the top one percent of my peers in the USA. This result, and some good SAT scores, later facilitated my admission to the MENSA society as a life member.

One of the accolades I garnered that year was the Science and Math Award from Rensselaer Polytechnic Institute (RPI), a highly regarded private school based in Troy, New York. I knew nothing of RPI at the time, but the fact that it was in my home state of New York piqued my curiosity. Research at the George AFB library revealed that RPI had a six-year Bachelor of Science/Medical Doctor combined program. I was intrigued enough to send in an application for that program, and a few weeks later was granted an interview. My father and I flew from California to New York for the event. I performed miserably: fidgeting in my seat, stammering answers, etc. I slunk out of the admissions office, and we flew back to California. Needless to say, I was not offered a spot in the six-year program, and I vowed I would never be unprepared like that again.

Just because I got good grades is not to say that everything came easily to me: I had to grind away at any subject to attain the knowledge base needed to get great scores. Though the dogged work ethic and lack of funds curtailed my dating life a bit during that senior year, I trusted that the academic effort would ultimately prove worthwhile. Needing cash to pay for gas and dates, I quit the VVHS tennis team in favor of taking a Red Cross Water Safety Instructor (WSI) course. The WSI certification allowed me to lifeguard and teach both kids and adults to swim at local swimming pools—and get paid for it. I also tutored the Base Commander's daughter in math at her home. She tried to repay me with marijuana, but I wisely demurred.

Early in 1972, I looked at the nation's top three Aerospace Engineering schools: California Institute of Technology (Cal Tech), Massachusetts institute of Technology (MIT), and Virginia Polytechnic Institute (Virginia Tech). Money for applications was tight, so I only chose one to apply to. Cal Tech was a great school, but a bit too close to my parents (my independent streak was coming out). MIT was also a great school, but having lived around New York and Cape Cod, I thought the climate there was too cold nor was I interested in attending a large school in a big city, with all its distractions. My choice was Virginia Tech. Situated in serene foothills at the southern end of the Shenandoah Valley, Virginia Tech had the first university-based supersonic wind tunnel in the USA. The director of NASA's Johnson Space Center in Houston, Christopher Kraft, was a Virginia Tech graduate and was sending much of the Apollo work to the Tech Aeronautical Engineering program for research and development. There weren't a lot of distractions at this remote academic outpost either, other than hiking in the beautiful mountains or tubing down the lazy New River. Off the application went, and several weeks later an acceptance letter returned.

"Senioritis" at VVHS set in by late April. The class went on weekend trips to nearby waterparks (yes, they made an artificial lake in the desert), our senior prom was held in the gym with *The Turtles* rock and roll group as our band, and our school was invited to "Grad Night" at Disneyland in Anaheim. Senior classes from several schools around southern California were invited on selected evenings to arrive at Disneyland at the normal closing time. Gentlemen wore suits and ladies wore beautiful long dresses for this formal affair. After a frisking worthy of the best TSA agents, looking for alcohol and drugs mostly, we gained admission to the park. All the rides and vendors were open for us until dawn the next morning. Unfortunately, it rained most of our night: we were all bedraggled but happy as we boarded the coaches to head home the next morning at sunrise. My date, Sheri Nolan (another USAF Brat), was a beauty, and a real trooper that evening, dragging her soggy white dress through the mud between rides throughout the night.

As my senior year wound down in the spring of 1972, it was announced that I would be the Valedictorian of my class. I prepared a ten-minute speech based upon John Donne's quote about *"No man is an island…"* and wrote everything neatly on a set of three x five-inch index cards for the big morning. The night before, I was invited to go party-hopping with several classmates. Unbeknownst to me, the mission for the partygoers was to get me drunk—I was still known as a strait-laced kid, and they thought getting me inebriated would be hilarious. I remember little, other than swimming pools, laughing, hopping around town, drinking lots of punch, and driving the Pinto back to George AFB in the starlit wee hours of the morning with the windows down, singing along to songs being loudly belted out by *Blood, Sweat, & Tears* on my 8-track.

After too few hours of sleep, I arose with a blinding headache. With a not-so-hearty "serves you right" from my mother and shake of the head from my father, we were off to graduation. The morning event was held outdoors on the football field facing the parents and family filling the bleachers. My wait to address the crowd seemed interminable, sitting there in the front row in my green cap and gown with my head in my hands. After my introduction, I staggered up the stairs to the podium. Snickers from my classmates behind me on the field abounded, as word had spread about getting Doug plastered a few hours before. A minute into my speech, I was silently thinking to myself, "I've got this." Just then, a sudden breeze came up and blew away my stack of index cards. In disbelief, I watched the last nine minutes of my oratorical masterpiece flutter across the gridiron. I remembered but a third of it. I finished my abbreviated speech, received hearty applause (especially from my chuckling classmates), and sat back down. Graduation was over, and everyone filed neatly out.

I learned an odd but useful lesson that graduation day: *No one ever complains about getting out of a meeting early!* I adopted that wisdom throughout my ensuing professional life—it is far better to finish a lecture or meeting early, than to ever exceed an allotted speaking time, even by a minute. As a corollary, *one should think before speaking so to be both precise and concise in communicating.* These skills served me well down the road in my medical profession, leadership roles, and in the cockpit.

After lifeguarding and teaching swimming lessons during the summer of 1972, we packed up the car to trek back across the USA. Destination: Virginia Tech.

CHAPTER 11

Virginia Tech

Ut Prosim, artistic painting, and a nice long fall

1972 was a time of turmoil in the USA and world at large. The unpopular Vietnam War continued, and things were not looking good for the South Vietnamese. The military draft was still in place and having just turned 18, I was eligible. In addition, eleven Israeli Olympians were murdered by terrorists at the Summer Games in Munich. On a brighter note, President Nixon and Soviet Leader Brezhnev signed both the SALT I and Anti-Ballistic Missile Treaties in May. In a mere footnote for many, President Nixon in January ordered the development of what later would become NASA's Space Transportation System—better known as the Space Shuttle. Into this turmoil I landed at Virginia Tech.

Virginia Tech proved to be all that I had hoped: an excellent institution of higher learning specializing in the sciences and engineering, situated in a pastoral setting. A land-grant university established in 1872, Virginia Tech's motto was "*Ut Prosim*" (That I may serve), a motto assigned by University President John McBryde in 1896. Tech had historically been an all-male enclave with a very active Corps of Cadets, many of whom ended up serving in the US military. By 1972, however, the Corps represented but a minority of the student body, and Virginia

Tech had become co-ed. Despite those changes the philosophy of *Ut Prosim* still permeated the fabric of the school and fit well with my long-term aspirations.

After dragging a footlocker containing my worldly possessions up to the sixth floor of Lee Hall on move-in day, my parents and sister bade me farewell and began their long car ride back to California. The next day, I traipsed across the Drill Field for a meeting with my faculty advisor in Aeronautical Engineering. A man of few words, his greeting is forever etched into my memory: "Son, what are you doing in Aerospace Engineering? Haven't you heard, they just cancelled the Apollo program? You won't be able to get a job in this field for the next ten to fifteen years! I suggest you find another major."

I stumbled from the Randolph Hall Engineering Building in a daze minutes later. So much for my plans for a NASA career! Before stewing on that, however, I needed to find another major quickly, as classes were to begin just two days later. I wandered past the Architecture Building and into another large building nearby. A bearded graduate student dressed in a loose open shirt, ratty shorts, and sandals was crossing the lobby carrying a tray of Petri dishes. I asked where I was, and he smiled and replied that I had entered the Biology Building. My mind raced as I stood there: perhaps NASA would need biologists or doctors down the road for extended space missions. I asked how I could become a Biology major. He guided me to the administrative offices, and thirty minutes later, the deed was done. My kaleidoscope had turned again…

Thus, by the time my parents made it home to Victorville three days later, I had switched to an entirely different career path. As I relayed this news over the dormitory hall phone later that week, my mother was in stunned silence, and I could just imagine my father shaking his head again. After recovering from my bombshell announcement, though, they were both supportive and wished me luck.

My collegiate life was sedate and focused—with my new track I knew I needed to ace my classes if medical school was ever to be a possibility. Fortunately, I had great teachers and loved the biological sciences. I was in an honors track, and as an enrichment benefit met with a professor and other honor students for a weekly supplemental Colloquium Seminar in which we would discuss a variety of topics. The class required that we extensively research and publish an article on a "hot topic" (keep in mind this was before Google, the internet, or computers), so once again the library became my refuge and haven that year. In the end, the school published our papers: mine was entitled *"Euthanasia—A Sociological Overview"* (Ref3). I discovered that I loved researching topics and writing up investigations. This affinity for research later guided my medical life to a large degree.

In late 1972 the whole topic of euthanasia popped to the surface of public discussion and remained so for the ensuing two decades. When, if ever, was it justifiable to take another human's life, or assist him in doing so? A healthy but depressed citizen, certainly not, but how about a terminally ill cancer patient in excruciating pain? Controversy raged: was it murder or compassion? Doing in-depth research on the topic revealed valid points on both sides of the argument. I realized a truism in life: *"Things are usually never black and white; one should strive to openly and objectively view all sides of an argument before arriving at a conclusion."* I have tried to follow that epiphany to this day.

I wasn't a total academic recluse that first year at Tech, however. I enjoyed several fraternity parties during my freshman year but realized that the Greek life was not for me. Few girls were even willing to speak to freshman boys, so dating was off the radar screen. Imagine my surprise, then, when during dinner one evening in the huge Dietrich Dining Hall, an attractive young lady upperclassman stopped at my table and asked if I was Doug Johnson. Totally bewildered and surprised, I sheepishly admitted that I was. She laughed at my discomfort and said that she'd seen me from across the cafeteria on several occasions and had thought I looked familiar. Finally, she had remembered that I'd been friends with her younger brother during sixth grade in Omaha! What a small world...

In the spring of 1973, many of us huddled around a radio in our dormitory as the latest set of Selective Service draft numbers were drawn. Mine was thirty-three, as I recall. That was not good, as at least the first one hundred or so had been called up after the prior year's draft lottery. I sweated bullets for several weeks, when President Nixon unexpectedly announced that he had cancelled the draft. Hallelujah! I could now focus on my studies without fear of being called away to Southeast Asia.

Days later, while walking through the Student Union, I noticed a brochure soliciting members for the Virginia Tech Skydiving Club. That sounded interesting, so a few days later I caught a ride out to nearby Pulaski Airport to investigate the skydiving school located there. Sure enough, there were several Virginia Tech students learning to jump. In addition to parachuting activities, this school provided my first introduction to civilian general aviation. I had a chance to examine the cockpit of the Cessna-182 jump plane, and once again felt a yearning for flight. Regular flying lessons were too expensive for my meager budget, but each jump was only three dollars! I signed up for skydiving lessons and then returned to my dormitory to concoct a way to pay for them. Perusing school newspaper want ads, I saw an opening for an apprentice in the dining hall.

I entered the dining hall with the ad in hand and was interviewed by the head chef. He asked me if I had any cooking experience. "Not a lick," I replied. "No sweat," he retorted. "I appreciate your honesty." He hired me on the spot as an "assistant head chef" and two days later I was in the vast kitchen cooking for the masses under his direction. I will never forget my first shift, during which I cooked 570 pounds of shrimp. Of course, after cooking for hours, I spent more hours cleaning up. I abhorred fried chicken nights, as grease was splattered everywhere in the kitchen at the end of those evenings. Nevertheless, that small paycheck gave me enough cash to return to the Pulaski Airport to begin my parachute training on weekends.

After completing the course in the spring of 1973 as a newly minted member of the United States Parachute Association, I was ready for my first static line jump, also known as a "hop and pop." With experience,

I would switch from static line jumps to free-fall jumps, when I would pull the ripcord to open the chute after descending to 2000 feet above the ground (an altimeter was strapped to our reserve chutes).

My first jump occurred on a calm April day, after we loaded up the plane with 4 students, a jumpmaster, and the pilot. The side door of the plane was removed to save weight and make exiting the aircraft easier. I had asked to sit in the position closest to the pilot to see just how he was operating the controls. At the selected jump altitude, the pilot slowed the plane to eighty knots and headed upwind over and past the jump zone on the airport. The jumpmaster estimated the wind drift and hurled a weighted streamer from the cockpit to confirm or adjust his estimates. The plane then swung around for another upwind run, and the jumpmaster instructed the first student (me) to climb out onto the starboard tire of the plane while holding onto the wing strut, after first clipping my static line to the pilot's bottom seat post. At the appointed time, the jumpmaster yelled, "Go, Go, Go," and I pushed off and away. After falling about thirty feet below and behind the Cessna, the taut static line released the chute strapped to my back, and I floated toward the jump landing zone. These days were well before the highly maneuverable rectangular parachutes that are universal today. We were instead using round-chute DL and TU military surplus equipment (think of the D-Day movies you've seen with paratroopers), with T10-A reserve chutes. Once under an open canopy, you could change the direction you were pointing by tugging on the risers, but only adjust your direction of drift a bit. Any landing within a quarter of a mile of the landing zone was considered a great jump!

My turn to jump always seemed to come up too soon. Though for me the best part of each jump was watching the pilot maneuver the plane during the climb, the pilot always made me get out at the top… Surprisingly, there was never any feeling of falling during a jump—the wind was in your face as you stood on the wheel and hung onto the strut, and was still in your face as you let go and descended. The feeling was more akin to lying on a soft mattress. A few seconds after that static line jump, however, a sudden jerk interrupted that cushiony feeling as the chute deployed and you slowed precipitously. Once you were under an open canopy, a sense of peace and calm ensued as you slowly drifted to earth. You could hear conversations on the ground five hundred feet below and could hear a bird's wings flapping as it flew calmly by. Landing successfully involved use of something called a PLF, or Parachute Landing Fall. In essence, you tried to spread the landing shock out over your ankles, knees, hips, and shoulder, in turn, before coming to a rest. Once the chute deflated, you stood up, gathered the chute in your arms, and trudged back to the landing zone, sometimes having to climb fences or ford streams depending on the accuracy of the drop.

A rule at the Jump Center was that they would pack your parachute for you the first three times, but after that you had to pack your own chute after every jump. Jumps took place from higher and higher altitudes to allow more time to practice new free-fall maneuvers such as turns, somersaults, and tracking. Once in stable free-fall, the so-called terminal velocity of the fall was 125 mph when in a spread-eagle position. Jumping at 5400 feet, for example, gave you a full twenty seconds of free-fall before you had to pull the ripcord. All went well until jump number twenty, when I packed the chute for my second jump of the day.

It was late afternoon by the time we took off, and it took us a while to climb to altitude. The jumpmaster went through his routine and eventually told me to prepare to jump. Out on the tire and wing strut I climbed, and when looking down noticed that it was getting dark. Building lights and streetlamps were coming on across the countryside. I got the okay to jump and pushed away, watching the altitude on my altimeter unwind until I pulled the ripcord at 2000 feet. Nothing happened: no jerk and no chute opening. Time slowed in my mind, and I had time to consciously review all my emergency procedures. I lowered my shoulder to reach for my emergency chute, and as I did so, my original main chute opened after all. I landed in the dusk, barely able to see the ground or prepare to do a PLF.

The jumpmaster was waiting to debrief me. He said that he had watched me the whole way down and could see what had happened: As it turns out, if a jumper is in a perfect spread-eagle position during free-fall, a small vacuum is created over the center of his back. When the ripcord is pulled in that situation, the tiny spring-loaded drogue chute on those old rigs might not be strong enough to overcome the vacuum: the entire drogue and main chute system would just burble around close to the harness. That is what happened to me. When I eventually lowered my shoulder to reach for my reserve chute, the vacuum dissipated, and my main chute finally deployed. I landed in the dark, about a quarter mile from the drop zone, and had a nice long trek back to the jump base.

During my debriefing, I told the jumpmaster that I had had plenty of time to review emergency procedures as I fell. He asked me how long I thought the whole episode took and I vowed that it must have been ten seconds. He chuckled and told me that it was all over and the chute fully deployed in only four seconds! Time dilated for me, to be sure. All he wrote in the comments section in my logbook for the jump was, "Nice long fall."

It was reassuring to me that I had not panicked under duress. That confidence helped me greatly in the ensuing years, as thorough and thoughtful preparation, be it in the air, in the operating room, or in a painting competition would usually carry me through stressful times.

Shortly before my freshman Virginia Tech year ended, I was elected President of the Virginia Tech Skydiving Club for the ensuing year. My joy was short-lived, however, when my parents discovered my new hobby—they were not enthusiastic about my leaping from airplanes and threatened to cut off my tuition unless I quit the endeavor! Thus, my brief time as a skydiver ended in June 1973 after a total of only twenty-one jumps, and pursuing aviation activities was once again put on hold.

My family transferred that year from California to the Washington, D.C. area where my father was assigned first to Headquarters Air Force at Bolling AFB and later to the National Security Agency (NSA). I spent the summer at their new home in Alexandria, Virginia, and once again worked as a lifeguard and instructor, this time at Bolling AFB.

The ensuing two years at Virginia Tech were consumed with knocking out academic requirements, pursuing upper-level electives in a variety of sciences, and enduring heavy course loads. In one memorable lab experiment during a Comparative Physiology course, I inanely volunteered to have my metabolism compared to that of the class iguana. After I had stripped down to athletic shorts, the iguana and I were subjected to heat lamps and had our core body temperatures measured and compared. I then had to hop into a metal tub packed with bags of ice (the iguana had his own tub). Distressingly, the ice bags ruptured and began to leak. I was cold, numb, and miserable. Once again, temperatures were measured and compared. My classmates were having way too much fun watching me suffer and finally ended the experiment early when I threatened a one-man rebellion!

In my sophomore year the school found itself short of dormitory rooms for incoming freshmen, so kicked a number of upper classmen off campus to make room for them, including me. My roommate, Thomas Kent, and I rented a small apartment at the edge of town. Getting to and from campus was a potential stumbling block, but thankfully my folks allowed me to take the mighty Pinto to school. I became known in the apartment complex as the blond California dude with the chrome mud flaps.

I made some progress in my artistic endeavors that year. With meager funds for decorating our apartment, I got creative. A local crafts store oil painting kit contained all the materials I needed to create two "masterpieces" for only ten dollars! How hard could it be? I painted a mountain scene memory from our cross-country expeditions, and a desert scene that reminded me of Victorville. (Figure 7) Over the ensuing forty years, I would hone my artistic skills and techniques solely by reading books; it never occurred to me to take actual lessons.

Tom and I needed furniture for our new apartment, too, so with our meager budget I brought to bear some skills picked up back in shop class and the many base hobby shops I had frequented with my father. As noted previously, the Architecture School was immediately adjacent to the Biology building. They had an outstanding shop facility in their basement for the Architecture students to use for constructing all their class projects. One of those students confided in me that the shop was open at all hours for their convenience. Hmmm...

For several weeks I would wait until after midnight, when presumably all the teachers would be off campus, and slip into that basement shop, acting like I belonged there. I foraged for discarded wood scraps, and using all their equipment, managed to form, shape, glue, stain, and varnish several pieces of furniture. During the daytime, my projects were just stuffed in a corner of the shop, and no one in authority ever questioned their presence. After completing those creations in the wee hours, they were transported one by one to our apartment. We eventually had coffee tables, end tables, bookshelves, and room dividers!

By the time I began my junior year at VT, I had decided I would definitely pursue a medical degree. Considering my miserable interviewing debacle at RPI two years previously, I thought it made sense to do a "trial run" at a medical school application. My hope was to be granted an interview to become familiar with the process and standard questions asked, so that when I applied in earnest in the fall of my senior year, I would be better prepared. I filled out an application to the Medical College of Virginia (MCV) in Richmond, a three-hour drive away, and to my delight was granted an interview. Thus, in November of my junior year, I motored to Richmond and met with two staff physicians conducting candidate interviews. I frankly explained what I was doing: trying to gain interview experience. One asked if I thought I was ready for medical school. I responded that, indeed, I had already completed all my prerequisites at Virginia Tech and was just "spinning wheels" until my real application the following year. Perhaps because there was no real pressure during those interviews, I was very relaxed. After the interviews concluded I thanked them for their time, hopped back into the Pinto, and drove up another two hours to Alexandria for dinner with my folks.

In the excitement of the day, I had forgotten that I had a mandatory class the next morning, so once dinner was over, I hopped back in the car for the four-hour trip back to Virginia Tech that night.

Driving at night through a remote rural area of Virginia near Culpepper, a large stag leapt from the side of the road and charged, colliding with the Pinto's driver's side, careening off the front fender and down the whole left side of the car. After bending back my rear bumper, he got up and staggered off into the woods. I was pretty shaken up and proceeded to the Culpepper Police Department to report the accident. At that time of night, the only concern of the sole trooper on duty was whether or not I wanted to eat the deer. I wasn't interested in that, so he left me alone to try to go find it to feed his own family. After thirty minutes I realized he probably wasn't returning anytime soon, so I climbed back into the wounded Pinto and continued my drive to VT. (The deer had smashed the entire left side of the car—I could only get in and out from the passenger's side.)

It had been a long and tiring day, with eight hours of driving behind me and two more to go, as well as the time spent at interviews in Richmond and the police station in Culpepper. Fatigue set in that I tried to counter with loud music and the rushing wind from open windows. About an hour later, I was jolted by a loud noise and screeching sound. I had fallen asleep at the wheel going 70 mph on interstate I-81. Drifting across the fast lane, I had scraped to a stop against the one stretch of guard rail within ten miles of that spot. If not for that rail, I would have careened down a steep embankment into the heavily forested median strip. I climbed out of the passenger side of the car to inspect the damage, which, like the deer collision just hours before, was also on the driver's side.

After several minutes, no one had stopped to help, so I got back in, started the car, and completed the trip to Virginia Tech at about 3 a.m. I stumbled upstairs into my townhouse bedroom and fell fast asleep. Tom, who had an early class that morning, left the apartment to head to campus just after dawn. A minute later, though, the front door crashed open, and he raced up the stairs into my bedroom, yelling, "Who did you kill?" I stumbled groggily back down and outside with him to see what he was talking about. In the light of day, the driver's side of the Pinto was sporting dents, scrapes, and streaks of blood from the front fender to the rear bumper. Several weeks and many dollars later, the car was repaired.

At quarter's end, I made the return journey home to Alexandria for the Christmas break. Just before New Year's Eve, a thin envelope arrived from MCV. Opening what I expected to be a rejection letter, I was surprised to see that the letter was instead congratulating me on my acceptance and admission to the MCV Medical School class beginning eight short months later! My initial joy was soon replaced by apprehension, as it dawned on me that I hadn't even graduated from college yet and wasn't scheduled to do so for another eighteen months! I spent the remainder of the holiday wondering how I was going to sort out the predicament.

In January of 1975, I trudged across the Drill Field at Virginia Tech to enter the massive stone edifice known as Burruss Hall, the administrative center of the University. I marched into the Dean's office and asked his secretary if he would see me. The Dean graciously welcomed me in and listened to my entire story about the "practice" medical school application that had unexpectedly become an actual admission offer. I was mortified, and asked what I should do. He thought for a moment while looking out his window over the snowy campus, then turned back to me and smiled. He said, "I'll tell you what. You go off to MCV this fall, and if you pass all your first-year medical school classes, I will count those as your senior year of college and let you return to graduate with your class in 1976." I will never forget those words or his kindness at that moment. I promised to make him proud and headed back to class with my head held high and spirits soaring.

Before the holiday, I had signed up for a grueling twenty-one hour schedule consisting of mostly advanced science courses. As my future four years had just come into focus with my medical school acceptance, I opted to scale back the load and enjoy life a bit for my last two quarters. I dropped several tough courses and substituted astronomy, archery, art history, and the like. I also saw a course on oceanography, thought "Gee, I'd like to learn about fish," and signed up. Days later I found out (and too late to drop it) that the course had nothing at all to do with fish but was instead a highly mathematical theory class using tons of calculus. Except for organic chemistry, it was the toughest class I took at Virginia Tech. So much for loafing off during my final months…

The other momentous event that early January in 1975 was meeting Susan Knorst Friedman, my future bride. On my way to cancel an advanced literature class in the English Building, I saw a gorgeous brunette in a powder blue ski jacket climbing the stairwell. I thought she was the most beautiful girl in the world and followed her into the class I was about to cut. In my hormone-directed state of mind, I determined that I wouldn't cut the class until I had gotten her phone number. Pressure was on, and with only one day left to cut the class without penalty, she gave it to me.

With my tight finances, I looked around for an inexpensive place to take Sue for a first date. As it happens, there was a free concert a few days later in the large Burruss Hall auditorium. I got two tickets and our date was set. As we sat in the audience that evening, I was surprised to hear that the concert was being sponsored by the Campus Crusade for Christ, a religious evangelical group. Now, I am a Christian, but not a fervent Holy Roller, and was fearful that Sue would get an inaccurate first impression of me. At intermission, she and I broke away and had a long chat about our take on religion.

Sue had been raised Catholic in her early years. Her mother divorced when she was young, but later met and married a wonderful man, Daniel Friedman, who, in turn, adopted Sue. Dan had been raised Jewish. When they married, both Dan and Sue's mother converted to become Methodist, as did Sue. Thus, Sue had a broad exposure to a variety of faiths during her formative years.

My father grew up in a Lutheran family, and my mother in the Baptist tradition. In the military, however, every installation merely had one common Base Chapel that served all religions. Under the same roof, from the same pulpit with congregants sitting in the same pews, services were all held in the same spot. The time you arrived for service determined which of the three options you would participate in: Catholic service, Protestant service, or Jewish service. Items in a large recess behind the altar would allow a statue of the Virgin Mary to be traded out for a golden Cross or a Torah and Arc, as needed, before each worship service. For Protestants, there was no splitting into sects: some years you might have a Presbyterian minister, other years a Methodist or Episcopalian, etc. We called all the preachers Chaplains and couldn't tell their religion by their looks or their uniform. Indeed, a military Chaplain's charge was to minister to anyone who walked through the Chapel doors or who might need guidance or support. Military personnel and their dependents all worshipped God under one roof, literally and figuratively. For that reason, my parents and I were tolerant and accommodating of all faiths and appreciated the unique contributions of each. My personal approach to spirituality has been to pray faithfully to God every day, asking for forgiveness and guidance, and to let my actions in life reflect my Christian ethos and values, rather than proclamations about them to others.

During that concert intermission, Sue and I were relieved that our views and outlooks matched so closely. We also found we had similar feelings about the number of kids we wanted to rear (two), and the importance of instilling in our offspring the virtues of education, frugality, honesty, kindness, common sense, and family. All in all, we covered an astounding bit of discovery for a first date. After three hours, we knew more about each other than most couples learn in months of courting. We soon began looking to the future as fast friends in love.

Also, during that concert evening Sue revealed that she had noticed me in a class we had shared the previous semester. What she remembered of me was not my devilishly handsome good looks (Hah), but rather that I would frequently pop up and ask questions of the professor if I didn't understand something. I wanted to have a clearer explanation of something before moving on, even if I was the only one who hadn't understood. She told me that after I asked all those questions, many other students would be madly taking notes, as they too had similar questions but were too embarrassed or timid to speak up. Sue was impressed with my courage to query the professor unabashedly.

Sue had attended Gettysburg College for her freshman year. Her parents then moved to Centreville in northern Virginia to follow a government job. Her boyfriend during her Gettysburg year had decided to apply to the Virginia Tech Architecture School program for his sophomore year, so Sue decided to transfer as well to follow him. Ironically, Sue was accepted to Virginia Tech, but her boyfriend was not. Finances decided it for her: she was now eligible for in-state tuition at Virginia Tech. To save her parents a bundle, she ditched the boyfriend and came to Virginia Tech without him. Eighteen months later we met in that stairwell, she with her beautiful long hair, winning smile, and powder-blue ski jacket.

We began dating exclusively a couple of months later and were pretty much inseparable. Adventures to Italian and Lebanese restaurants were mixed with a caving trip in the nearby mountains, a ski trip to the nearby Snowshoe resort in West Virginia, hikes, tubing on the New River, and eating scores of donuts. (Figure 8) Money was tight, but we were creative. At the end of our junior year in June 1975, we returned to our folks' homes in northern Virginia and continued to see each other regularly.

I had had a discussion with my father earlier in the spring to explore how I was going to afford medical school. He had discovered that the military had a program called the HPSP (Health Professions Scholarship Program). To apply to the HPSP, one had to first be accepted to a medical school. From that pool of candidates, the HPSP program selected top applicants for a full scholarship at any USA medical school, including tuition, books, fees, and equipment, and even provided a monthly stipend. Accepted applicants would be commissioned as 2nd Lieutenants during medical school, and upon completion and receipt of their M.D. diploma, would be promoted directly to Captain and begin residency.

Upon completion of a residency, a commitment to the awarding military branch would begin: one year owed for every year of medical school they paid for. Having already been a military dependent, I already knew that life well and would gladly serve time to pay back such a commitment. It was not easy to get the scholarship, as they only took the top ten percent or so of applicants, but I decided to try for an Air Force HPSP position. To my great relief, I was selected for the program, and my immediate financial concerns were alleviated! In a special moment together, my father arranged to perform my Air Force swearing-in ceremony. (Figure 9)

One sad event transpired in 1975—the passing of my maternal grandmother, Amy "elefante" Rosborough. Amy was the ideal grandmother everyone wishes for: kind, compassionate, funny, and smart as a whip. We had lived with her on and off over the years in Newburgh during my father's deployments. There was a long history of cancer in her family, and she ended up developing advanced breast cancer. Cancer wasn't openly discussed by her generation: she had noted a big breast lump months before, but didn't seek help until the cancer had broken through the skin and spread across her upper chest. Though she bravely put up with prolonged and toxic chemotherapy, it was to no avail and the cancer progressed. Several months before her passing, Amy came to live with my parents in Alexandria and refused to see anyone but close family because she was too embarrassed by the smell of her infected chest wall.

Unfortunately, Sue never got to meet Amy, though she was only one room away when Sue came over to visit me and my family. Amy did call me into her room, however, near the end. Knowing I was about to start medical school, she took my hand, looked into my eyes, and said, "Doug, be a good doctor, and don't let this ever happen to anyone else if you can help it." How impactful those words would be five years later: they would give me the courage to make a major career shift, and treatment of cancer would ultimately consume my long medical career.

In the fall of 1975, I set up an apartment on the south side of

Richmond with Sue's help and the assistance (and station wagon) of my Aunt Donna and Uncle Dan Ludwig, who helped transport my Blacksburg apartment goods to the new digs. By mid-September, Sue was beginning her senior year back at Virginia Tech, and I was a freshly scrubbed first year medical student at MCV.

CHAPTER 12

MEDICAL COLLEGE OF VIRGINIA

"Education is one thing no one can ever take from you."

—ANDREW L. JOHNSON

1975 was a watershed year in the USA, as Saigon fell and the Vietnam War came to a messy end. Bill Gates and Paul Allen partnered to form a software startup called Microsoft and two new television series debuted: *Wheel of Fortune* and *Saturday Night Live*. On the celebrity front, Cher filed for divorce from Sonny after 10 years of marriage, and one month later filed for divorce from Greg Allman after only 10 days of marital bliss.

Classes began at MCV for the 180 or so new medical students in late August. The sheer volume of information to be absorbed daily was enormous, but I loved every minute of it. The first two years were consumed by classroom work and the anatomy lab, where we spent a semester dissecting cadavers in the pungent atmosphere of formaldehyde emanating from the cadaver vats, and learning to identify different tissues under the microscope. After the first several months, our hair, skin, and clothing were almost as pickled as the corpses. The entire first year at MCV was devoted to learning how a body normally works, while the second year involved learning everything that could go wrong in a body.

The MCV campus was a conglomeration of four adjacent hospitals and several office and education buildings located in the heart of inner Richmond. A typical day would involve driving downtown by 7 a.m. and walking up the hill from under the railroad tracks where we all parked, usually stepping over one or two vagrants sleeping there, to enter the education buildings by 7:45 a.m. After a full day of learning, studying, and eating on campus, I would head home about 8 p.m. and continue studying until about 11 p.m. nightly. I found it hard to "turn off" my mind at night, knowing that I had to repeat the entire process the following day. My insomnia resolved, however, when I began painting landscapes at night from 11 p.m. until just after midnight. Cares dropped away as I laid paint on canvas, and once I put the brush down, sound sleep followed in minutes. I would awaken in the morning fully refreshed and ready for a new day. I like to think I was an early adopter of "art therapy" which decades later would become a recognized relaxation technique. Thus, I did get to pursue creating some artwork during my medical school years, but there was still neither time nor money to seriously consider any pilot training.

Eventually, we were assigned to interview and examine a real hospital patient and document a complete history and physical examination: a pivotal day in our training. As my appointed day to complete the task arrived, I anxiously wrote copious crib notes on my hands and wrists, wore my freshly unpacked white coat with the creases still in place (I don't think I owned an iron), and carried my shiny new black doctor's bag filled with newly unwrapped diagnostic tools. I took the elevator to the designated floor and sought out my assigned room, that of a patient awaiting a heart transplant. I cautiously entered after knocking, introduced myself, and tried not to stare at the huge mound of flesh sitting on the bed, replete with corn-rowed hair, large bare breasts, and a wandering gaze. Truthfully, I was not even sure if the patient was male or female. I sat stiffly upright in a bedside chair and self-consciously began my interview. After a few minutes, I noticed that he (the chart revealed he was indeed male) was not looking directly at me. I queried him about that, and he said he was blind.

Oh, happy day for me! I could relax, as he couldn't overtly critique my appearance. I slouched a bit in the chair and pulled out my complete multi-page history forms and just started casually jotting down each answer directly on them. After ten minutes of this, a nurse stopped at the door to the room and waved a can of Coca Cola. Without hesitation, the patient said, "No thanks, I'm not thirsty." "Wait a minute," I cried, "You told me you were blind!" He replied, "Yes, but only in one eye!" Gulp—my cover was blown. I got through the rest of the exam and sheepishly left the room to complete my report. A valuable lesson was learned that day: *Be precise in your questions and never make assumptions about responses.*

Two weeks later, I returned to the patient's room to check on him, as he had indeed had a successful heart transplant in the interim. Blessedly, he was making a good recovery and had no memory of our prior interaction.

To raise some cash during those first years, I worked as an EMI-Scan tech on nights and weekends. EMI (yes, the same British company that produced the Beatles records) had developed one of the first commercially available Computed Tomography (CT) scanners on the market, and MCV bought one. Unlike modern CT scanners today that complete myriad images and reconstructions in seconds, the old EMI was totally manual: only the patient's head could be imaged, and a water-filled bag needed to be inflated around the head before starting the scan. The table had to be manually cranked to each ensuing scan position, every image took about ten-fifteen minutes to acquire, and once an image appeared in the control room booth, I had to swing a Polaroid camera in front of the screen to snap a picture of it. After developing each Polaroid shot, I had to manually staple the photograph onto a blank sheet of paper in the patient's chart. A complete scan only acquired six-eight images and took well over an hour to complete. On a good day we could scan five or six patients, but there weren't many good days: not only would the equipment fail regularly, but women with hidden bobby pins in their hair would routinely pop the balloon, thus rendering the machine useless until another balloon was sent over from England. Despite all that, the EMI was considered leading-edge high-tech equipment, and Richmond was lucky to have one.

I also scraped together some cash by working as a radiology technician, snapping portable x-rays on bedridden patients throughout the hospital as ordered by attending physicians. My last hospital job was less noble, as I became a "plasma prostitute" for several months, selling enough of my plasma to the blood bank to buy three new tires for the Pinto. After that, my aversion to those huge needles was so strong that I couldn't stand the idea of returning to the blood bank again—I never bought a fourth tire.

Sue would occasionally catch a ride from Virginia Tech to Richmond on weekends during my first year, and we had fun exploring the city's attractions and sampling the local cuisine. Our donut-eating tradition continued as well. We would buy a dozen donuts to eat while watching Saturday night "creature features" on television. Dunkin Donuts had a promotion during that first year: for every dozen you bought, you got a card punch. After twelve punches, you were awarded a free dozen. We were awarded two free dozen during that promotion, and never gained an ounce…

In June of 1976, first year classes wound down and I headed back to Virginia Tech for my college graduation ceremony. Sue and I walked together in the procession and afterward our families got to interact a bit. It was a proud moment for both families, as Sue and I were the first on either side to graduate from college. Shortly thereafter, Sue left her dorm and moved to Richmond, where she had landed a job as a tenth-grade English teacher in a local public high school. Meanwhile, I got a haircut, donned my Air Force uniform, and went off for six weeks of USAF active-duty training. An annual summer active-duty stint was repeated throughout my medical school years and included assignments to Andrews AFB, Maryland (Family Practice), Lackland AFB, Texas (Internal Medicine), and Sheppard AFB, Texas, to learn how to be an officer in the USAF (including classes on leadership, saluting, marching, and proper wear of the uniform).

Sue and I knew early on that we were soulmates. Only true love could account for her being willing to sit in the formaldehyde smog permeating the gross anatomy lab, waiting for me to finish an intricate dissection. In the fall of 1976, I asked Sue to marry me (over a box of donuts, of course). The USAF determined our wedding date, as I had a very short window between classes ending and the start of an active-duty period. On July 23, 1977, we were wed in a small chapel in Centerville, Virginia, which had been used as a hospital during the Battle of Bull Run in the Civil War just over a hundred years previously. My sister Susan played the flute and my former college roommate, Tom Kent, was my best man. After the ceremony we flew to Jamaica for a wonderful but short 3-day honeymoon at the Runaway Bay resort. It was Sue's first time abroad, and the first of many foreign adventures to come.

Back in Richmond, we nested in a modest townhouse close to her school. We earned enough money now between us to put good food on our table, buy some new furnishings, and pay off the note on Sue's beloved bright orange "Love Bug" Volkswagen as well as her federal student loans.

During the third and fourth years of medical school, our large class was divided into smaller pods of around fifteen students. These pods then moved together on different rotations such as Cardiology, GI, OB/GYN, Pediatrics, Family Practice, Orthopedics, Surgery, Urology, etc. Our group of fifteen became close, and we still travel with one couple from that group, Bob and Anne Silverman, forty-five years after graduation. The hands-on education at MCV during each of those rotations was outstanding.

Beyond pure book-learning, we experienced daily real-life triumphs and tragedies during those rotations. On my OB/GYN rotation, I witnessed many young women coming in with unwanted pregnancies, but who were too poor to travel out of state for an abortion (abortions were tough to get in Virginia, but not as hard in nearby Maryland), and too uneducated to practice contraception. Late one late night I delivered a baby to a thirteen-year-old girl. When I asked her why she was having a baby at such a young age, she said it was to keep her baby brother company—she had already delivered another child the previous year at age twelve! When I asked another child mother the same question the following week, her reply was that "I really wanted a baby doll, but dolls cost money, and real babies are free!" Neither mother had any idea who the father was. These interactions shaped my views on abortion rights, and my feeling that the government should stay out of the fray and leave abortion decisions to the patient and her doctor. Period…

An experience during my Veterans Administration hospital (VAH) rotation taught me a lesson about clearly documenting observations. One afternoon, I saw one of my assigned patients angrily flipping through his chart at the nursing station. Upon seeing me, he rushed over and grabbed me by the collar, shouting, "You called me an SOB!" After a quick look at the offending entry he was referring to, I clarified that SOB was merely my abbreviation for Short of Breath. That was the last time I entered that particular notation in a patient's chart.

We had more free time during those electives and were able to attend numerous parties and social events throughout the year. One of our favorite holidays was Halloween, when Sue and I would create costumes from whatever we had in the townhouse (no store-bought items allowed) to come up with zany outfits. Sue was also a true partner in my medical career, helping me study for tests with books, notes, and flashcards. She took pride in our joint efforts when I got high marks, and we still laugh remembering how I got "Honors in Endocrine" and other specialties. With her support, I did well enough to be elected to the Alpha Omega Alpha national medical honor society—an achievement limited to the top ten percent of medical students.

In early 1979, most fourth year students nervously awaited the results of "Match Day." The Match was a nationwide process in which senior medical students interview for internships and residencies at different programs around the United States. They then rank their preferred programs in order, and at the same time the programs rank their applicants. On a single momentous day across the country, the best matches are announced, and the applicants know where they will be heading after graduation. The thirty or so of us in the military HPSP programs (Army, Navy, and USAF), however, were spared that. We had applied to one or two programs in each service and knew before the civilian students where we were to be assigned.

I received active-duty orders to report to the Wilford Hall USAF Medical Center on Lackland AFB in San Antonio a few short weeks after graduation, where I was to begin a three-year Internal Medicine residency. Cardiology staff at this same hospital ten years previously had told me I hadn't a prayer of ever flying with the USAF. Happily, I would later prove them wrong.

With two weeks free before my MCV graduation, Sue and I drove to San Antonio to look for housing. We purchased our first home, a small but new three-bedroom ranch in a subdivision a few miles from Wilford Hall. We hadn't enough savings left to pay for complete backyard landscaping, so bought half a pallet of sod and laid a strip of it every 3 feet or so crosswise on the dirt slope behind the house to cut down on erosion. I also broke up discarded rocks from other home sites with a sledgehammer to make some crude "mulch" around our sparse bushes. Several other medical residents purchased homes in the same subdivision, so the wives had a built-in support network while their spouses were at the hospital.

With several days remaining until graduation, we pulled out the trusty Rand-McNally Road Atlas to look for another spot to visit. Neglecting the scale of the map, we noticed that the Grand Canyon was only about three inches away. Off we went, westbound on a whim. After an eternity, we found the Grand Canyon, still swathed in snow in late May. The south rim was beautiful as we got there at dusk. Unfortunately, the Lodge had no room for us, so we set up our tent in the snow next to the parking lot and hung around the Lodge's cozy lounge until they kicked us out later that night. After a quick breakfast the following morning, we took a hike down into the canyon.

For us flatlanders, the effortless one-hour trip down was offset by a nearly three-hour rigorous return climb back up, requiring frequent rest stops to catch our breath in the thin air. We were ill-prepared for the hike: improper clothes, no food, no water, and no sunscreen. After a second miserable night in the tent, we realized that we needed to make a beeline back to Richmond to make it to graduation. We hopped back into the Pinto and raced over twenty-two hours non-stop from New Mexico to Richmond. What a miserable trip. We vowed never to be that unprepared for a trip again. That hard-won wisdom follows us to this day, and I always check the map legends for distance scales!

The MCV graduation ceremony went off without a hitch, shortly thereafter the movers packed us up, and once again we headed back to Texas to begin our next adventure.

Packed away were not only my rarely used paint brushes, but also any thoughts of flying for the next year, as my medical workload was about to explode. Little did I realize then that I would finally climb into a cockpit only eighteen months later, but my paint brushes would remain stored away for another decade.

CHAPTER 13

INTERNSHIP

Air Attacks, the Shah, and Desert One

Wilford Hall USAF Medical Center in San Antonio was the largest USAF hospital in the world with over 1100 inpatient beds and several outpatient clinics. It also sponsored the largest USAF post-graduate training program for residents and fellows in a multitude of specialties. The facility was called the "quaternary" USAF referral center (akin to Bethesda in the US Navy, and Walter Reed in the US Army); the most difficult cases from around the world were flown to Wilford Hall for evaluation and treatment.

My internal medicine internship schedule for the first year was grueling: 7 a.m. to 7 p.m. the first day, 7 a.m. the next day for a full shift and overnight stay in the hospital (a full twenty-four hours that middle day), and from 7 a.m. to 2 p.m. on the third day. This schedule repeated every third day for the entire first year in a seemingly endless and relentless cycle. Only two internal medicine interns and a resident covered the entire 1100 inpatients overnight; sleep was rare on those nights. In addition to the current inpatients and those admitted at night via the emergency room, the Aeromedical Evacuation flights from around the world would usually land in the evenings—not uncommonly you would get thirty minutes notice that ten admissions or more to your service would be arriving shortly. Ambulances transported these newest charges directly from the flight line to our Emergency Room entrance, often with minimal accompanying medical information. Instead of "Air Evacs," we in the trenches referred to those nightly flights as "Air Attacks." In addition, we cared not only for general medical ward patients, but also all those in the Intensive Care Unit (ICU). The grueling schedule unmasked one's true "inner self" during those gauntlets, when all the veneer of safe and sane working hours was ripped away. Life and death decisions had to be made on the fly several times a night. The learning curve was steep, but the sheer variety of patients and support of the nurses and ward staff was outstanding and made it tolerable—barely.

Embedded in those long hours spent in-house daily, several clinical anecdotes from that internship year are seared into my memory.

Two stories involved visiting allied troops from other countries who were training in Texas beside their USAF counterparts. In the early fall of 1979, a peculiar rash of Emergency Room admissions of Saudi Arabian troops occurred: they were being brought in with full-blown grand mal seizures. Of course, each seizure admission necessitated a full multi-day workup including brain CT scans to rule out tumors or cerebral bleeds and also painful spinal taps to culture fluid to rule out infection. Every one of those evaluations came up empty. The Saudis would be fine by the next day in the hospital and would return to their units upon completion of their lengthy complex negative evaluations. One day, a Saudi interpreter supplied a key piece of information: It turns out that having a seizure for a Saudi is the same as having a migraine would be in an American—it was a cultural thing! Said conversely, when a Saudi was under stress, he didn't get a headache, he got a seizure. From that time forward, we scaled back our evaluations of these "Seizing Saudis," as they were thereafter described behind closed doors. We learned the true value of an embedded translator to bridge cultural gaps.

Another enigma baffling residents and staff that year involved visiting Egyptian troops. Whenever an Egyptian troop was admitted for anything, standard lab and urinalysis samples were run on him just as they were routinely for all patients. The quirk was that *every one* of the Egyptians had microscopic blood in their urine—something rarely seen in Americans. Standard hematuria evaluation required kidney intravenous pyelograms (IVPs) and invasive bladder cystoscopies to rule out tumors or infection. No tumors were found, nor were any common urinary tract infections. What they all did have, however, was a rare parasitic infection called schistosomiasis. These parasites were endemic in the Nile River, where most Egyptians swam and bathed. Lengthy hospital stays to administer prolonged and often toxic anti-parasitic treatments were required to clear these infections. Not uncommonly, the weeks of treatment were so long that by the time we cleared up their parasites, the Egyptian troops were immediately rotated back to Egypt. What's one of the first things they did upon returning to Egypt? They, of course, resumed swimming in the Nile and were probably re-infected within days. New guidance eventually came out from our internal medicine department head: we were NOT to check a urinalysis on any admitted Egyptian from thence forward!

We learned over the year to expect the unexpected, especially when it came to strange infections: With the daily Air Attack flights from around the world, Wilford Hall saw everything from antibiotic resistant venereal disease to leprosy, tuberculosis, and scrofula.

Another medical and life lesson resulted from these examples: *Know your audience. Time researching the background of your co-workers, acquaintances, and patients is well spent, and facilitates quick and effective communications.*

One clinical episode leaned toward a biblical theme, and became legendary over time—I wouldn't have believed it had I not been there that night… On one routine overnight shift in the hospital, a rather corpulent psychiatry intern was paired with me to staff the hospital. This huge fellow loved to eat, could barely fit in a uniform, and was known on the wards as "Big Ed." Just before heading to the cafeteria for an 11 p.m. snack that fateful evening, Ed was called to a patient's room to pronounce him dead after a nurse couldn't arouse the patient or feel a pulse. Miffed at possibly missing a meal, Ed stormed quickly into the patient's room armed with his stethoscope, performed a cursory listen to the patient's chest, and plopped down on the bed, facing the grieving family to express his condolences. As he was in the midst of his speech, the family gasped and cried out as he felt movement on the bed behind him. He spun around to see the patient awake and sitting up in the bed. Not missing a beat, Ed yelled, "It's a miracle, it's a miracle," after which he ran out of the room and off to the cafeteria, leaving the family, patient, and nurse shell-shocked. News of Big Ed's escapade traveled quickly, and his ward moniker was changed instantly to Lazarus! Not unexpectedly, Lazarus was fired soon thereafter and left the residency.

Just prior to my arrival at Wilford Hall, the Shah of Iran was deposed and exiled in February 1979 during the Iranian Revolution, when the monarchy was overthrown to create the Islamic Republic of Iran. Because he had been a former friend and military ally of the USA, the Shah's fall from grace with Muslim clerics was mirrored by a similar fall of the USA's reputation in Iran as well. During the fall of 1979, Shah Pahlavi traveled to the USA to receive medical care for cancer in New York City. In New York he unfortunately suffered post-operative complications following a surgery that required prolonged hospitalization and recovery. Concerns for his safety in the metropolis arose so the White House looked for safer medical housing away from the limelight of New York or Washington, D.C. To that end, the Shah was air-evacuated for his continued medical care to Wilford Hall in December 1979, where his security could be better insured on a military installation. Ahead of his arrival, the Shah's advance team paid for renovations to a whole floor on one wing just to meet his lavish needs and lifestyle. Military security was beefed up around the hospital, including sharpshooters on the roof, guards posted around the facility and in the hallways, and armored personnel carriers on the front lawn. Everyone entering the hospital, including doctors, had to be hand-searched.

The Shah had been diagnosed with chronic lymphocytic leukemia (CLL) and required ongoing treatment for that at Wilford Hall.

A routine check to assess the status of a patient's CLL included a bone marrow biopsy. That painful procedure involved numbing up the posterior iliac crest (the "hip bone" that helps keep your pants up), inserting a large-bore Jamshidi needle through the skin and muscle at that site, and boring into the bone itself for about a centimeter. Suction would then be pulled on the needle hub, the whole needle twisted and turned, and the hollow needle then removed. If done correctly, a nice core sample of the bone marrow held inside the needle could then be sent to the pathologist for staining and analysis.

Senior residents performed these bedside procedures routinely. When it was determined that the Shah needed a bone marrow biopsy, however, he refused to let a "mere" resident touch him: he instead insisted that the Chief of the Hematology-Oncology service do the deed. Well, the Chief probably hadn't done a bone marrow in years. The residents took the Chief behind closed doors an hour or two before the scheduled biopsy and trained him by having him repeatedly stick the Jamshidi needle into a grapefruit.

At the allotted time, the nervous Chief marched down the hall and carried the sterile biopsy tray through the guarded swinging doors of the Shah's wing while we all waited anxiously down the hall. Thirty minutes later, the frazzled Chief emerged from the wing soaked in sweat with his shirt untucked and a used tray setup in his hands. Once reaching us, he cracked a huge smile, loudly announcing, "Ladies and gentlemen, I just poked the ass of the King of Persia!" Sighs of relief mingled with our laughter.

In April of 1980, international events would again directly impact Wilford Hall. In November of 1979 Iranian anti-US Muslim students overran the US Embassy in Tehran, capturing and holding sixty-six American hostages. A secret plan to rescue those hostages, code-named Operation Eagle Claw, was formulated and rehearsed at Hurlburt Field, Florida, and other sites in the USA over the ensuing months. The plan was executed in April of 1980 in a joint military operation involving both fixed and rotary wing aircraft operating in marginal weather conditions.

The rescue attempt ended in flaming disaster when two aircraft collided and burned at the staging site known as Desert One on the outskirts of Tehran. Many servicemen were killed, wounded, and burned. The wounded and burned patients were transported by the USAF aeromedical evacuation service to San Antonio, with some brought to Wilford Hall and others directly to the Burn Service at Brooke Army Medical Center. Although I did not directly care for any of those patients, I was one of the doctors in the hospital the night they arrived, and in a hastily formed receiving line at the hospital rear entrance the next evening when sitting President Jimmy Carter made a surprise visit to the survivors. As he passed down the hospital's line and shook hands with each of us, he looked as though he had aged ten years overnight. He took the tragedy personally. At that moment, none of us were Democrats or Republicans—we were all Americans mourning an awful loss.

Though I hadn't realized it until then, I had had another cross-link with Operation Eagle Claw a month previously. In early March 1980, a forty-year-old USAF LTC Special Operations pilot was admitted to me with a pathologic fracture of his humerus (upper arm bone). A humerus fracture in an otherwise healthy forty-year-old is extremely rare, and evaluation found that he suffered from an advanced kidney cancer called renal cell carcinoma. The kidney cancer had spread to his bones and caused a fracture at a weakened spot in his arm—his prognosis was dismal. When I sat to discuss his treatment options, however, his only concern was whether he had at least six weeks to live, and how soon he could be released. He confided that he was involved with an ultra-secret and urgent critical mission involving national security that he could not discuss with me. He was assigned to Hurlburt Field, FL, and was going to check out of Wilford Hall shortly, with or without my permission, and whether we could help him or not. Our Orthopedic Service placed a rod through the fracture site and forty-eight hours later he was gone. I can only presume he was integrally involved with planning and executing Eagle Claw a few short weeks later.

I never forgot that selfless patient or his unusual presentation with renal cell carcinoma. Later in my career, while at Stanford, I picked up two more identical cases and began teaching colleagues that one of the first studies to get in a young adult presenting with a humerus fracture not associated with trauma was a renal ultrasound to look for an unexpected cancer. My peers labeled this clinical axiom "Johnson's rule."

Despite the incredible workload during internship, Sue and I still had a great year in Texas. Sue taught tenth grade English at John Jay High School in southwest San Antonio. When not working, we explored the Spanish Missions, River Walk, museums, and many other attractions in the area, and even slipped away for a brief Colorado ski vacation with another resident and his wife. To keep Sue company during my days away from home, we adopted our first "starter child," a Samoyed puppy we named Katy. A pure white Nordic breed probably wasn't the greatest choice of pet for a new home with a dirt backyard and a blisteringly hot Texas summer. We had to give Katy a bath almost daily and still loved her even after she ate all three of my newly planted banana trees, roots and all.

Many memorable patients from my internship year come to mind, including a General Officer with hiccups who refused to blow into a paper bag (yes, that works), and a middle-aged woman with pulmonary problems. During her exam, I noticed numbers tattooed on her left forearm. We had a lengthy emotional discussion as she related her experience thirty-five years before as a prisoner in a Nazi concentration camp. She described the medical experiments performed on her—she had been repeatedly placed in an altitude chamber, taken to a simulated high altitude, and exposed to multiple explosive decompressions to see how her body reacted. She had suffered burst eardrums, "the bends" in her joints, and collapsed lungs, among other things. The effects of those gruesome experiments still haunted her decades later.

Some encounters in the hospital were just, well, bizarre… One day I was asked to see an attractive young lady who had just flown in for a psychiatric evaluation for nymphomania. Upon entering her room, she immediately launched into why she needed to have sex daily, even to the point that she had corralled a man in the aircraft lavatory on the way to Wilford Hall the day before—on each leg of her flight. Why was I, an internist, consulted? She was complaining of pain in her groin and lumps in each breast and wanted to be examined—thoroughly! My internal red flags screamed out. I got two female nurses to chaperone a quick and cursory exam to make sure there were no masses or indication of appendicitis and then fled the ward after making a quick call to the referring psychiatrist stating that he needed to get to work, pronto!

One aspect of internship involved rotating through a variety of medical wards every four-six weeks over the year. As it happened, I was assigned to multiple oncology wards over those months, as a lot of cancer treatment for USAF active-duty, dependent, and retired personnel took place at Wilford Hall. Many of those cancer patients were on national clinical research trials. As opposed to the crude experiments conducted during WWII in concentration camps, these oncology trials were carefully created, controlled, and administered by the National Cancer Institute (NCI) or its designees. Scientific as well as ethical review boards were involved with each proposed trial, often years before the trial was approved to enroll patients. I was intrigued by these trials and the brave and selfless patients who agreed to participate, all hoping to improve their lot while simultaneously advancing knowledge in the attempt to eradicate cancer.

As low man on the totem pole, it was my duty as an intern to help order tests and record the results and physical exams for enrolled patients in conjunction with the clinical research associate assigned to each patient. Forms needed to be precisely and accurately completed for submission to the NCI-affiliated organization responsible for the trial (there was a virtual alphabet soup of these organizations, including the NSABP, RTOG, ECOG, etc.).

I learned that there are four types of human clinical trials. Phase I trials involve new medicines or procedures that are fresh from the laboratory and have shown promise in animal models. The main objective of these trials is not to treat a particular cancer, but rather to determine how best to administer the medicine or procedure. If testing a drug, for instance, how high a dose and how frequently can it be given before the toxicities it causes are prohibitive? As you can imagine, patients on Phase I trials need to be evaluated thoroughly and frequently around the clock; they can often only be enrolled where special unit beds are available for that purpose. Although risky, these trials are imperative.

If a safe drug schedule is determined by the Phase I trial, it can be considered for a Phase II trial. These trials use the new drug at the maximum safe dose to test its effectiveness against a particular cancer. All patients on the Phase II trial get the same drug.

If data collected from a Phase II trial suggests that the drug is indeed helpful in treating a particular cancer, it might be considered for a Phase III trial. These trials are large and often conducted across many Cancer Centers around the nation. In the Phase III scenario, the best current standard of practice treatment is compared to a program incorporating the new drug or therapy. Treatments on one research arm or the other are assigned randomly and a Phase III trial is thus appropriately called a "randomized clinical trial." These trials often enroll hundreds of patients and involve massive data collection, collation, and review efforts by large organizations. They are the acid test to see if a new drug or technique will improve the lot of a cancer population, and often take many years to complete and analyze.

Finally, if a new drug is approved for cancer treatment, the Food and Drug Administration (FDA) might still require the drug manufacturer to perform a Phase IV trial, also known as an "aftermarket" study. In this case, the manufacturer will continue to collect outcome data on treated patients for years.

By far the most common studies we conducted at Wilford Hall were of the Phase II or III type. Although they involved significant extra work and meticulous charting, I became intrigued with this realm of clinical research, and the pursuit of advancing knowledge through these trials later became a lifelong pursuit.

In contrast to the excitement of being on the leading edge of oncology research on the wards, I found the weekly outpatient internal medicine clinic both frustrating and boring. In those clinics, we saw patients with routine medical problems like colds and flu, as well as complex issues involving hypertension, diabetes, kidney failure, arthritis, and obesity. As the year wore on, I grew unhappy practicing that kind of medicine. No one ever really got rid of those chronic medical problems: they were merely managed. For example, once you became diabetic, you remained a diabetic; once hypertensive, you were always at risk for hypertension, etc… Another frustrating management problem was obesity: One patient I saw week after week kept gaining weight despite all the dietary and exercise counseling I had provided. In frustration, I finally gave her a logbook and asked her to return in two weeks after recording everything she had eaten so that I could do a calorie count. She returned at the appointed time and handed me the logbook. After totaling the food calories she had recorded, it was clear that she should have lost weight. Our scales told a different story: she had put on another couple of pounds. Baffled as I sat with her adding up her caloric intake, she pulled out a Twinkie from her purse and wolfed it down. I scanned the diary and saw no mention of any other Twinkies. When I asked her about this, she looked me in the eye and said, "Well, a Twinkie isn't a food, it's a snack. I don't record my snacks!" I was dumbfounded. It began to dawn on me that perhaps internal medicine was not my cup of tea. With my personality, I needed a specialty in which I either cured a problem or didn't.

Nearing completion of a fourth month of Hematology/Oncology wards, I noted that although most of my patients were miserable from their cancers or the toxic chemotherapy we were administering, there was one completely different group. Those patients were disappearing daily down to the basement for radiation therapy treatments. Over a short time, their pain was going away, their tumors were shrinking, and they were smiling. What was this magic? I followed a patient down to the Radiation Therapy department one afternoon to find out.

In that clinic I met two radiation therapy physicians, known as radiation oncologists. These fellows explained the ins and outs of using radiation particles and beams to treat cancer and gave me a textbook about the specialty for me to read. They were enthusiastic and happy in their work, and the clinic had a very upbeat vibe.

Using radiation to treat cancer was not new: Madame Curie and her husband discovered radium in 1898 and only one year later used radium paste to treat a large skin cancer. In the decades since, x-ray beams had occasionally been used by radiologists to treat cancer, with progress largely made in Europe at the Curie Institute in Paris, the Royal Marsden in London, and the Radiumhemmet in Stockholm. By the late 1960's, radiation therapy in the USA split off from diagnostic radiology as a unique specialty, requiring three-four years of training after internship to become board-certified. In the 1970's and 80's, the preeminent training institutions in the USA for what became known as Radiation Oncology were the Joint Center in Boston (a partnership of five hospital teaching centers including Harvard and Brigham & Women's' hospitals), the M.D. Anderson Cancer Center in Houston, and Stanford University Medical Center in Palo Alto, California.

Over the next week, I read the loaned textbook from cover to cover and was enthralled: this was the specialty for me. It was very hands-on with patients but required a high level of expertise not only in clinical oncology but also in radiobiology and radiation physics. I had loved physics since my high school experience in Newburgh, and the science just made sense to me.

My kaleidoscope spun, and a new vision appeared—upon returning the book, I expressed my interest in becoming a radiation oncologist. The staff docs informed me that there were only six or seven slots in the entire USAF, but that I was in luck on two counts: first, at least two of those USAF radiation therapy physicians were approaching retirement, and second, I was speaking to the two USAF docs charged with approving any replacement applicants for training! The military had no residency programs in Radiation Oncology; an applicant would have to apply independently to the civilian programs, and if accepted, would need USAF approval to attend such a program. Although time was getting short, I made phone calls, wrote letters, and hopped on a plane to interview at the Joint Center and at Stanford (one of the docs at Wilford Hall had already been trained at M.D. Anderson, so he suggested I apply to one of the other powerhouses to round out the USAF expertise).

Both institutions were outstanding, and because my resume was solid and I would be a free body to either institution (the USAF was going to keep me on active-duty during the training, so the institution didn't have to find any extra funds to add me), I was accepted to both programs. Both residencies would begin a new training year within a matter of weeks.

Sue and I discussed our options: Boston or Northern California. She was happy with either, so it was up to me. My final decision was based on a hot dog…

A hot dog? Let me explain: When a resident candidate visits an institution, it is customary for more senior residents to take him or her out for lunch between interviews to get to know the candidate better. The Department supplies funds for these lunch outings. My first interview was in Boston, where lunch consisted of stepping out of the hospital entrance to a street corner hot dog vendor. It was a typical April day in Boston: windy, freezing, and raining. I think our "lunch" took about ten minutes. The very next week, I went the other direction to San Francisco and then down to Stanford in Palo Alto about twenty minutes south. The weather was also typical for there: seventy-two degrees, sunny, and delightful. Between interviews, the residents took me to the nearby Stanford Mall, where we dined for over an hour at Mama's Restaurant, where I ate Crab Louis and chocolate torte. There was no comparison in terms of quality of life.

Both programs were stellar in terms of training, but I couldn't pass up the lifestyle in the Bay Area. I accepted the position at Stanford and prepared to head west from San Antonio just six weeks later.

After a flurry of last-minute preparations, it was soon time for Sue and me to hit the road again, this time with Katy. In our two-car caravan

Chapter 13

we set out on I-10 in early June 1980. This was way before cell phones, so we talked to each other during the drive using those trusty walkie-talkies my dad had purchased for me long ago in Nebraska, the same ones I had used to talk to that RAF bomber aircrewman. Our trip was sidelined for two days in west Texas, as Sue was hit with an awful case of food poisoning. Once back in the saddle, we made good time to the southeastern California desert, up the central valley and over into the Bay Area. Until we could find a rental to live in, we were able to stay in the Navy Visiting Officers Quarters on NAS Moffett Field, near San Jose.

CHAPTER 14

STANFORD

Becoming a Radiation Oncologist and a Private Pilot

1980 saw new happenings in both the USA and abroad. The Union of Soviet Socialist Republic (USSR) hosted the Summer Olympics along with their mascot, Misha the Bear. The Carter administration elected to boycott those games for political reasons, so American athletes did not participate. Newly-elected President Ronald Reagan was sworn in in early 1981, and the Iranian hostages were finally released.

By 1983, world tensions increased as the USSR shot down a Korean Airline flight that had strayed off course, and World War III was only averted by an alert Soviet junior officer who believed an indicated launch alert against the USSR was a false alarm. He was correct, and a USSR retaliatory strike was not initiated. The rise of anti-West radical Muslim factions escalated as a suicide bomber inflicted massive casualties among US Marines at the Beirut barracks in Lebanon, killing and wounding over three hundred people. The only real bright note in 1983 was our return to space with the launch of the new Challenger Space Shuttle, over eleven years after I had abandoned my aeronautical engineering major in favor of the biological sciences.

In the San Francisco area, finding affordable lodging wasn't easy, as being saddled with a dog, lawnmower, and washer/dryer equipment precluded apartment living. We finally rented a small 900 square foot 1940's bungalow, replete with rusted shut windows and rats in the attic, for a monthly fee that was triple what our monthly mortgage had been in San Antonio for our new home!

Sue explored applying for another teaching position but found out that California required all teachers to have master's degrees. I found that ironic, as the high school education I had received in Texas and New York (where teachers only needed Bachelor's degrees) ten years previously had been clearly superior to what I had experienced in California. As we were paying both a mortgage in Texas and rent in California, though, Sue needed a job for us to survive. She eventually became a Civil Servant, working as a Technical Publications Editor for the Hydrology Division of the US Geological Survey (USGS) based in nearby Menlo Park. She loved that job, and we made a whole cadre of interesting friends outside the medical community.

Eventually, we sold our house in Texas, and miraculously didn't lose money on the deal. I was so relieved that I decided to finally resurrect an old dream—as a reward for surviving internship, and now with a few extra dollars in my pocket, I decided to finally take flying lessons at the Navy Flying Club on NAS Moffett. To my delight, Sue opted to take lessons with me. After completing ground school on nights and weekends after work, we both ended up soloing in the fall of 1980. Sue decided to end her training then, as she didn't feel comfortable with all the military acronyms being spouted over the scratchy aircraft radios near the Navy airfield. I persisted and was awarded my FAA Private Pilot certificate in early 1981. A major life goal realized at last! From that day forward, flying has always provided a welcome release from daily worries and a chance to see our world from a beautiful and different perspective.

After initial training in the petite Cessna-152, I worked up to more complex and larger Cessna and Piper aircraft. (Figure 10) Hours were spent exploring the airports and terrain all around northern California and travelling as far south as San Diego (and even back to the tiny high desert town of Victorville for my tenth high school reunion). I flew all over with Sue and other Stanford friends, and even flew songster Joan Baez' son for a night flight over the Bay area with Tony Howes, my Stanford colleague who had befriended Joan.

Over the next three years our medical life was also salted with non-medical mussel fests on the beach, backpacking in the Marble Mountain Wilderness, psychedelic Grateful Dead parties (I still have some Jerry Garcia ties), bluegrass festivals, and ski trips to the Lake Tahoe area. Every hike with the USGS folks included an educational tour of geological formations and local flora along the way. The mantra at Stanford was to work hard and play hard. Sue and I took that approach to heart, and when I wasn't in the clinic, we were off exploring California and the entire northwestern USA at every opportunity.

Locally, I also enjoyed exploring the beautiful Stanford campus itself, including its eucalyptus groves, the Stanford mausoleum, the athletic fields (we saw quarterback John Elway, later star of the Denver Broncos, play) and tennis courts (John McEnroe had recently graduated).

A curious event occurred one day when I decided to visit the grand Stanford Engineering Library. While perusing some remote stacks, I noted papers sticking out of a book. Succumbing to my "neatnik" tendencies, I pulled out the book from the stack to properly reinsert the pages. As I did so, some pages fell to the ground, emblazoned with the red stamps "Confidential" and "Secret" across the tops. Looking closer, they appeared to be blueprints and diagrams of portions of the Space Shuttle. Something was definitely wrong with this scenario. Being on active duty in the USAF at the time, and in the thick of the Cold War, my first obligation was to call the legal authorities at the nearest military facility to report this discovery. I held on to and later turned over the documents to the Naval Investigative Service from Moffett NAS later that day. They indicated that I had stumbled on a clandestine drop for foreign agents: A spy had somehow obtained classified material from the nearby NASA Ames Research Center and was about to deliver it to his/her handler. I am not sure what happened with the ensuing investigation but noted a few years later just how much the Russian Buran space plane resembled our Shuttle! The Naval agents had quipped the day I met with them that the safest place in the USA during a nuclear war with the USSR was Silicon Valley, as the Soviets would never bomb their biggest source of research and development.

My training program at the Stanford University Medical Center Department of Radiation Therapy was outstanding in all respects. The field of Radiation Therapy was exploding with new technologies and techniques at that time. Just a few years before my arrival, the first medical linear accelerator (now the backbone of radiation centers worldwide) had been developed just down the street at Varian Industries and installed at Stanford. By 1980, that first linear accelerator (LA1) had been donated to the Smithsonian Institution, but LA2 was still active in our department, and we also operated two even newer machines, as the close collaboration between Stanford physicists and Varian engineers expanded technological boundaries. Prior to linear accelerators (linacs), the only practical high energy machine available to treat cancer was the Cobalt-60 machine, a comparatively primitive instrument used in many centers around the world. With that device, treatment was administered by dragging a radioactive chunk of Cobalt-60 to an open window in the lead-shielded head of the machine. Gamma rays would then shine down on the patient lying underneath until the chunk was pushed back away from the open slot after a predetermined time. Linacs, on the other hand, generated even higher energy photon beams from scratch, using a small particle accelerator in the head to create highly focused beams. The beams could deliver the same dose to a tumor more accurately in a fraction of the time required by the old Cobalt machines, with far fewer side effects.

Many leading experts in the field staffed the Stanford department, including Dr. Henry S. Kaplan, who along with Dr. Saul Rosenberg had developed the first curative standard treatment programs for Hodgkin's disease and various lymphomas using a combination of radiation therapy treatments and a chemotherapy cocktail called MOPP. Patients would travel to Stanford from around the world for treatment of these diseases, and one of the resident's duties was to escort and navigate these VIP guests through the process. I helped care for a panoply of patients ranging from California central valley farmers to Italian judges, and even an elegant older woman from Brazil who spoke no English. Despite the language barrier, she and I got along well, and upon completion of her treatments, she presented me with a biography (in Portuguese) of her life. After her departure, I sought out a Portuguese translator at Stanford to reveal what the book was about and who she was. As it turned out, she was a close confidant and travelling companion of Ernest Hemingway in the 1920's, and was one of a group of disillusioned musicians, writers, and poets in post-WWI Paris described as the "Lost Generation" by Gertrude Stein. Sadly, through the years since, her book and name have escaped me.

The serious nature of our training and work in the department was occasionally salted with bits of humor from the patients themselves. Once I entered an exam room to examine a young breast cancer patient returning for routine follow-up care only to find two patients undressed and ready to be examined rather than one. They were both young women with breast cancer who had become fast friends during their treatment process and had decided to return to the clinic together afterwards. One had undergone a mastectomy while her friend had undergone a lumpectomy. As the appointment was winding down, one giggled to the other, "Should we tell him?" The other grinned and told me, "Guess what, Doctor J? We are writing a book about our different breast cancer experiences here. Want to know the title?" "Sure, what is it," I replied. "We're calling it *A Tale of Two Titties*. Our editor isn't too pleased with that title, but we've assured him that it will be a 'breast seller'." Ugh…

Other luminary professors in the department included the Chairman, Dr. Malcolm Bagshaw, who was internationally renowned for the development of radiation therapy as an alternative to radical surgery for the management of prostate cancer; Dr. Don R. Goffinet, who was pioneering new techniques of brachytherapy for head and neck and other cancers; Dr. Richard Hoppe, who was developing new research protocols for lymphoma, including a rare skin lymphoma called mycosis fungoides; Dr. Sarah Donaldson, a world-renowned Pediatric Oncology researcher and clinician; and Dr. C. Norman Coleman, a stellar physician who was board-certified in both Radiation and Medical Oncology and a pioneer in combining the two regimes to get a synergistic (1+1= 3) effect on various cancers. He was also instrumental in the development of various drugs to act as radio-sensitizers: drugs given to a patient just prior to a radiation treatment to improve the "hit" on a tumor.

Norm took a special interest in me and was a great mentor over the next three decades; he recognized in me a desire to develop and conduct leading-edge cancer clinical trials and guided me for years. Norm went on to become Chairman of the prestigious Joint Center for Radiation Therapy in Boston, and later a premier researcher and investigator at the NCI. While at the NCI, he co-founded the ICEC (International Cancer Expert Corps) and asked me to join their Advisory Board. The ICEC even today serves as a resource to the Third World and industry as it tries to improve the care of cancer patients in less developed nations around the world, and I am honored to have had a very small part in that initiative. A photo of the Stanford Radiation Therapy Department physicians in 1983 (including both faculty and residents) is shown in Figure 11.

In addition to my workload at Stanford, the USAF also sent me to specialized courses reflecting another side of the radiation world—the world of nuclear warfare. In the fall of 1980, I was selected to attend a course entitled "The Medical Effects of Nuclear Weapons" held at the Armed Forces Radiobiology Research Institute (AFRRI) in Bethesda, Maryland. Later, during my brief Stanford tenure as a professor, I was able to use some of that material (non-classified, and with approval) to deliver an hour-long lecture on the physics of what transpires during the first three seconds of a thermonuclear detonation to a packed auditorium at the Medical Center.

That AFRRI training also came in handy in the spring of 1989, when I was invited back to AFRRI as part of a quiet project to review results of the medical assistance we had provided the USSR immediately after the 1986 Chernobyl nuclear reactor disaster in Ukraine. We had sent teams to assist the Soviets with bone marrow transplants, etc., for the local heroes who selflessly subjected themselves to lethal or near-lethal doses of radiation while trying to contain the spreading radiation contamination at the site.

My academic interests flourished at Stanford, as I performed clinical research, wrote clinical trials, published numerous articles, presented at national meetings, made wonderful connections with international leaders in cancer research, and in general developed a life-long passion for being at the "bleeding edge" of the crusade to take down cancer. While there, I developed and patented a device to shave forty-five minutes off the operating room time for breast cancer patients in whom we were implanting temporary Iridium-192 seeds. For my invention, I earned a USAF Patent Award for Air Force Invention #15,157 (Johnson Adjustable Breast Bridge, or JABB) from Wright-Patterson AFB, OH, in 1983. Ultimately, US Patent number 4,682,593 was issued in 1987 for the JABB after years of effort, modification, and testing. (Figure 12)

As Sue learned early on in our courtship, I was never shy to ask a question, nor answer one, especially if I could infuse a bit of humor in my response. That trait could have landed me in big trouble on one occasion during my last year on "The Farm," as Stanford was called locally.

Every week, a large Head & Neck Tumor Conference was held in the ENT Department. The routine was to have several new or problematic cancer patients come to the clinic in the morning where they would be examined by the Radiation Oncology residents and ENT fellows along with the faculty, after which all the staff would adjourn to a large conference room to discuss treatment options for those difficult cases. There were perhaps thirty-forty attendees at those conferences including doctors, nurses, and ancillary staff.

Both the ENT Department and the tumor conference were chaired by a chain-smoking but brilliant ENT surgeon who was known to be merciless in his grilling of all involved staff about tumors, exams, presentations, and treatment options. The Chairman would work his way up that ladder of staff, until he left each, in turn, drenched in sweat from his verbal harangues and challenges.

One patient I had examined that morning was the matriarch of a wealthy and prominent San Francisco family. She had a long history of a rare slow-growing tumor in the mouth called an adenoid cystic carcinoma. I knew that those tumors didn't respond to chemotherapy or radiation treatments very well, and that even after surgical removal, they tended to recur. Indeed, that had happened to this woman each time after several surgeries the Chairman had performed in the past. There was also a legend that she was so appreciative of the surgeon's efforts over the years that she had given him a Ferrari sports car! Well, she was back now with another recurrence.

The Chairman stood chain smoking at the front of the conference room and as usual began grilling everyone in sight. As he ran out of victims, he looked my way and said, "Well, Dr. Johnson, would YOU treat this woman with radiation?" I stood up, and before my brain could put the brakes on my mouth, I blurted out, "Well, if she gave me a Ferrari I might!" After some sharp gasps in the audience, the room went deathly quiet as he stood there staring at me, motionless. He was motionless for so long that the ash on his cigarette fell unabated to the floor. "Oh brother," I thought, "There goes my residency." Just at that moment, he started to snicker. The snicker became a belly laugh, as he howled, "But it was only a used Ferrari!" Tension in the room broke and laughter erupted all around. I think I was the first person to speak back to him in recent memory. After that, he and I became good friends. Phew, I had dodged a bullet!

Thanks to the connections of a junior professor at Stanford, Dr. Anthony Howes, I had the opportunity to do a clinical rotation abroad at the Ludwig Institute for Cancer Research, housed at the Addenbrooke's Hospital in Cambridge, England, from January-April of 1983. This renowned facility, home of researchers Watson and Crick, featured their original wooden DNA model on display in the lobby. I was under the supervision of Dr. Karol Sikora, Director of the Institute, who was one day destined to become Chief of the Cancer Program of the World Health Organization, and a luminary in the cancer world. In addition to clinic duties, I participated in monoclonal antibody research, investigating using them to target advanced breast cancer. Karol and I published a paper together while I was there and like my Stanford faculty, he fostered my interest in clinical research.

British oncology care in those days was interesting; in many cases, patients wouldn't even be told that they had cancer, much less sign an informed consent. I always wondered just what they thought they were being treated for. When I queried attending consultants about this, they told me that their patients did not want to hear the word cancer; furthermore, some thought the practice of obtaining informed consent in the USA was cruel and uncalled for. Views on curability of cancer in general by some older consultants (who we would call attending physicians in the USA) seemed a bit archaic at times: On one occasion a 21-year-old fellow who had been treated successfully for testicular cancer a few years before was admitted for acute appendicitis. In the USA, this would have precipitated emergency surgery. On that day in Addenbrooke's, however, the attending consultant refused to operate. When I piped up to ask why not (to the utter shock of the local registrars, who would never think of questioning a consultant), he responded simply that there was no sense wasting resources on a cancer patient, as "everyone" knew that all cancer patients die. We had to treat the fellow aggressively with antibiotics alone over the next several days, hoping that his infection would come under control before his appendix burst. In the end, the attack subsided, and he did fine.

In contrast, the daily clinic experience was very civilized. Clinics would start early in the morning but would come to a grinding halt at about 9 a.m. when the coffee trolley rolled into the waiting room: Doctors, staff, and patients alike all stopped what they were doing to socialize over a "cuppa" in the foyer. After about twenty minutes of this, everyone resumed his or her place and the clinic work continued. The same routine was repeated at 4 p.m. every day, but with a tea cart. The registrars (as they called residents there) would regularly pop out at midday to a nearby pub for a pint and a ploughman's lunch. Teams of registrars (including me) would be assigned once or twice a week to travel to outlying clinics up to an hour away to serve the local patients. Addenbrooke's was so large that it had dedicated staff athletic facilities and a staff swimming pool. There were at least two physician lounges in the hospital, and both were equipped with a full bar! Surgeons would pop in between cases in their scrubs and boots for "a quick one to steady the nerves." To quote The Wizard of Oz, "we weren't in Kansas anymore…"

Sue and I rented a small flat in the nearby village of Trumpington. I would walk across the fens and over turnstiles to get to the hospital every morning in my Wellies boots. We rented a beat-up stick-shift right-hand drive Volvo from an ambulance driver at the hospital so we could tour the countryside. Every weekend, we would slip away to another corner of the United Kingdom, visiting Portsmouth along the southern coast, London, Brighton, Dover, Bathe, Stonehenge, Stratford upon Avon, the Lake District, Hadrian's Wall, and Edinburgh, in addition to myriad small villages, cathedrals, and castles throughout the region. We had a routine in that reverse-controlled car: the driver in the right front seat would steer and handle the clutch, brakes, and gas pedal, and when an upshift or downshift was needed, he would call out to the front passenger to move the shifter while he held the clutch in. Not an elegant solution, surely, but it made sense to us at the time, and it served us well as we put thousands of kilometers on the car over those months.

At end of my externship in Cambridge, we left chilly England via hovercraft from Dover to Calais, and then journeyed by overnight train to Venice for a few days of sunshine and relaxation before heading back to Frankfurt, and a flight home to the USA. The trip from Venice to Germany took place over the Easter holiday and our train stopped in Innsbruck, Austria, for a few hours, affording Sue and me an opportunity to walk around the town and window-shop (everything was closed for the holiday). On the walk, we saw a beautiful set of etched crystal glassware through a window. On the shop-front sidewalk, Sue drew a sketch of the glassware that we carried back to Stanford. Once in

California, we wrote a blind letter back to the shop indicating our interest in buying a set of the crystal and included a large bankers draft for a bunch of Austrian currency along with Sue's sketch. Weeks later, an entire set of crystal glasses arrived at our home, all delivered without a scratch.

Unfortunately, travelling from Frankfurt to the USA turned out to be a lot easier for the crystal shipment than it was for Sue and me. Our plan had been to both fly back to the East Coast on a USAF space-available (Space-A) cargo flight. From there, we would travel to Alexandria, pick up our dog Katy who had been my parents' guest during our Cambridge time, and then fly commercially back to San Francisco. Unfortunately, the USAF sergeant staffing the Air Mobility Command transportation desk at Wiesbaden Air Base in Frankfurt was not so enamored with that plan.

To back up, I had been allowed by the USAF to attend the Cambridge training rotation on what is called a Permissive TDY (temporary duty) status: I would remain on active duty and still receive my monthly pay and benefits but would have to pay for travel expenses out of my own pocket. After dropping off Katy in Alexandria in early January, my parents had driven us to Dover AFB, Delaware. We had then flown from Dover in the belly of a giant USAF C-5A Galaxy transport, sharing the space with cargo headed for European bases. The price was right, something like $10 each for the ticket and another $1.85 for an in-flight box lunch. We landed in the United Kingdom at Mildenhall Air Base on a frigid January morning, walked out the front gates to a nearby bus stop, and rode from there to nearby Cambridge. Our plan was to reverse the process in April from Wiesbaden Air Base back to the USA.

To fly Space-A, the active-duty service member (me, in this case) must be in uniform for the flight. The sergeant manning the desk at the Wiesbaden AFB terminal, however, told me that Sue couldn't fly back Space-A, as spouses were not entitled to fly with someone on a Permissive TDY status. When I tried to make a stink, claiming that since they'd already flown both of us to Europe months earlier, they we obligated to fly us both back home, he was not amused. As tempers flared he threatened to back-charge us several thousand dollars for that initial trip to Europe she had taken with me in January!

Our only option was to get Sue on a civilian flight back to somewhere on the USA East Coast from the civilian Frankfurt Airport terminal, situated on the other side of the runway (the Air Base and civilian airport shared the runway). We hopped in a taxi and headed around to the civilian terminal where we were luckily able to get Sue a last-minute ticket to New York City on Lufthansa. I was nervous at the civilian terminal, as Americans were being targeted by extremists in Germany, and we had been warned by the Defense Intelligence Agency before heading overseas to never wear our uniform in public while off base in Europe. Nevertheless, I saw Sue safely to the gate and rushed back to the military side of the field hoping to snag a seat on an evening flight back to the USA; there was a C-141 Starlifter due to leave in a few hours, destined to land at McGuire AFB, New Jersey, not too far from New York City. The transportation desk had previously told me I had high enough priority to get a Space-A seat on that plane, but when I checked back in, they announced that the plane was not going to take either passengers or cargo when it headed out. This was a potential disaster logistically, as I had no way to let Sue know what was going on (this was way before cellphones, and she had already taken off, anyway).

I persevered by asking why the flight status had changed and was told there was a problem with the pressure seal on the rear cargo hatch, and the heaters in the main cargo area were inoperative, too. It was considered too risky to carry cargo, much less people, and the plane was limping home to McGuire with just a minimal aircrew to a get to a repair depot. I stressed the urgency of the situation to the desk person, who eventually took sympathy on me and agreed to talk to the pilot. The pilot, in turn, agreed to take me onboard as long as I realized the risks. "No sweat, just get me onboard," I replied. Thus, three hours later I was winging my way back to the USA in the bowels of a crippled cargo transport along with another passenger who'd also talked his way on. We sat there in sling seats along the side of the cavernous empty fuselage in a space big enough to hold several city buses.

The plane never lost pressurization, but it started to get cold. Really cold. My fellow passenger and I opened the suitcases at our feet and started donning every pair of slacks and shirts we could fit into to keep warm. For the last five hours of the flight, it was below freezing in the cargo hold. Eventually, the crew chief took pity on us and let the two of us rotate fifteen-minute stretches in the cockpit to warm up, as they had a separate heating system there. We landed safely in New Jersey, and either because of hypoxia, hypothermia, or stress, to this day I don't know how Sue or I got back to the Washington, D.C., area.

After a few days with my parents, we boarded a civilian flight back to San Francisco and Stanford, arriving just weeks before completing the program. One last hurdle stood in my way before obtaining board certification in Radiation Therapy: the dreaded Oral Boards. The Board process for our specialty required successfully passing two sequential exam parts—the Written Boards and the Oral Boards. The multiple day Written examination the previous fall was composed of one-third clinical medicine, one-third radiobiology, and one-third radiation physics questions. All three parts of that Written exam had to be passed before an applicant was allowed to sit for the Oral Boards the following June. I had passed all three parts of the Written Boards without issue and had then studied assiduously with my fellow residents several nights a week for nine months to prepare for the upcoming Oral Boards.

The Orals involved flying to a central location in Kentucky, where residents sitting for the exam from around the nation congregated. One floor of a hotel was set aside for the exam, and each candidate was assigned a start time at a particular room. He or she would then rotate through six adjacent rooms every thirty minutes to be grilled by different examiners on a one-to-one basis. Each examiner covered a different topic such as Pediatric cancer, GI cancer, Lung cancer, Head & Neck cancer, GYN cancer, etc. After completing the gauntlet, applicants departed for home while examiners tallied their scores. To achieve board certification, the applicant had to pass ALL six sections. The flight I took into Kentucky was abuzz with the chatter of anxious candidates. The flight out the day after the Orals was as quiet as a tomb.

In 1983, the Radiation Therapy Boards were the toughest in the nation: fewer than thirty percent of candidates passed. In the prior year, known as the year of the "West Coast Massacre," no one from Stanford or the University of California-Berkeley passed. No one… That was unheard of, and pressure was on all of us to excel.

Two weeks later, an envelope arrived in the mail announcing that I had successfully passed and was now a board-certified radiation therapist (the formal name was switched a few years later to radiation oncologist). Even better, my five other co-residents had all passed as well: Dr. Harvey Wolkov soon left to join the Sutter Radiation Oncology Group and became heavily involved with both Pediatric Radiation Oncology and the governance of various Radiation Oncology national committees. Dr. Mark Schray became faculty at the Mayo Clinic in Rochester. Dr. Ken Russell went to Washington state, where he came to hold leadership positions at the Fred Hutchinson Cancer Center in Seattle as well as the University of Washington Medical Center. Dr. Mary Austin-Seymour left for Harvard University, where she became faculty on the Proton Radiotherapy Project at the Massachusetts General Hospital. And finally, Drs. John Wells and Shyam Paryani, my future partners, headed east to private practices in and around northern Florida.

I had been told by the USAF to expect orders back to Wilford Hall in San Antonio in early July 1983. Upon returning from the Board exams in mid-June, however, a surprise awaited me. My orders had been rescinded and reissued with only ten days' notice. Rather than returning to Texas, the USAF assigned me just ninety minutes up the road to head the Radiation Oncology Department at the David Grant USAF Medical Center on Travis AFB, California, close to Vacaville.

To arrange for movers to get us to Travis on short notice, I needed help from the Travis AFB Finance and Housing offices. To expedite a meeting with those offices, I rented a small Cessna-152 from the

Moffett Navy Flying Club and flew it up to the huge runway at Travis. Travis AFB was a vital hub of the Military Airlift Command (MAC) and housed scores of large C-5A and C-141 transport aircraft, as well as KC-135 and later KC-10 tankers. The day I landed at the base to check in with the finance office, the tower controllers (who had probably just noticed that a "Navy plane" was inbound and probably hadn't worked with such a small and slow civilian trainer before) cleared me to approach and land. Increasingly anxious voices over the radio told me to speed it up, as there was a B-52 bomber setting up to land only three miles behind me, rapidly overtaking me at twice my airspeed! I dove for the runway and stopped so fast that I exited the concrete strip at the normal runway entry ramp where the typical massive transport or bomber aircraft performed pre-flight checklists before taking off. After the huge bomber whizzed by me mere seconds later and landed further down the runway, the tower came on frequency to ask me if I knew where I was going. I responded, "It's my first time here." The tower instructed me to stay put until a "Follow Me" truck came to lead me. Minutes later, a massive vehicle (about the size of a fire engine, and at least twice the size of my Cessna) with a large sign saying FOLLOW ME emblazoned on the back, found and guided me to a spot in front of Base Operations. My plane resembled a tiny gnat behind it. I was even more embarrassed when a contingent of four servicemen jumped from the truck as I stopped to place chocks around the wheels, carry a fire extinguisher just in case, and signal me to kill the engine. They had brought out the same team they used to park the massive C-5's (capable of carrying six city buses and towering over seventy feet in the air). Through the windows of Base Ops, uniformed folks in their flight suits were peering out at me, pointing and laughing at the scene. I sheepishly climbed out of the cockpit, raced over to the Finance office to arrange for our move, and then departed the base as quickly and quietly as I could.

Several days later, and in our cars this time, Sue and I cruised up the road to Vacaville to find a new home, and to don the uniform in earnest once again.

CHAPTER 15

TRAVIS AFB

Gateway to the Pacific, rebuilding, and flying adventures

Travis AFB lies halfway between San Francisco and Sacramento, California, just southeast of I-80 and only eight miles as the crow flies from Napa Valley. Sue, Katy, and I purchased another small ranch home in nearby Vacaville, a small agrarian community known for growing pecans and onions. The medical center on Travis AFB, named David Grant USAF Medical Center, is one of the five largest USAF hospitals in the world, serving as the tertiary referral center for the fourteen western United States and the entire Pacific basin including our bases as far west as Thailand, Korea, Japan, and the Philippines. For that geographic reach, Travis is known as the "Gateway to the Pacific."

Running my small department was quite an adjustment after leaving Stanford's nurturing womb surrounded by titans in their field. Despite its prominence in the USAF medical hierarchy, the radiation facilities upon my arrival in 1983 were archaic. The only megavoltage radiation equipment they had was an old Cobalt machine: a device I had read about in history books but had never actually seen. I had been spoiled with all the linacs at Stanford. Imagine graduating from the Sebring Racing School driving the latest racers and then having to compete in a dilapidated Model A jalopy. My predecessor had unexpectedly retired and moved to Alaska, leaving the staff in turmoil, so my first order of business was to get the department organized and the clinic up and running. As a pleasant incentive, I had just pinned on the golden oak leaves of a newly-promoted Major.

We were able to requisition a more refined Cobalt source that yielded tighter margins on the delivered treatment beams, which, in turn, reduced the side effects inflicted on our treated cancer patients. Through this and other equipment tweaks, we were ultimately able to provide decent treatment to a wide variety of patients.

Simultaneously, I put in request after request for the USAF Medical Service to purchase linacs for all five USAF hospitals providing radiation therapy services. I obtained letters of support from all the other USAF radiation oncologists as well and was essentially the squeaky wheel (or thorn in the side, depending on your point of view) that ran the request all the way up to the Pentagon. Cobalt units were relics from a bygone era, and I made that point in no uncertain terms up the chain. I knew I was either going to be lauded for my efforts or fired.

Luckily, the brass eventually came around, and linacs were purchased not only for David Grant, but also for all the other USAF facilities (Wilford Hall already had one by that time but needed a second). Though ultimately successful in my efforts to upgrade and enhance the external-beam equipment in the department, I was disappointed at the glacial pace of the government acquisition process; indeed, linac installation at David Grant was finally completed less than a year before I was to finish my four-year duty commitment.

Another necessary safety enhancement I pushed strongly for had to do with our Hot Lab's large inventory of tenuous and potentially dangerous Radium-226 needles. Titanium-encapsulated radium-filled rods had been used for brachytherapy implants since early in the twentieth century (brachytherapy means "close therapy" in Latin and describes treatments in which radioactive elements emitting alpha or beta particles, or low-energy gamma rays, are placed adjacent to or within tumors rather than using a high-energy external gamma ray or photon beam from a Cobalt unit or linac).

Radium is a natural radioactive element that decays over time to toxic radon gas, a radioactive gas that can easily spread around a room, contaminate surfaces, and be inhaled. Several times every year, a physicist had to inventory the sources and perform "swipe tests" on the outside of these radium needles to make sure there were no leaks. These checks had been going on for decades in an isolated room we called the Hot Lab on a workbench where a bulky lead chest housed trays filled with these needles. As the inevitable decay of radium occurred, radon gas pressure built up inside the needles until they burst. This was an accident waiting to happen and represented an unacceptable risk to my staff and my patients.

Elsewhere in the USA, radium needles had already been largely replaced by needles containing a far safer isotope called cesium-137. Cesium does not decay to a gas, so there was minimal risk of leakage. I went on another crusade to replace the entire stock of radium needles, having no idea what a firestorm this seemingly simple swap was to engender. The acquisition process to acquire new cesium needles took ages, as expected, but the real problem was getting rid of those old dangerous radium needles.

Radium was tightly controlled by the Nuclear Regulatory Commission (NRC), and all sources had to be routinely accounted for—we couldn't just throw these things out. By the time the USAF granted us permission to dispose of the radium, all radiation disposal sites in the country had closed, with one exception. The Hanford site in Washington State was still accepting radiation waste, but the process was detailed and laborious. I give great credit to my physicist and chief radiation therapy technologist for relentlessly bird-dogging the project through the various federal chains of approval to make it happen.

After months of choreography, the removal day came. An entire hospital parking lot was evacuated and cordoned off, surrounding a lone semi-truck and flat-bed trailer, a cement truck, and a stack of empty

55-gallon drums. Armed guards were placed at the crowd line to keep people away from the action. A hazmat team and my physicist checked off our inventory as they removed two needles at a time from the Hot Lab, placed each pair in a 55-gallon drum atop the semi-trailer, and then witnessed the cement truck fill each drum completely with concrete. After filling each container, the drum was sealed and proper paperwork attached. Keeping in mind that we had well over fifty needles in our lab, the event took all day.

As the last of the inventoried needles was checked off the list and the operation was about to wind down, I asked my physicist if he had gone over the lead containment box in the Hot Lab to make sure we hadn't left anything behind. Although he assured me that the inventory was complete, he begrudgingly agreed to pass a Geiger counter over the box. Ten minutes later, he returned flustered and red-faced: the box was still hot.

We eventually were able to turn the heavy receptacle upside down and out fell several more needles: needles that had not only escaped the inventory process sometime in the preceding decades, but needles that had not been swiped to look for leaks over that entire time! Several more barrels filled with these "extra" needles were added to the group on the trailer by day's end. We had dodged a bullet…

Our department was not very popular for the next week due to the inconvenience we caused by hogging all those parking spaces: the concrete-filled barrels had to cure before they were allowed on the roads to be hauled to the disposal site in Washington. Portable lights and guards twenty-four hours a day guarded our disposal inventory, and the huge parking lot remained closed to staff and visitors. I was ecstatic the day the truck was able to pull away and our hospital could resume a state of normality. A small mission, but huge headache, was over at last.

A careful inspection of the rest of the department soon unearthed another surprise: buried behind some boxes in the simulation room, I discovered a somewhat rare French Papillon device and all its supporting equipment. This device was being used in Europe for trans-anal endoscopic irradiation via intracavitary brachytherapy for rectal cancer, to avoid massive surgery and colostomies otherwise required even for early-stage patients. When I asked my longstanding Civil Service physicist about the unit, he stated that it had been requisitioned years previously by another radiation oncologist but had not been delivered until long after that doctor had left the service. My physicist had duly installed the machine when it arrived and calibrated it yearly, but it had never been used and was lost in time. I had never even seen this machine before, but after reading more about it, and the progress in avoiding colostomies in France, I decided to try it when an applicable case came along. Over the next two years, I treated three patients with a series of these treatments, all of whom had complete disappearance of their tumors and who were able to avoid major surgery. Unfortunately, during a room renovation in 1986, a worker dropped the unit and bent some irreplaceable parts. The machine was scrapped.

Over time, I enacted these and other initiatives to change the culture of the department as we strove for excellence. I encouraged my staff to be creative in bringing solutions to internal problems that they had seen but not commented on before. I had their backs and encouraged open communications about all things, be they good or bad. I put into practice a saying of my father's: "*Take care of your sergeants, and they will take care of you.*"

I told my staff, "Strive for perfection but realize we will never quite get there: All humans make mistakes, and all machines will occasionally hiccup, but if issues are recognized and taken care of promptly, we can minimize untoward results." Rather than assign personal blame for errors, we tried to identify system errors that could be improved. With this positive "can do" atmosphere, the morale and comradery of the staff improved dramatically. The number of treatment errors dropped precipitously from about 1 in 1000 to 1 in 10,000, and the clinic's efficiency rose commensurately.

Once we were on the right track, I announced that I was going to get us recognized and registered to participate in regional and national clinical trials. This was a very high bar and tough gauntlet to navigate, but we were successful in becoming an affiliate organization of several trial groups, including the regional Northern California Oncology Group (NCOG) and the national Radiation Therapy Oncology Group (RTOG), a rare feat for any Radiation Oncology practice, much less one at a military facility. Staff exuded pride as we offered world-class leading edge treatments to our patients. I even carved out time to author three clinical trials for these groups, related to the use of radiosensitizers to accompany daily treatments for prostate cancer.

Over the ensuing four years, I accepted more leadership responsibilities: I served on many David Grant hospital committees, including the Cancer Committee (Chairman) and Tumor Board (Chairman), and the Institutional Review and Radiation Safety Committees. In addition, I was appointed to several positions within the NCOG, including the Breast Committee (Co-Chairman), as well as the Radiation Sensitizer, Lung, Genitourinary (GU), Radiotherapy, and Lymphoma Committees. Nationally, I was the Principal Investigator for the RTOG at our institution. Finally, the American College of Radiology (ACR) asked me to serve a three-year term on the Manufacturers Liaison Committee on Radiation Oncology Equipment Development commencing in 1986.

On another academic note, Stanford appointed me as a Voluntary Clinical Faculty member for Radiation Therapy, a position I held for the ensuing four years. I had the opportunity to teach residents and attend clinics several times a month at the Stanford Radiation Therapy department and also served as a ward attending physician for six weeks yearly (I was only able to do the latter after we got a second David Grant radiation oncologist around 1985).

Ultimately, I was awarded a USAF Meritorious Service Medal for my efforts in the department but accepted it on behalf of our entire team's efforts, not just mine.

While at Travis AFB, Sue and I took full advantage of the on-base amenities, one of which was the Travis AFB Aero Club. I got checked out in several club aircraft, including Piper Archers and Arrows,

Chapter 15

Cessna-172's, Grumman Tigers, and even a Beechcraft T-34A Mentor. We used these Aero Club birds to travel all over the state, especially around Monterrey, the Bay Area and Lake Tahoe. I flew a plane for my weekly trip to/from Stanford for my faculty duties, as the weather was usually excellent, and enjoyed carrying my David Grant colleagues for fly-out lunches to area airports.

On one such trip, Sue and I flew to the Monterey airport an hour southwest to visit her former college roommate. She and her Naval-officer husband were assigned to the Defense Language Institute in that beautiful seaside community. After a pleasant day with them, we departed Monterey and headed back up the coast toward San Francisco. Air traffic controllers gave us permission to fly above the Golden Gate Bridge as we turned east and headed over the San Francisco Bay and Alcatraz penitentiary, enroute to Travis AFB. Unfortunately, this was one of those rare dicey weather days in northern California that dictated we dodge several storms before arriving safely home. Sue was not a happy passenger, and that trip planted the idea that someday I would get my instrument rating.

Sue and I developed a wonderful set of military friends and neighbors, and there always seemed to be fun activities in the area. Many small farming towns in the region held annual fairs to celebrate their local produce, and Vacaville was no exception; the annual Onion Festival featured local cuisine that was eye-watering, literally! We enjoyed winter ski trips to Lake Tahoe resorts and both spring and fall off-road adventures to explore ghost towns in our new International Harvester Scout sport utility vehicle.

After six years of marriage, our life was now stable enough to consider starting a family. In April of 1984 we were blessed with a beautiful daughter, Danielle Annette Johnson. We laughingly remember that during Sue's labor late the night before, we watched Tiny Tim and Vickie's nuptials on *The Tonight Show starring Johnny Carson* in the hospital delivery room. Danielle arrived in the wee hours of the following morning. There was no concept of paternity leave for fathers in those days; I had come to the hospital with Sue in my uniform, and after the delivery slept on the floor of my office for two hours. At 8 a.m., my routine clinic day began.

In January 1986, we mourned with the nation when the Space Shuttle Challenger exploded shortly after takeoff. Spirits in the Johnson household rose immeasurably just a few months later, when we were blessed with the birth of a healthy baby boy in June 1986—our son Michael Andrew Johnson. Mike also arrived in the wee hours of the morning but wasn't very patient: we barely made it to the hospital before he was born.

Just before Michael's arrival, however, another event rocked the world. In late April 1986, I was on a weeklong ASTRO Young Investigator Travel Grant Award sojourn to the renowned Radiumhemmet Cancer Center in Stockholm. While there, I had a chance to meet local relatives for the first time, and just before my departure they took me to dinner at a well-known restaurant in the city's old quarter. Fem Små Hus (The Seven Cellars) was serving a delicious reindeer meat special that evening. "When in Rome," I thought as I ordered that meat. Upon my return home a day or two later, US newspapers were plastered with headlines about the Chernobyl nuclear plant meltdown in Ukraine. The event had occurred on April 26 but was only disclosed by the Russian government after being challenged by the Swedes. The Swedish government had picked up radioactivity 1) in the air as part of their nuclear early warning system, and 2) in reindeer meat. Hopefully that reindeer restaurant special was a mere coincidence…

The Chernobyl event resurfaced in 1989, when I received unexpected orders to report to AFRRI for a special temporary duty tour. Shortly after the 1986 explosion, a unique international collaboration had transpired; although relations between the USA and the Soviet "Evil Empire" were still icy, that extraordinary radioactive disaster resulted in the USA (and other European allies) offering assistance to the Soviets to contain the situation. It was truly a time for "all hands on deck" in the civilized world. US military and civilian colleagues ended up quietly helping staff overseas medical facilities caring for injured and irradiated Soviet first-responders. In 1989 it was time for AFRRI to review the results of our efforts and codify what to expect and how to respond should another similar disaster arise down the road. I was one of a conference group "think tank" involved with briefings on those results. Our work was ultimately published by the Defense Nuclear Agency in a monograph entitled *"Treatment of Radiation Injuries,"* and my name is listed along with others on the roster of participants (Ref4).

Many Soviet citizens had heroically and selflessly entered lethal high radiation zones to try to stem leakage at the exploded reactor site. Several of the exposed died of radiation sickness within weeks, but some may have been saved by the bone marrow transplant teams and assistance we provided. Templates that the US military had developed to assess radiation exposure on a nuclear battlefield (documenting certain physical signs and symptoms and measuring various blood tests) were used to help differentiate which Soviet citizens could potentially be saved from those who were the walking dead.

On the domestic front, Sue and I had long before decided that the world was made for families of four (four-passenger cars, four-place restaurant tables, etc.) so our nuclear family was now complete. Both our children were officially Military Brats, having been born on a military base to a military family, but neither was destined to live the nomadic life I had so many years previously.

Our parents treasured any time they had to visit with grandchildren, so were only too happy to watch them given an opportunity. In early 1987, Sue and I dropped the kids off in Washington, D.C., with both sets of grandparents and shortly thereafter were winging our way to Nairobi, Kenya, for a two-week photographic safari and medical facility tour. Grandparents and grandkids had some wonderful bonding time, and Sue and I had a marvelous journey into the remotest parts of Kenya. During a chance meeting with a Maasai tribe member in the bush, he inadvertently jabbed himself in the eye with a spear while showing us the weapon. No one seemed to be rushing to attend to him, so I asked the six passengers on our van to give me what medical supplies they had. After debriding the eye as best I could (there was a deep gash in the sclera, or white part, of his eye), I rinsed it with sterile water and applied some topical antibiotics. (Figure 13) After we applied a crude dressing, our guides sent the poor fellow off on a two-day trek to the nearest hospital. I never heard if he made it, or if he kept his vision. The harshness of austere life in remote Africa was on full display that day.

We saw amazing medical work being done with the limited resources the Kenyans had available, but conditions were grim if you needed cancer treatment; they didn't have any regular supply of chemotherapy and the sole Cobalt radiation machine I saw contained a source so old that it often took sixty minutes of beam time just to treat one patient (as opposed to the normal ten minutes in USA centers). In remote clinics, we saw references on wall posters to what was obviously the AIDS epidemic (often passed heterosexually in Africa), but there was no open discussion about that with us.

In the desert-like wilderness of northern Kenya, just below Somalia, lies the large Samburu National Park. It was there that I was out of commission for four days with an extremely high fever, aches, and chills. I slowly recovered to the point that I could resume the trip but missed most of the park as I lay prostrate under a mosquito net in our hut, with melting wax dripping from my feverish ears. Doctors later told me that I had probably contracted Dengue Fever.

A week later, another guest became gravely ill at a stop in the Maasai Mara National Reserve. She did not improve, so required a medical evacuation flight back to Nairobi. Sue and I volunteered to accompany her back, and I was pleased to be the co-pilot for that flight. A few days later, we headed back to the USA, picked up Katy, Danielle, and Michael and returned home to California.

My commitment to the USAF was ending by mid-1987, after eight challenging but rewarding years of active duty. Options going forward were to remain on active duty, leave active duty for a civilian job but stay in the USAF Reserves, or quit the USAF altogether.

Chapter 15

I was conflicted: On the one hand, I had a young family and had to think about our future from a financial standpoint. My entire yearly salary at that point was around $47,000. We were frugal, but even so that income wasn't going to help pay for a bigger home or college education; the attraction to higher-paying civilian jobs was a logical choice. On the other hand, my David Grant predecessor and I had a hand in laying out the Radiation Oncology department for the entirely new David Grant Medical Center scheduled to be built in the late 1980s, and I wanted to see the completed project results. In the end, I decided to compromise—I would leave full active duty but stay in the USAF Reserves and continue to serve active-duty yearly stints at David Grant.

The next decision I had to make was whether to stay in academia or join a private practice. I was fortunate to have options. Stanford urged me to come back to the Medical Center on their faculty; and my former Stanford professor Norm Coleman, who was now Chairman of the Joint Center in Boston, asked me to join his Harvard Faculty. I would have been honored to join either of their programs, but the reality was that their salaries were not stellar, and both practices were in some of the highest cost of living areas in the USA. To top it off, mortgage interest rates in 1987 went through the roof, making it difficult to buy a home in those areas.

About the time I was contemplating these academic positions, my former Stanford residents Shyam Paryani and John Wells asked me to consider joining their private practice in Jacksonville, FL. They had originally started at different practices in the southeast (Shyam had grown up in Jacksonville, and his father was a radiation oncologist in practice there already; John was from Georgia and had joined a practice there). John had later moved to join Shyam in Jacksonville after the elder Paryani had become ill. Their practice had grown, and they needed help after Shyam's father passed away. The chance to practice with my old Stanford chums was appealing, and Florida offered a wonderful quality of life for our family: a cheaper cost of living, better salary, nice weather, and lower taxes than either California or Massachusetts. Florida was also on the East Coast, so we would be closer to our families. The main drawback was that it was a private practice rather than an academic one.

After many conversations with Sue and others, I reached out to Shyam with a proposal: I would come to Florida to join the private practice if we agreed to run it up to academic standards, including participating in national clinical research trials. The practice would bridge those two types of practice by essentially creating an academic practice in a private setting—a concept unheard of in 1987. We all pledged to make the concept succeed, and I agreed to join the group.

In May of 1987, Sue and I, along with our dog Katy, 3-year-old Danielle, and 11-month-old Michael, piled into our cars and set off for our final move east and new adventures in the Sunshine State.

CHAPTER 16

FROG

Rise of the FROGS, Clinical Research, and Collaboration

The "mothership" of our practice was the Williams Cancer Center located within Baptist Medical Center (BMC) and situated on the south bank of the St. Johns River in Jacksonville. The practice had been co-founded back in the 1960's by a superb triple-boarded Harvard-trained physician, Dr. Walter P. Scott, and Shyam's father, Dr. B.T. Paryani, a quiet but caring physician beloved by his patients and staff. These two pioneers were well-respected by their peers throughout northeast Florida.

By the mid 1980's, the population around Jacksonville and surrounding communities was exploding. The trip downtown for daily radiation treatments was becoming more arduous for many patients from outlying areas as traffic and the number of traffic lights grew. Smaller community hospitals and physicians asked if the group couldn't somehow bring treatments closer to their rural patient populations by building satellite clinics. We, in turn, presented these requests to BMC administrators, who replied that they didn't have the budget for such undertakings but wouldn't stand in our way if we decided to build them. I suspect the administrators also thought we were going to lose our shirts on any such ventures as well, and they wanted no part of that risk. They did agree, however, to lease us Baptist employees to staff any clinics we built, and to allow the patients to come to BMC for all their treatment planning. Dr. Shyam Paryani was convinced we could build the clinics and run them successfully.

Undeterred by the risks inherent in delving into a completely foreign aspect of medicine, the group's partners took out loans and got into the clinic-building business. We were literally and figuratively breaking new ground. Just before my arrival, the first satellite clinic opened in St. Augustine, Florida, followed shortly thereafter by another in Orange Park and a third in Jacksonville Beach. Eventually, Memorial Hospital in Jacksonville also asked us to run the center at their facility, and a bit later the medical community of Palatka invited us to erect a center sixty miles to the south.

These clinics not only succeeded against all odds, but thrived, for a variety of reasons. First, we had not forced our way into any area: rather, we had been invited to come by local doctors and hospital administrators. They were all too happy to refer their patients to our new local centers and thereby keep their patients' care within the community. Secondly, we made a conscious decision not to wear a "Baptist" hat in any of the satellites; when in Orange Park, for instance, we were "Rah, Rah" Orange Park docs and when in Palatka, we were Palatka docs, etc. All clinics were named for their local area, such as the Beaches Cancer Center or St. Augustine Cancer Center. Thirdly, there were no competitors in these market spaces. Until our group figured out how to share the "back door" resources of physics, dosimetry, research support, and staffing, no one had ever predicted that satellite radiation therapy clinics could be economically sound. Finally, through our nationwide contacts, we were able to purchase reliable but used linac machines to install in our centers for a fraction of a new machine's price.

As we built satellite clinics, we added more physicians. The letterhead on our correspondence started to sound like a law firm, with "Scott, Paryani, Wells, Johnson, and Chobe." Something had to be done. In late 1987, in the back room of a local Indian restaurant one night, the doctors decided we needed a new simpler name; ideas were written on paper napkins and traded around the table. In the end, the new name I had scribbled down for the group was chosen: the Florida Radiation Oncology Group (FROG). That name would over time become nationally known and would brand the organization until the group's dissolution in 2014.

We eventually had six Stanford-trained radiation oncologists in the group: the largest enclave of Stanford graduates east of the Mississippi River. The Stanford Medical Center Radiation Oncology Department in Palo Alto even began referring to FROG as "Stanford East," and would refer us patients moving to the East Coast for follow-up care. Several well-trained colleagues from other great training programs joined our group as well. Interestingly, the big reason we were able to attract such great talent was the decision we had committed to upon my arrival: to create an academic level private practice. That premise appealed to some brilliant minds and set us apart from other groups.

To that end, I helped set up and run our FROG clinical research program. BMC had another research champion in the person of Dr. Neil Abramson, a Medical Oncologist of national repute who served with several national clinical trials groups such as ECOG (Eastern Cooperative Oncology Group) and the NSABP (National Surgical Adjuvant Breast and Bowel Project), both supported by the NCI. Neil was happy to have a kindred spirit at Baptist and arranged for me to be accepted as a Principal Investigator for both of those organizations. FROG physicians also became members of and Investigators for the RTOG, POG (Pediatric Oncology Group), and COG (Children's Oncology Group). The latter were important, as BMC's affiliated hospital on our campus, the Wolfson's Children's Hospital, had, in turn, attracted the Nemours Clinic to Jacksonville. The Nemours Clinic was like a "Mayo Clinic for kids," employing a host of pediatric subspecialists to serve the pediatric needs of the southeastern United States. The Nemours Clinic was heavily involved with pediatric cancer research, and FROG became the main provider of pediatric Radiation Oncology services to Nemours for decades, helping care for children whether they were on clinical trials or not. Finally, I also served as an Investigator for the North Central Cancer Treatment Group.

Taking on clinical research in a practice is no easy task, as I had learned previously at David Grant Medical Center in California. Protocol guidelines are stringent and outside oversight and reviews are constant. Whether the research is done at Stanford, Harvard, M.D. Anderson, or even in a FROG clinic, the rigorous standards are the same. Staff needed to devote extra time, care, and caution to "dot the I's and cross the T's." They were not paid to do so but rather did so out of an innate sense of responsibility to improve the lot of patients in their care as well as those of future generations.

Over time we noticed that the quality of care for *all* our patients, not just those on clinical trials, improved dramatically. Staff morale improved in all corners of the FROG network, as the team realized they were contributing directly not only to routine patient care but also expanding the knowledge base of cancer care in general. In addition, patients on clinical trials often were able to receive leading-edge treatments and drugs not available to the general public. Patients were reassured that they didn't need to travel far for state-of-the-art treatment, as we were locally offering the same opportunities for patients as the leading academic treatment centers in the nation.

Performing research made me a better clinician. Perhaps because of my research bias, and not just accepting things at face value, I strove to improve the lot of my patients in any way possible. I was an aggressive radiation oncologist, as I believed there was only one chance to cure a patient. I understood that "standard" doses of radiation treatment were relative rather than absolute. Whereas some of my colleagues took dose schedules listed in texts as Gospel truth, I knew that those regimens were developed and based on a sliding scale of risks.

My aviation background played into my approach to medicine. In the aviation world, it is accepted that risk can never be eliminated, but it can be managed in a way to minimize risk for any flight scenario: Is the plane in good shape? Is the pilot in good shape? Is the environment cooperating (weather, terrain, the enemy, etc.)? So too with patients—risks of any medical procedure can be managed.

A concept called the LD5/30 was used in radiation research to determine the dose resulting in a five percent risk of death within thirty days of treatment, and an LD50/30 was the dose that would result in a fifty percent risk of death within thirty days, for instance. In most cases the "upper dose limit" used for cancer patients was the more conservative lower number. In certain dire situations, though, it was reasonable to consider increasing the dose to a higher level and accepting a higher risk if doing so resulted in a much higher probability of cure than that expected from a more conventional lower dose.

Before committing to administration of a higher-than-standard radiation dose I always had a long frank conversation with the patient and family. If conditions were appropriate, and they were game, we would sometimes reach into this higher risk realm together. Fortunately, this approach worked out in the cases I treated, and I am confident that more patients were "pulled from the fire" because of it. Many cohorts didn't support this concept, however, and rarely colored beyond the lines…

I was aggressive, but not flippant, in choosing my patients' dose regimens, and became the "go-to" guy in my group for risky or difficult patients at our main campus. For my accomplishments in the academic and research arenas of radiation oncology, the American College of Radiology awarded me Fellowship in the College in 1994, an award bestowed on only three percent of radiologists in the USA. (Figure 14)

In my role as Chairman of Radiation Oncology at BMC, visiting residents and newly hired physicians initially oriented for a time with me at our department to instill in them the FROG way of doing things, before sending them off to other clinics in our system. Upon the arrival of new physicians, I would invite them to my office to discuss basic FROG Rules. Rule 1: The patient always came first, and we served as the patient's ombudsman in the larger cancer system. Rule 2: The patients, their families, and our staff were to be treated with the utmost respect.

Rule 3: We would do anything in our power to provide superior service and opportunities to our patients. Rule 4: We never did something TO our patients, we did it WITH our patients—the patients were an integral part of the team.

After the orientation chat, I asked the new doctors to shed their white coats and ties and escorted them to the patient waiting room for the rest of the morning, where they were to sit and carefully observe the interactions there. In the afternoon, they would return to my office and tell me about the patients they saw: their confidence or their fear, their concerns voiced to family or others, the amount of time they had to wait, their interaction with the front desk personnel, etc. It was an eye-opening experience for most of them and gave them a better understanding of just what the patients they were soon to be caring for were going through. They became more empathetic. Years later, some would still remember that experience.

I also set appearance standards for the physicians. Rule 5: In an era where some practices were allowing doctors to dress in polo shirts or scrubs, I insisted that all the male physicians wore nice slacks, a dress shirt, and a tie. All females were to wear either a dress or suitable slacks and blouse set. Rule 6: Clinicians were to always wear a white coat when in the clinic. Patients respected our counsel, and I expected my staff to display a well-groomed appearance as a courtesy to the patients and to demonstrate our professionalism.

Behavior standards were important for FROG's, too. Rule 7: I instructed new folks to look any patient in the eye when first introducing themselves, to sit on a stool in front of them, and to just listen to them for several minutes before writing anything down. Rule 8: I expected them to do a complete physical exam, no matter what part of the body we were anticipated treating—it amazed me over the years how many unrelated but serious problems we picked up in the clinic that way. Patients were uniformly grateful for all this, and nearly always gave us outstanding ratings for honesty, compassion, and care.

One example I recall was an elderly fellow who came to me for consultation about an eye issue. During my exam I noted that he had a loud cardiac murmur. I asked him about that, and he said he'd never been told he had a murmur previously; he admitted to being short of breath for several days, though. I told him I suspected he had ruptured his aortic valve and sent him by ambulance from my clinic to the hospital emergency room. Four hours later a cardiothoracic surgeon was replacing that sick valve in the operating room. The family and patient were eternally grateful.

I instituted workflow processes to streamline and standardize our care delivery. When patients complained that they weren't being told how long the interval would be between my consultation and their treatment, for instance, we decided to resolve that nebulous area. Patients were being told that the steps would take "a while," and that they would start "sometime in the next two weeks." That was unacceptable, as patients needed advance notice to properly arrange work and vacation schedules, get babysitters, and the like.

My solution was to adopt a NASA-like launch routine: I first had my staff break down the tasks needed to get the patient underway, from initial consultation to the first actual treatment, and the time required for each step. Just like NASA preparing for a launch, we used that data to set a "T minus" daily schedule; for example, to plan for a complex external beam treatment course the initial consultation day might be "T minus 5," obtaining insurance authorization "T minus 4," simulation day "T minus 3," plan completion "T minus 2," physics approval "T minus 1," and first treatment date would be "T minus 0." After staff overlaid this decision tree on a calendar, the patient knew exactly the date they were to commence daily therapy, and the staff knew their deadlines for each step.

As social media platforms debuted, some physicians were leery for fears that an upset patient might leave a bad rating on one of the healthcare rating sites. I took the opposite tack, suggesting that we encourage ALL of our patients to give a rating on those sites for two reasons: first, if a patient had a legitimate beef, we should know about it so we could correct it; and second, if it was just a spurious comment by a disgruntled outlier, the vast majority of "great" ratings we garnered would put that one "poor" rating in context. We gave all the patients links to the sites and asked them to provide an honest and anonymous rating of our service. Patients loved the opportunity to give ratings, and the overall process was a wonderful complement to our organization over the ensuing years.

To facilitate research in the realms of cardiology, cancer, and other specialties, BMC had an oversight committee called the IRC (Investigational Review Committee). Composed of both medical experts and lay members of the public, the IRC met monthly to review the ethics and feasibility of any proposed research trials or activities to be conducted within BMC's walls. I ended up serving on that committee and eventually chaired it for many years.

Although our FROG nurses were critical in the initial thrust into the clinical research arena, with the tomes of paperwork engendered, it quickly became apparent that the group needed to hire a dedicated CRA (Clinical Research Associate) to assist me in my role as the FROG Director of Research.

To that end, one of the finest CRA's I've ever had the pleasure to know agreed to join us, Ms. Jan Peer. Although new to the CRA environment, Jan was perfect for the job: meticulous, extremely well organized, friendly and patient-oriented, and a stickler for following the myriad rules imposed by the various clinical trial groups over the years. Jan was indeed a Superwoman, able to juggle the varied research needs of multiple clinics while preparing voluminous documentation and data submission tasks required of us and keeping up with the new trials I wanted to open. Jan was literally the glue that held our research program together. Under her care, our data quality submission audits by various NCI-based trial groups routinely placed us in the top five percent in the nation, and often the best in FL. We were also lucky to have the commitment of our FROG physician and nursing staff, and many of them were major contributors to our efforts over the years.

As our enrollment numbers to national trials steadily increased, leaders of the trial groups and various large academic institutions started to take notice of FROG. We were invited to the table, so to speak. I was asked to sit on several national research committees including the Chemical Modifiers and Gynecology Working Groups within the RTOG and the Thoracic Site Committee for ACRIN (American College of Radiology Imaging Network).

As our record of NCI-based clinical trial group participation and quality grew, we began receiving solicitations from industry to beta-test new equipment, medications, and techniques. At the risk of falling too far into the weeds, some notable examples follow to give an idea of the scope of FROG's endeavors.

We investigated the use of a radio-protector called WR-2721 (later FDA approved under the trade name of Amifostine) to protect normal tissues during head and neck radiation treatments.

We were early investigators in the use of injected anti-androgen therapy to complement external-beam irradiation in the treatment of prostate cancer—injecting patients on RTOG protocols with the experimental medicine years before it was to become standard practice in urology clinics.

The Stanford Radiation Oncology Department had pioneered the use of total skin electron beams to treat a type of lymphoma called mycosis fungoides. We were able to duplicate that technique at BMC and became the regional referral center for treatment of those rare cancers.

Bone marrow transplant (BMT) was commonly used in the 1990's-early 2000's to treat several types of leukemia, a common pediatric tumor. Our Baptist center was certified as one of the few centers in Florida to offer total body irradiation to both children and adults as a part of their preparation for BMT.

The FROG group had a strong background in brachytherapy—the administration of radiation by placing sources close to or within tissues, either temporarily or permanently. Although we used different brachytherapy techniques for a broad variety of issues, several were unique or pioneering.

One example for which we used brachytherapy was the use of a superficial beta applicator applied to the sclera (white part) of an eyeball immediately after surgical removal of a benign tumor called a pterygium to reduce the chance of it recurring from almost eighty percent down to five percent (Ref5).

Another unique use of brachytherapy involved patients with heart disease who needed to have a stent placed to open clogged coronary arteries. Early "bare-metal" stents were effective in the short term, but over several weeks had an issue with re-stenosis, an inflammation-induced re-narrowing of a blocked vessel at the site of the new stent. Research showed that the temporary placement of radiation sources within a freshly implanted coronary artery stent in the heart (so-called intracoronary radiation) via an arterial catheter in the groin could reduce the risk of re-stenosis in the stent area from roughly sixty percent to twenty-five percent. We performed between 100-200 of these applications. Although proven effective, the need for this cumbersome and time-consuming procedure was later obviated by the introduction of "drug-eluting" stents.

These intra-coronary radiation applications required careful coordination between cardiologists, thoracic surgeons, radiation oncologists, and radiation physicists. Things did not always go according to plan. One memorable afternoon while on vacation, relaxing at a pub overlooking the Rhine River in Germany and enjoying time with my extended family, my cell phone chirped. Upon answering the call, a voice on the other end said, "Dr. Johnson, we are ready for you in Room 2." I put my beer down and asked for clarification. Apparently, the Cardiac Catheterization lab techs were so used to seeing me in their domain they had written my name and personal phone number on the side of a machine console in the Cardiac Cath Lab. Presuming I was to be doing the case, they thoughtfully rang me directly to give me a heads up. I quipped, "Houston, we have a problem" before explaining my circumstances and suggesting they call my department telephone number to determine who was actually supposed to attend the case. The techs were amused that they were talking to me in Germany, and laughter was heard throughout the Cath Lab as they spread news of their faux pas.

Another radiation technique we used routinely involved the use of I-131 radioactive capsules. Patients would ingest these capsules orally to treat hyperthyroidism or after surgery for thyroid cancer. Again, significant coordination between doctors, nurses, physicists, and patients was required. Patient education before an I-131 treatment was imperative so that the recipient knew how to self-quarantine to protect other people from radiation exposure for a time after swallowing the pill.

FROG physicians also pioneered the use of injecting radioactive yttrium (Y-90) coated microspheres via a hepatic artery catheter to treat cancer in the liver. This effort, too, was a highly choreographed affair, involving diagnostic radiology, interventional radiology, and radiation oncology teams. We were one of only three sites selected and approved to perform this research technique in Florida.

The largest pioneering effort involving brachytherapy, however, pertained to its use in the treatment of prostate cancer. Historically, prostate cancer had been treated with either an aggressive surgery called radical prostatectomy or with external-beam radiation treatments. The latter treatment involved returning for a daily outpatient treatment for nine weeks. Each radiation treatment was delivered in a shielded vault while the patient lay on a radiation treatment table.

Advantages of surgery included the fact that it was all done in one sitting, and that the removed prostate could be examined pathologically along with nearby removed lymph nodes. Disadvantages included the fact that it was a major surgery, with all the attendant risks of bleeding and infection, as well as prolonged healing over several weeks and months. Up to forty percent of men had some degree of urinary incontinence after a radical prostatectomy and virtually all had impotence (the nerves that "run the erection room" lie adjacent to the prostate and usually were cut to ensure complete tumor removal). Even worse, if the pathologist found that tumor had penetrated the edge of the prostate, a full course of radiation treatment was still needed in addition to the surgery to try to prevent a tumor recurrence at the surgical edges left in the pelvis.

Advantages of external-beam radiation treatment included avoiding all those risks of bleeding and infection associated with surgery, the fact that it was all delivered in a fifteen-minute daily outpatient session so that working men could continue their jobs throughout treatment, and the fact that it could treat not only the prostate but also all the surrounding tissues. Urinary incontinence was rare afterwards, and about half the treated patients still retained their potency. Disadvantages included the fact that the radiation oncologist had to "pull his punch" somewhat, as the radiation had to traverse a bunch of normal tissue to reach the prostate: to limit normal tissue damage, the total dose delivered to the prostate was limited as well. A side effect not seen with surgery included the long-term development of something called telangiectasia (small abnormal blood vessels like those seen in the face of elderly folks who have spent years out in the sun) in the lining of the rectum or low bladder. These tiny blood vessels would form over the two years following external beam treatment and might bleed if nicked or irritated. Thus, some rectal or urinary bleeding was seen in about five to ten percent of patients down the road.

Various European programs had tried to combine the advantages of both external-beam radiation and brachytherapy to treat prostate cancer over the years. Brachytherapy, like surgery, was performed in one sitting by inserting small radioactive pellets into the "meat" of the prostate. The radiation emitted by the implanted seeds would decay (fade away) over a period of months, thus radiating the prostate "from the inside out." Because the prostate itself was not removed, the risk of bleeding or infection was dramatically reduced, and because the radius of action of each seed was only about one cm, there was relatively low exposure to the normal tissues around the gland. This, in turn, allowed a much higher dose of radiation to be applied, with a corresponding increased chance of eliminating all the cancer cells. Instead of months of protracted healing, the patient was up and about within about a week. The risk of incontinence was only about five percent, and more than sixty percent were able to keep their potency and active sexual life.

If this all sounded too good to be true, it was. The theory was fine, but there were many technical challenges to delivering the seeds. Until the advent of rectal intra-operative ultrasound machines in the 1990's, it was difficult to know where the prostate was minute by minute, where to deposit the seeds, or even how many seeds of what type and what strength to use. Placing the seeds was problematic, and early papers suggested that many improperly placed seeds would migrate away from the prostate area to other parts of the body. Better applicators allowing more accurate placement of the seeds at precise spacing needed development as well.

The Stanford-trained FROGs had some experience with early seed implant techniques, but it was not until we actively pursued research in Jacksonville and our surrounding communities that things finally evolved. The transrectal ultrasound equipment came of age and was incorporated by our urology colleagues; we could not only measure the size of the prostate in advance, which allowed us to calculate the number of seeds required to treat the gland, but could use that same machine in the operating room to locate the exact position of the prostate at the time of seed insertion and watch each seed being deposited in the correct position in real time. Seed migration to other parts of the body became a thing of the past. Computerized dosimetry allowed better calculation of the ideal number and strength of seeds to order. We helped evaluate different needles, templates, insertion "guns", and seed cartridges to allow accurate deposition of the seeds as well (in a manner akin to the JABB device I had patented years before). We also helped standardize the upper safe dose that could be administered with I-125 seeds. A bit later, during a national shortage of iodine I-125 seeds (created from byproducts of commercial nuclear reactors), we also explored the use of another isotope called palladium (Pd-103). Pd-103 had some theoretical benefits over I-125: it delivered most of its radiation over only three months, compared to twelve months for I-125, and its radius of action was smaller than I-125. That smaller radius helped better protect tissues outside the prostate. In the early 1990's, I performed the first Pd-103 implant in the state of FL, according to the vendor who attended the procedure.

Ultimately, two FROG radiation oncologists who had trained at the Mt. Sinai Hospital program in New York, along with several other FROG doctors who performed these implants, put an integrated package together with a system incorporating real-time intraoperative dosimetry. They amassed a huge database of long-term patient outcomes treated with a customized program including combinations of anti-androgen hormone blockage, seed implantation, and/or external beam radiation treatment. Over 15,000 patients pooled between the FROG and Mt. Sinai programs have been followed for in some cases over two decades and have definitively shown not only fewer side effects but also better survival and cure rates than seen with standard surgery. Subsequent articles, including one in the Journal of the American Medical Association, confirmed their findings (Ref6). These same two doctors, Drs. Mitchell Terk and Jamie Cesaretti, traveled abroad to train French and Japanese physicians in the use of these techniques.

Sadly, widespread adoption of the real-time intraoperative dosimetry prostate brachytherapy technique across the USA has been a challenge for three reasons. First, it takes training and experience to become good at it, as does any surgical procedure. Second, it takes teamwork crossing many disciplines and schedules, including a urologist, a radiation oncologist, a dosimetrist, and a physicist all converging with their equipment and talents simultaneously in a reserved operating room with the assigned operating room staff—a bit like herding the proverbial cats. Not many institutions are willing to dedicate resources to this labor—and time—intensive effort. Third, the procedure does not make much money for the hospital or provider: they can realize a greater profit by recommending a full nine-week course of external-beam radiation treatment, or by performing a prostatectomy. I consider myself lucky that our team routinely put the patient's wellbeing above profit.

Chapter 16

Starting In the 1990's, the FROG team also became pioneers in the use of a technique called radiosurgery: using intense highly focused radiation beams to remove tumors and treat isolated areas of the body without any incisions at all. We staffed special radiosurgery machines with such space-age names as the Elekta Gamma Knife, Accuray Cyberknife, and Varian Industries Novalis TX to successfully treat a broad variety of conditions, including a "benign" but devastating condition known as trigeminal neuralgia.

The group's reach expanded beyond just treatment of disease. A pioneering imaging advance called PET (positron emission tomography) scanning began to revolutionize imaging of cancers: unlike CT or MRI scanners that visualized an abnormal swelling or lump, the PET looked inside a tissue to see if it was too metabolically active (as many cancers are). Thus, the PET could often detect cancer in a tissue even before it caused any structural changes or enlargement. We knew this could have an enormous impact on determining just what tissues we needed to irradiate, and which we could safely spare. We were invited to participate in a huge NCI and CMMS (Centers for Medicare and Medicaid Services) federal effort to determine just how important the technology was, and what cancers it worked best for.

The isotope used in PET scanning, called FDG, was a positron emitter attached to a glucose molecule, and had a very short half-life once produced (this was the first clinical use of anti-matter; *Star Trek*'s Captain Kirk would have been proud). No one was producing the isotope in northern Florida, so FROG decided to remedy that problem by converting an old clinic to house the first privately-owned isotope reactor in the United States: Our General Electric Mini-Trace was installed in 1998. We at one time provided the FDG not only for our own use, but for most of the hospitals in northern Florida. As the regional hospitals were slow to adopt PET/CT scanning, Dr. Paryani worked with industry to develop mobile PET/CT scanning trailers so that we could move them from site to site on a rotational basis. This, in turn, required us to create a whole transportation department within the group, including tractor trailers, vans, delivery trucks, and the staff to man and schedule them.

The effort was worth it: after ramping up to a maximum of over 7000 PET/CT scans annually, we were able to demonstrate that the PET/CT images changed our radiation fields in an incredible forty percent of our patients! Dr. Larry H. Wilf, a diagnostic radiologist who headed the Imaging Services branch of FROG, was recognized by industry leaders as one of the most experienced PET/CT interpreters in the nation.

Recognizing our developed expertise in many of these fields, the Mayo Clinic asked us to become an integral part of their fledgling Radiation Oncology residency program in Jacksonville. Several of us were awarded Mayo Clinic faculty appointments through the Mayo Clinic Medical School in Rochester and for several years Mayo residents spent up to six months with us, learning our techniques and advanced procedures.

At the end of my medical career, I became involved in an exciting international research study, thanks to an introduction to an Israeli investigator, Dr. Nir Peled. Nir had a strong interest in the use of nanosensors to detect lung cancer from just a breath. He had put together a team in Jerusalem and the Technion Institute in Haifa to investigate breath samples along with his colleague, Dr. Hossam Haick. The idea showed great promise locally, but they needed more patients to verify their results. Thus began an international collaboration between investigators in North America, Europe, and Southeast Asia. I was the Principal Investigator for the United States. We launched a supportive research trial in Jacksonville and accrued newly diagnosed lung cancer patients to volunteer their breath. The breath and the collected research data were sent for analysis back to the Technion. In the end, a paper was published in 2017 that included 1407 patients worldwide and was considered a landmark in the field. The breath test paradigm researched was over ninety percent effective in detecting early-stage lung cancer (Ref7).

I cherished my time at the helm of the FROG research program. Through our team's efforts, we were able to publish extensively in the literature: I personally wrote over sixty-five accepted publications and many others in the group published extensively as well. For a private practitioner, that was satisfying! The biggest key to success in all these endeavors was the dedicated collaboration across multiple specialties we were able to pull together over many years.

By the early 2000's, practices were responding to outside influences, and our FROG organization was going to have to make some radical changes. Turbulent waters lay ahead.

FIGURES

Figure 1. T-shirt tail hung in NAS Moffett Flying Club 1980

Figure 2. Andrew Johnson in first integrated squadron in the USAF 1950

Figure 3. Doug and Andy playing near home in Salina, Kansas 1956

Figure 4. Shepherd tending flock in Spain 1960 (oil painting)

Figure 5. *"Cockpit memories"* of the F-102 in Zaragoza, Spain (oil painting)

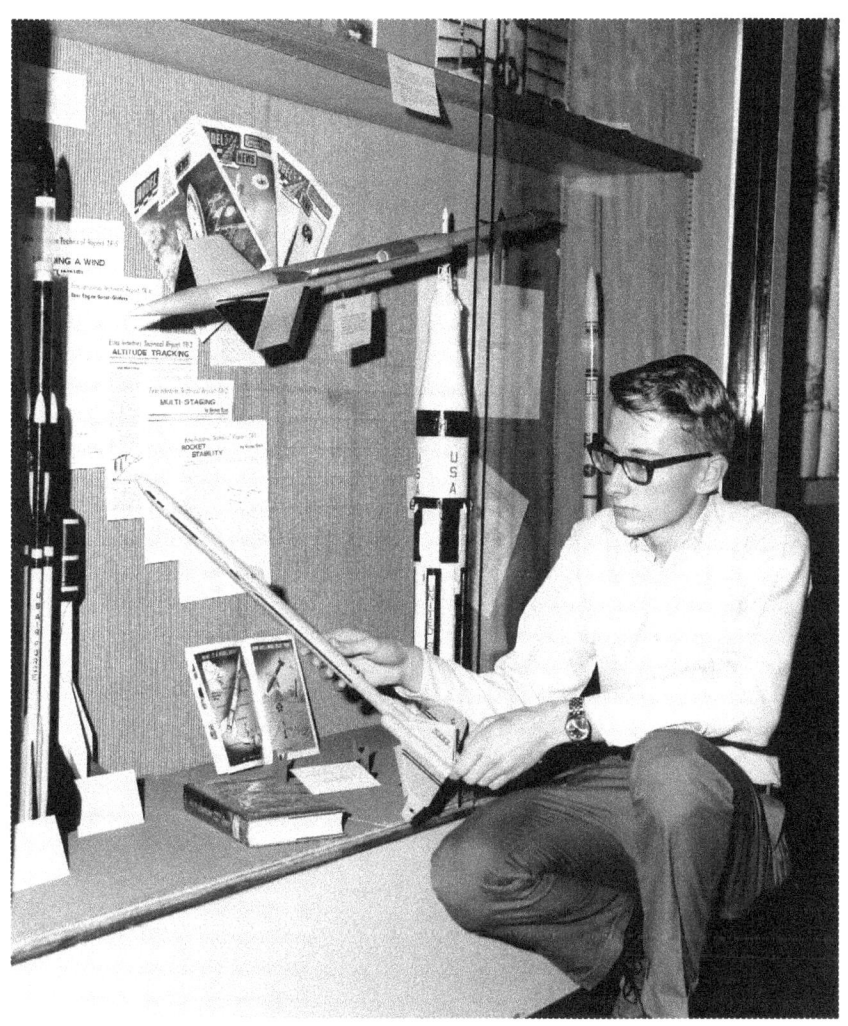

Figure 6. Library display of rockets and technical papers at Randolph AFB 1970

Figure 7. An early painting, depicting a *"Mohave Desert sunset"* 1974 (oil painting)

Figure 8. Doug and Sue enjoying weekly donut night in 1975

Figure 9. Doug's father, LTC. Andrew L. Johnson, swearing him into the Air Force just prior to medical school in 1975

Figure 10. Flying a Piper Archer out of NAS Moffett, California 1981

Figure 11. The Stanford Radiation Therapy Department in 1982-83. Standing, left to right: David Schreiber, William Morrison, unknown, Richard Hoppe, Donald Goffinet, Mark Schray, Thomas Pedrick, Marc Crnkovich, C. Norman Coleman, Kenneth Russell, Anthony Howes, Peter Fessenden, unknown, Douglas Johnson. Sitting, left to right: Sarah Donaldson, Francine Halberg, Henry S. Kaplan, Malcolm Bagshaw, Mary Austin-Seymour, Linda Chak, Harvey Wolkov

United States Patent [19]
Johnson

[11] Patent Number: **4,682,593**
[45] Date of Patent: **Jul. 28, 1987**

[54] **ADJUSTABLE BREAST BRIDGE FOR USE IN MULTIPLE-PLANE INTERSTITIAL BREAST IMPLANTS**

[76] Inventor: Douglas W. Johnson, 8265 Riding Club Rd., Jacksonville, Fla. 33216

[21] Appl. No.: **435,514**

[22] Filed: **Oct. 20, 1982**

[51] Int. Cl.⁴ A61B 17/00
[52] U.S. Cl. .... 128/303 R
[58] Field of Search .... 128/316, 319 R, 303 R; 33/21 R, 21 B, 21 D, 42, 9 R

[56] **References Cited**
U.S. PATENT DOCUMENTS

899,202	9/1908	Byrd et al.	33/9 R
905,723	12/1908	Longnecker	33/9 R
1,254,986	1/1918	Conlon et al.	33/42

Primary Examiner—Edward M. Coven
Attorney, Agent, or Firm—John R. Flanagan; Donald J. Singer

[57] **ABSTRACT**

An adjustable breast bridge includes a pair of upright members, a rectangular span member, adjustable fasteners connecting the support members and span member together in an inverted U-shaped configuration in which the bridge is adapted to straddle a breast of any size. Each support member has a vertically adjustable slot which can be raised or lowered as desired to any desired distance above the base of the bridge, as indicated by millimeter calibrations on the outer sides of the support members. The marking tool can be inserted through the support member slots and used to draw a line on the breast surface a precise distance above and parallel to the base of the bridge.

9 Claims, 10 Drawing Figures

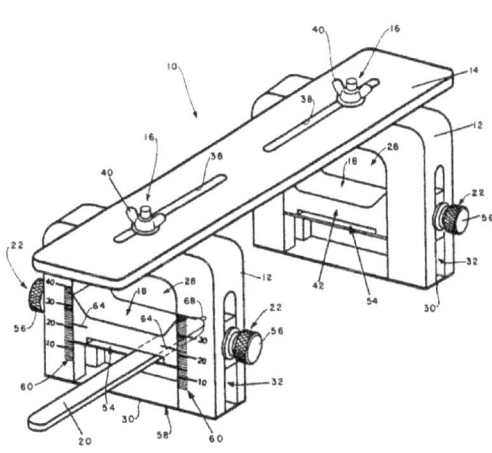

Figure 12. The JABB patent for a device used in breast cancer surgery; awarded in 1987.

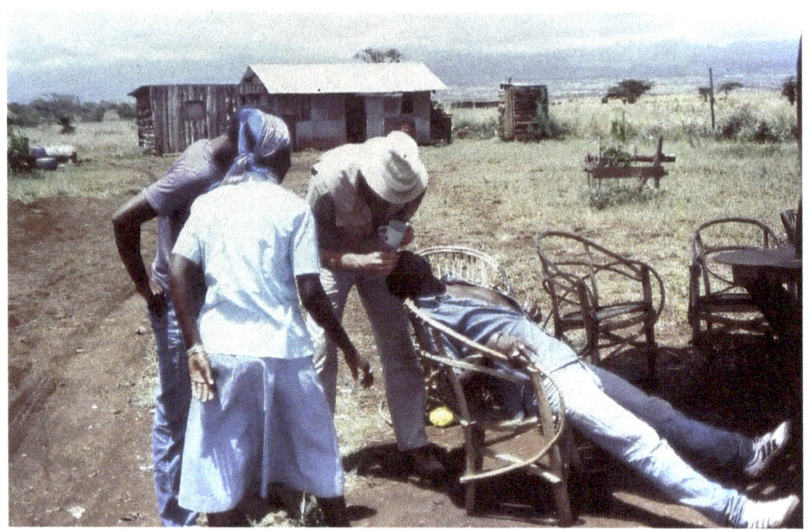

Figure 13. Doug debriding and cleaning a spear injury scleral laceration in Kenya 1986

Figure 14. Doug recognized in the Jacksonville Magazine June 2004. Photo by Bradley Stookey

Figure 15. The new David Grant USAF Medical Center, which Doug was later to command as an IMA 1995

Figure 16. Colonel Doug Johnson official photo 1996

Figure 17. Doug (right) after a strenuous
F-16 night mission and feeling it

Figure 18. Digger and Doug in Navy flight gear

Figure 19. The Johnson's and Cessna HWZ at Redcliffe, Australia 1994

Figure 20. Herding cattle in the Outback by motorcycle

Figure 21. Danielle and Mike snoozing aloft

Figure 22. Climbing Ayers Rock (Uluru)

Figure 23. Outback salt flat landing strip

Figure 24. Opal mine shafts at Coober Peedy

Figure 25. ASCAN interviewees relaxing after a long day of tests. Houston 1995

Figure 26. Touring the simulation building, Johnson Space Center 1995

Figure 27. Prototype NaNose breath sensor 2012

Figure 28. Plein air painting during the Westcliffe retreat

Figure 29. N654DM on display at Udvar-Hazy Center of the National Air & Space Museum 2009

Figure 30. Unloading Haitian relief medical supplies. Dominican Republic 2010

Figure 31. T-42 on display after an eventful journey. Oshkosh 1995

Figure 32. Maneuvering the Lancair with the new glass panel 2015. Photographer Will Page

Figure 33. Doug and Sue outside Cuzco, Peru 1998

Figure 34. Doug and Brad Mottier in the highlands during the 2003 Scottish Malts Endurance rally

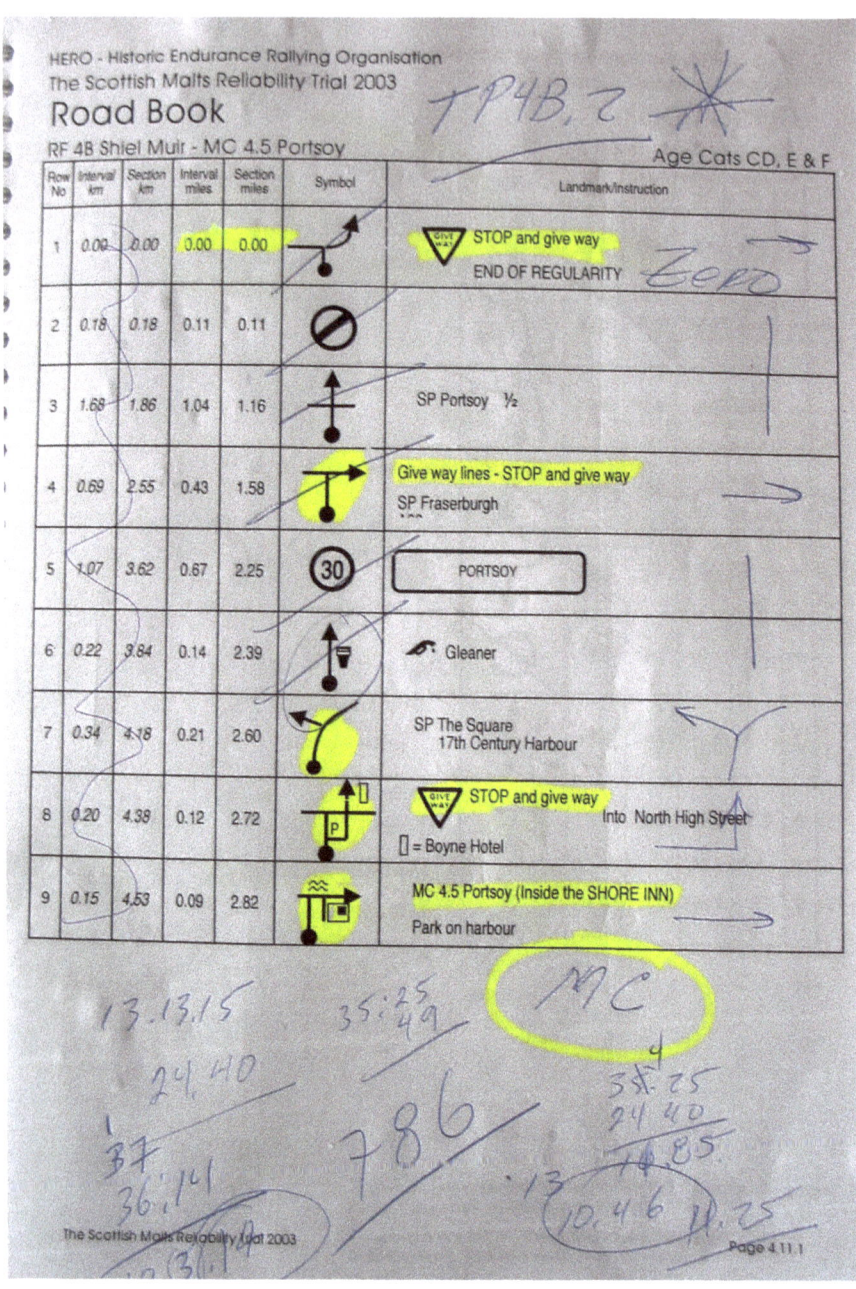

Figure 35. Tulip directions during the Malts. Scotland 2003

Figure 36. After the flight in a dual-control WWII Spitfire at Biggin Hill, UK 2024

Figure 37. *"Happy feet in old Havana"* Cuba (oil)

Figure 38. *"Raising the sail"* on the Nile River, Luxor, Egypt (oil)

Figure 39. *"Destination Hagia Sophia"* Istanbul, Turkey (oil)

Figure 40. *"Winter Marsh"* Florida (oil)

Figure 41. *"Listening for spirits"* Mesa Verde, New Mexico (oil)

Figure 42. "*Fishing off the ramp*" (oil)

Figure 43. "*Icelandic Cliffs and arctic terns*" (oil)

Figure 44. "*Eiffel tower before the Games*" 2024 (oil)

Figure 45. *"Rendezvous at the Ice Plant"* (oil)

Figure 46. *"The old seafarer"* (oil)

Figure 47. Plein air at Old Rhinebeck, New York 2022

Figure 48. Pelican attack

Figure 49. *"A stroll through history"* Barcelona, Spain (oil)

Figure 50. "*The Alcomabar Gates*" Ronda, Spain (oil)

CHAPTER 17

USAF Reserves

Back in uniform, call sign "Laser"

After leaving active duty in 1987, I transitioned to the USAF Reserves (USAFR) as an Independent Mobilization Augmentee (IMA). The thought behind IMA positions was that a reservist would be an "echo" of a critical active-duty position. If a conflict arose and that critical person was sent off to war, his IMA would be activated to replace him at his original duty station. Historically known as weekend warriors, active reservists usually drilled for one weekend a month at a local USAF facility and then spent two weeks on active duty per year.

I had two immediate problems with that routine: First, there was no nearby USAF medical center in which to do my active-duty time, and second, there were few places in the USAF that could use my skill set. In addition, I was working hard all week and wanted to spend as much time with my family on the weekends as possible.

As it happens, the nearby NAS Jacksonville was home to a large regional Naval Hospital. That facility had had a Medical Oncologist stationed there for years who had recently been transferred to another Navy Hospital in Virginia. Without his presence, not only was there no one at the Naval Hospital to assist the staff with treatment recommendations for newly diagnosed cancer patients, but any formerly diagnosed active-duty cancer patients couldn't be stationed in the southeastern USA. Why not? The Navy had a rule that active-duty personnel with a history of cancer needed to undergo an annual examination and Medical Evaluation Board to determine their continued ability to serve. On top of that, the rule stated that the examiner had to be located within a certain geographic range. The geographic hole created by the Oncologist vacancy in Jacksonville was directly impacting the mission of several bases in the region.

I was able to coordinate with both the USAFR (I was technically assigned to the 9019th Air Reserve Squadron in Denver) and the US Navy to work out a win-win solution for all of us: I would hold a weekly afternoon clinic at the Naval Hospital to see active-duty, retired, and dependent folks with either newly diagnosed or previously treated cancer to help direct their care, and would attend their monthly tumor boards as well as perform the Medical Evaluation Board exams on active-duty troops. These four half-days a month replaced weekend duty, and I am forever grateful to my FROG colleagues who granted me the time away from the office to perform them in uniform. There was no free lunch; however, my two-week annual tours were still performed at the David Grant Medical Center in northern California, and that time away was deducted from my annual FROG-allotted vacation.

This routine worked well over the ensuing thirteen years, and I was able to assist many newly diagnosed cancer patients at the Naval Hospital Jacksonville. To avoid any appearance of impropriety or self-referral while wearing the uniform, I provided all patients requiring radiation treatments a complete list of local treatment facilities, FROG or otherwise, and would help coordinate their appointments anywhere they wished. Rather than competition, other radiation oncologists in town eventually thought of me as an unbiased referral source for them.

1989 was marked by international rejoicing as the Berlin Wall fell and the Soviet Union—the "Evil Empire" as described by President Ronald Reagan—crumbled. There was talk of a "peace dividend" in terms of a draw-down of US military forces now that our Cold War enemy had fallen. Quiet harmony was to rule the world for the foreseeable future. Unfortunately, no one told that to the nations of the Middle East or radical Muslims…

Just one year later a large international coalition launched a military reprisal to counter Saddam Hussein's invasion of nearby Kuwait in August of 1990, and the first Gulf War was underway. Uncle Sam sent word that I was to be recalled to USAF active duty along with a cohort of two hundred other physicians within a few weeks. I was poked with fourteen inoculations for various pathogens at the Naval Hospital, and I knew things were really serious when I had to get prescription lens inserts made for my gas mask! I had my will updated and coverage for my clinics arranged. No one knew how long I would be away, but my family and the FROG partners were very supportive. All packed and standing by for orders on the Thursday prior to my anticipated Saturday call up, I received a directive notifying me that the war was ending, and the call up canceled. Army General "Stormin' Norman" Schwarzkopf had routed the Iraqis in a swift series of attacks that laid waste to all resistance in record time, and Kuwait's invasion was over.

The following week found me back in clinic seeing my patients for their routine on-treatment visits. One elderly fellow, noting that I seemed a bit glum, asked me what was going on. Realizing that he was part of the WWII "Greatest Generation," I confided that I was feeling a bit guilty about not being recalled to active duty during the Gulf War. After all, wasn't that what I had signed up for all those years ago, to protect and defend our American way of life? He told me to shut the door and sit down and then related a story that has stuck with me ever since. "Doc, let me tell you about WWII. All your friends were enlisting in the military, but if you were rejected for whatever reason, you felt guilty because your friends were all in uniform. If you got in but were stationed stateside, you felt guilty because your friends were heading overseas. If you got overseas but were stationed in the rear, you felt guilty because your friends were heading to the front lines. If you got to the front lines and survived unscathed, you felt guilty because your friends were getting wounded. If you got wounded but your friends were dying, you felt guilty. Face it, Doc—the only ones who didn't feel guilty were dead." What a stunning but obvious truth. I reflected on those words years later while standing on the once-bloody sands of Omaha Beach upon the 80th anniversary of the D-Day invasion.

Returning to David Grant each summer over the next few years, I spent time in the Radiation Oncology Department in the newly constructed hospital—it was a treat seeing it become a state-of-the-art reality. (Figure 15)

I kept in touch with my old colleagues at Stanford as well, sometimes even lecturing there. One day in early 1991, I accidentally dialed a wrong number when attempting to reach Stanford to discuss an upcoming "medical effects of nuclear weapons" lecture I was slated to deliver. The fellow who picked up the phone, however, was intrigued that a radiation oncologist had called his office talking about medical radiation effects. As it turns out, I had inadvertently called an unlisted number within a classified section of the Lawrence Livermore National Laboratory, a site secretly developing nuclear capabilities for the military.

This chance interaction ultimately led to an invitation to lecture Lawrence Livermore staff about the medical effects of high-energy radiation exposure and ways to mitigate harm. A date was set, and they met me at an off-installation hotel meeting room. I didn't ask and they didn't volunteer exactly what their roles were, but it seemed the talk went well. Days later I received a phone call from my contact at Lawrence Livermore expressing his appreciation and asking if I would like to undertake some accident investigation work for the government. Intrigued, I said, "Yes."

That misdialed phone call eventually led to my performing ad hoc work for the Nuclear Regulatory Commission Office of Nuclear Material Safety and Safeguards (NMSS) radiation accident response team, under contract to the Idaho National Engineering Laboratory. During my tenure over the next three years, I was fortunately only asked to mobilize and investigate a single radiation accident: one involving misadministration of radiation seeds at a major Ivy League hospital.

After my site visit, I prepared a report on the probable medical sequelae of the accident for the patient and hospital personnel, and suggestions for improved quality control, prevention, and mitigation to reduce the risk of similar scenarios arising in the future.

Over the next few years my career path in the USAFR evolved. I obtained my Flight Surgeon's wings and now was a rated airman—finally able to fly in a military cockpit and proving those cardiologists at Wilford Hall all those years ago wrong. After a long and tortuous road, I had achieved a workaround and realized my dream to fly in the USAF.

To further my military leadership education, I remotely completed the Air Command & Staff College over eighteen months, and later Air War College over two years via the Air University at Maxwell AFB, Alabama. For the uninitiated, completing Air War College is the military's equivalent of earning an MBA.

There is an old saying among military pilots that "if you stick around long enough, you'll fly a desk." That held true for me as well. I gradually moved up the chain of command at Travis and eventually became the IMA to the Medical Center Commander, 60th Medical Wing. Over these years I was promoted twice on a fast track, reaching full Colonel in 1994, at age thirty-nine. (Figure 16)

Some amazing leaders at David Grant during the 1990's inspired me, including Major General Lee Rodgers, who later went on to command Wilford Hall in San Antonio, and Major General Leonard Randolph, who ultimately served as Deputy Assistant Secretary of Defense for Health Plan Administration, Health Affairs and Chief Operating Officer, TRICARE Management Activity, Washington, D.C., in 2003.

I will never forget a piece of leadership advice General Randolph gave me one day while chatting in his office: "*Give your staff responsibility and empower them.*" He embodied that philosophy in his morning staff meetings with the Department heads overseeing the 2000+ David Grant employees, saying "*Don't bring me a problem, unless you also bring me the solution.*" His subordinates usually were first to recognize a problem and often knew what the best remedy would be but needed the confidence and authority to make corrections. I took that advice back to my practice and leadership positions at BMC and tried to carry that message forward for the remainder of my career.

Being the IMA Wing Commander and a Flight Surgeon had its privileges: I could ask to be added to the manifest on local flight missions when my time allowed. I had the opportunity to stand in the cockpit of the massive C-5A Galaxy while junior pilots jockeyed behind aerial tankers to refuel at high altitudes with only twenty feet between the jets, and to lie or sit in the tail of KC-135 and KC-10 tankers while we refueled a variety of aircraft, from the huge C-5A to the much smaller A-10 Thunderbolt (or "Warthog" as it was called by its crews). Knowing I was a pilot, some aircrews even gave me some right seat stick time, including one sortie in a C-141 Starlifter on a low-level training mission in the canyons of the desert Southwest. I also had the chance to see the operations of the real "line USAF" in action: as a Wing Commander, I was expected to engage in the weekly classified "Hollywood Squares" staff meetings with the other Wing and Base Commanders. These meetings were held in a special secure conference room, one side of which had a bank of television monitors connecting similar conference rooms in the Pentagon and other bases around the world, so that information could be passed between leaders at a moment's notice. Think of this as a massive weekly secure Zoom call, more than twenty years before Zoom existed.

Between active-duty stints back in Jacksonville, I would also periodically don my uniform to help in the Flight Surgery Clinic at the 125th Fighter Interceptor Group Florida Air National Guard unit when their own docs were deployed to Southwest Asia. While those docs were over in "the sandbox," I conducted clinics and sick calls for pilots, navigators, and their families. As a reward for my help, I occasionally was given a ride in the two-seat versions of their tactical jets.

On one memorable night training mission over the moonless and inky black Atlantic in an F-16B, my pilot sent the second ship of the element back to base after the wild maneuvers of the training mission were complete, saying that he would be twenty minutes behind. The veteran in the front cockpit then proceeded to engage in a favorite game amongst jet jockeys of "let's get the doc sick!" After requesting me to look down at my right hip to switch to a different radio frequency, he suddenly whipped the plane into a 90 degree bank and pulled a prolonged 9G maneuver as he completed a minimum radius turn in afterburner. Let me tell you, 9G's hurt: my normal 180lb body weighed over 1600lbs, and my head weighed over 135lbs. I initiated my strain maneuver to try to keep the blood in my brain as the G-suit inflated to squeeze the blood in my legs and abdomen upward as well.

After he rolled out of the turn, his quiet voice came over the intercom, whispering, "Are you still with me, doc?" Fortunately, I hadn't passed out (barely), but as I caught my breath I replied, "Yes I am, but just remember if you do that again, I have a six-inch spinal needle awaiting you back in the clinic!" He chuckled. I had passed my initiation rite and was one of the guys from then forward. He let me fly the jet for a while, doing turns and aileron rolls, but then asked for the controls back.

I relaxed in the seat for a few minutes, when the dark sky overhead suddenly lit up with a blazing sun seemingly just above us. Unbeknownst to me, he had called for an aerial refueling. We had moved right behind and just underneath the massive tanker, and as refueling lights speared the cockpit, I could see the face of the tanker boomer (or "gas-passer" as he was called) staring down at me from a window just a few feet away. The refueling probe came down to connect to our F-16 with a loud "thunk" just inches behind my head. After refueling, we headed back to the airport and finally landed. A maintainer snapped a photo of the pilot and me just after we clambered down from the cockpit. Minutes later I shed my flight gear and headed for the Base Operations parking lot, where I reclined the seat in my car and rested for a while before driving home. A week later, when the planeside picture was processed, I had to laugh—I was as white as a sheet standing next to the pilot late that night. (Figure 17) Before the mission, our complexions had been the same…

The morning after the F-16B flight, I got a call from one of the other flight surgeons, asking if I had "G measles." "What are you talking about?" I replied. He asked me to go into my bathroom, remove my shirt, and look at my back in the mirror. Sure enough, it looked as though I had red measles spots all over my back. He explained that when pulling high-G maneuvers, blood rushes to your back and pops the capillaries in the skin, yielding the rash. He said not to worry, as they would fade over a week or two, and after a few more flights I wouldn't get them anymore, because I'd have already burst all the vessels. Jeesh! If that was going on in my skin, what was happening in my brain?

Colleagues and friends often ask me what it feels like to pull all those G's with the G suit. My terse reply: "It's like getting hit in the stomach with an axe, over and over and over again."

A few years later, the 125th switched from F-16's to F-15's and once again I had a chance to ride along in an F-15B during a daylight practice mission, this time with the Group Commander in the front seat. For this exercise, a six-ship formation of F-15s from the 125th were to attempt to "bomb" the Marine Corps airfield in Beaufort, SC. Midway up the coast, our flight was to be intercepted by a "hostile force" of Marine F-18's out of Beaufort, who were going to try to prevent our attack.

My Group Commander's strategy as the designated "bomber" was to quickly escape the dogfighting melee by diving under the gaggle of sparring aircraft to hopefully proceed undetected to the target. We all departed Jacksonville, climbing to over 20,000 feet in the Warlord military warning area off the coast, and turned north. Sure enough, we soon detected the hostiles on radar. As the others proceeded to the attack and aerial combat maneuvering encounter (dogfighting), the Commander and I rolled inverted and dove for the sea.

Rolling out about one hundred feet or so above the waves (after pulling more of those fearsome G's), we accelerated to supersonic speeds skimming the sea surface and under the fur ball of turning and twisting aircraft far overhead. As we ran north, we passed a fishing boat. I clearly remember seeing the skipper leaning back in his lawn chair on the flying bridge, reading a newspaper as we flashed past him only about three hundred feet away from his stern. He never heard us until the sonic boom hit him a moment after we passed. Craning my neck around, I distinctly remember his paper thrown into the wind as he dove for cover. Minutes later, we were over our target, mission complete. My pilot gave me the stick and I flew back to Jacksonville. The mission was quite a thrill; I got some F-15 stick time and didn't get sick at all!

Rounding out my series of fighter flights, I was offered a flight in a US Navy F-18B based out of Cecil Field NAS, Florida, just west of Jacksonville. Cecil housed a training element providing F-18 Hornet pilot transition training to naval fleet pilots. I had cared for one of the instructor pilot's relatives in our Orange Park clinic and knowing my status as a USAF flight surgeon, he was able to get permission to take me up, provided I passed the rigorous water survival training required of all Naval Aviators.

Held at a large facility at Jacksonville NAS, the water survival training day was quite an event. After morning lectures on water survival techniques and equipment, it was time to head to the pool. Dressed in our full flight suits, helmets, gloves, and boots, we had to complete various tasks like swimming underwater, clearing away from parachute shrouds while in the water, and learning proper ways to be lifted to a rescue helicopter from the sea after ejecting (hint: never touch the cable lowered from the chopper until it has grounded itself in the water, lest you suffer a lethal shock). The final task of the day was surviving a torture device known as the helo-dunker; a device meant to simulate the actions of a helicopter full of people crashing into the ocean, turning upside down, and sinking thirty feet.

Each time the training rig full of pilots splashed into the water, we had to wait until it had turned turtle one way or the other and hold our breaths until completely submerged, after which we were to make our way "in an orderly fashion" out the side door and swim to the surface. Each of the three dunkings we had to undergo got progressively more difficult, and rescue scuba divers were stationed around the submerged vehicle with each event. The final challenge was getting out while blindfolded, wearing a helmet with an opaque visor. Talk about disorientation! Blindfolded, upside down, rotating, and with water filling your nose, ears, and sinuses, you were to feel your way along the inverted bench, reach for the door frame, and then get yourself out, after which you were to follow your bubbles to the surface. In my case, matters were even worse, as I had been randomly chosen from the ten of us to be the last man out—I was positioned furthest away from the door.

The cardinal rule for escape when submerged and inverted in the dark was to NEVER let go of your bench seat edge, as that pointed the way to the door. So, what was the first thing I did in that actual test? I let go of the seat edge… Immediately disoriented, I forced myself not to panic and started groping futilely around. What saved me was getting kicked in the face by someone next to me. I figured he had to be closer to the door than I was, so I headed toward the kick. Fortunately, I found the door before I drowned, swam up, and broke the surface gasping. Two of the other Navy pilots had to be helped by the rescue divers. As I weakly climbed the ladder out of the pool, receiving congratulations from the trainers, I asked just how long this training was good for. They replied that the training had to be repeated every four years. I paused, looked them in the eye, and said, "Gentlemen, I will fly with the Navy for the next four years, but I ain't never doing that again!"

Once past that hurdle, I was ready for my F-18 flight on a two-ship bombing mission over a military range in central Florida. "Digger" Van Dyke did a fabulous bombing job, hitting the bullseye on each attack, and then let me fly the plane back to Cecil Field. I even executed two acceptable touch-and-go landings in the bird before we parked at the ramp. The most difficult part of the mission for me was not the flight, but getting suited up for it; the Navy G suit had a lot more belts and straps than the USAF equipment, plus we also had to don all the water survival equipment. (Figure 18)

Aside from the tactical fighters, I also had a chance to fly a military Cessna T-37 trainer at Randolph AFB and rode in the back of several

C-5 Galaxy flights with Sue on Space-A status: twice to/from Europe, and once to/from Hawaii on TDY or vacation.

I'm often asked whether I ever had a call sign. Call signs were historically given by squadron mates or leaders, and often were bestowed after some inept performance, embarrassing incident, or even a quirk of their names. The abbreviated names were used in flight while on missions and were more commonly used in the US Navy than the USAF. I fortunately had not done anything too stupid in a military cockpit and had avoided sexual references related to "Johnson," so was initially just called "*Doc*" by my USAF pilots. My ultimate call sign, however, was ironically bestowed by a US Navy instructor pilot.

There was a civilian company at one point offering aerial combat maneuvering training near Atlanta, Georgia. The instructor pilots were all active-duty, reserve, or retired US Naval aviators and flew/taught the curriculum in old but reliable Beechcraft T-34 Mentors. I had signed up for a couple days of that training to enhance my civilian piloting skill set. During my initial preflight brief, the lead instructor, knowing I was a USAF flight surgeon, asked if I had a call sign already. When I announced that I was only known as "Doc," he shook his head and said that would never do. He stopped the brief and asked me to describe my specialty of radiation oncology. For about five full minutes, I enthusiastically regaled him and the other instructors with stories about high-energy physics and particle accelerators, radiation beams, and radioactive seeds. As I got into full fever-pitch descriptions, an instructor's hand shot up: "Stop, doc, that's enough. Henceforward, I dub thee *Laser*." The mission brief continued, and that was that. The name stuck. It wasn't very cool, as in my mind it distilled eight years of hard complex training into one simplistic word, but hey, it could have been worse.

While at Travis AFB performing my annual two-week tour during the summer of 1999, I received an unusual call from a USAF Reserve General on the East Coast. He said that he and a colleague wanted to meet me for lunch two days hence at Travis. I asked if he'd like me to make reservations at the Officer's Club, but he said no, they would reach out to me upon their arrival.

On the morning of the appointed day, my secretary fielded a call from the General with directions to the lunch meeting. To my surprise, the spot was a secluded restaurant a few miles away from the base. I arrived at the appointed time and was escorted to a dark table at the back of the nearly empty restaurant, where I was greeted by not one but two General Officers, both of whom were physicians in the USAFR. The meeting and its location were disquieting.

After a few pleasantries, they got down to business. "Colonel Johnson, I am sure you are wondering why we called you here today. Well, your name has bubbled up for promotion consideration to Brigadier General. Before submitting your name, however, we wanted to speak with you to let you know what you'd be getting yourself into with that promotion." He went on to relate that there were but a handful of USAFR Generals, and to be a success in that role a candidate had to agree to give up about one-quarter of his private practice and pony up about $100,000 per year.

When I balked at that and asked them to explain, they further stated that the role of a Reserve General medical officer largely consisted of conducting spot IG (Inspector General) inspections at USAF medical facilities around the world. These duties usually required about one week a month of time away from home. Furthermore, these inspections were often at the last minute: you might receive a call on Friday morning in Florida, instructing you to be in Seoul, Korea, on Sunday morning, for instance. "Notice is usually so short that there is no time to go through the usual routine of having a military travel office procure your tickets, so you must buy them at full fare just before you take off, out of your own pocket. To make matters worse, when you return and apply for reimbursement to that travel office, they will only compensate you for the cheapest fare they could have obtained in advance with several weeks' notice. Your unreimbursed total costs can easily exceed $100,000 per year." These constraints had not deterred the two Generals sitting before me: they were highly compensated semi-retired surgeons who really didn't need money from their civilian practice. I, on the other hand, had two young teenagers and a spouse to care for back at home. I thanked them for making the trip, and said I needed to discuss the situation with my wife.

Upon my return to Jacksonville, Sue and I sat down and had a long chat. Although I loved the USAF and the military, at our current stage of life and with college costs looming we just could not afford to accept a promotion with those constraints, and by declining it, I would have reached the ceiling of my USAF career.

Shortly thereafter, I submitted my notice of separation. After twenty-five years as a USAF Brat, followed by another twenty-four wearing the uniform myself with eight years of active duty and sixteen years in the reserves, my days in the military were ending. Though I had never borne arms in battle during that entire time, I had served in the background during the Cold War and supported the conflicts in Iraq. By early October 1999, I was retired from the USAFR, and a major chapter in my life had closed.

CHAPTER 18

Flying higher

Slipping the surly bonds of earth…

After moving to Florida in 1987, my flying activities continued unabated. I had previously rented a variety of single-engine airplanes at both the Moffett NAS Flying Club and the Travis AFB Aero Club. There were many advantages to renting rather than owning a plane including lower costs, fewer headaches having to deal with renting a hangar, not paying separately for maintenance, and the ability to fly a broad variety of planes based at the clubs. Balanced against those advantages were the hassles of always having to schedule the plane far in advance, club limitations on the distance away they could be flown, and seemingly constant maintenance issues due to their older airframes and heavier workloads, etc.

Jacksonville NAS also had a Flying Club, so after transferring my credentials and a few check outs with club instructors, I was free to explore the area. The main difference between flying in Florida vs. California was the flat terrain and frequent cloudy or stormy days in the Southeast. The latter put a frustrating crimp in my aviation activities, so after almost ten years of strictly fair-weather flying, I decided it was finally time to earn my instrument rating. The didactic and practical skills challenge was difficult but rewarding, as the instrument rating opened a whole new world of capabilities and options for travel. That training also started a cascade of additional training and ratings over the next few years. I decided to reach for a higher level of pilot license; after additional training to much more rigorous standards and successfully completing an FAA check ride, I earned my Commercial Pilot license. The Commercial ticket theoretically allowed me to carry passengers or cargo for hire, tow banners, do aerial photography, and the like. I earned endorsements for complex aircraft and technologically advanced aircraft (think glass cockpit) and later my high-altitude endorsement. As we began taking longer trips, the idea of having a second engine appealed to me as well, so I earned my multi-engine rating in a Beechcraft Dutchess. On the fun side, along the way I also added a tail-dragger endorsement and seaplane rating.

A few misadventures on commercial flights, though, eventually led me down an unexpected path in my civilian aviation journey—building my own airplane.

Commercial cross-country airline flights from Florida to California normally carried me to and from my annual active-duty tours. In both 1991 and 1992, unfortunately, the airlines lost my luggage on those flights. Now there is nothing worse for a reservist than showing up for duty without uniforms—it was considered unprofessional and inexcusable. I was mortified each of those years and spent a lot of time, effort, and money upon arrival at Travis AFB scrounging around for replacements.

This embarrassment and the fear of a repeat debacle the following year led me to wonder about the possibility of flying myself across the country. The clapped-out Flying Club aircraft I had been flying wouldn't do for a few reasons. First, the Club wouldn't release one of their rental aircraft to a member for three weeks at a time. Second, I wasn't confident that the Club planes could make the nearly five thousand mile round trip without some type of breakdown along the way. Finally, the Club planes just weren't fast enough to get me there in a reasonable amount of time; even the fastest of the bunch I was flying, a twin-engine T-42 Beech Baron, would require sixteen hours of flight time each way, plus stopovers for meals, fuel, and rest.

My first thought was to explore buying a newer aircraft to perform the mission. Newer and more reliable piston-powered planes were available, but they were too slow. I looked at small jet aircraft. They would fit the bill in terms of speed, but the price tag and operational expenses of a jet were completely beyond my means.

I was about to give up on the idea of flying myself to California when a pilot friend suggested I look at a new aircraft that had just been written up in an aviation magazine: the Lancair IV. I located the article, and this new airplane was impressive indeed—it was constructed of strong space-age carbon fiber that wouldn't rust, it carried up to four people in the cabin and was fast because of its powerful dual-turbocharged engine and sleek laminar-flow wings. The plane was designed by Lance Neibauer and manufactured in Redmond, Oregon, on the dry eastern side of the Cascade Mountain range.

After a call to the factory to schedule a test, I flew commercially to Portland and was picked up by their chief test pilot in the factory demonstrator plane. The plan was to depart Portland and fly east over the mountains to reach Redmond. Once there, I would have a factory tour and demo flight. Well, that was the plan, anyway… After takeoff in the factory Lancair IV, the pilot boldly climbed eastward toward the mountains and right into a layer of clouds. After a few minutes of this I noticed two things: first, the pilot was not talking to anyone, and second, there was ice forming on the leading edges of the wings.

When piloting an aircraft, one of two sets of rules apply. In clear weather with at least three miles of visibility one can fly under Visual Flight Rules (VFR) at one's own discretion. Talking to flight controllers while flying VFR is optional as it is the pilot's responsibility to see and avoid any conflicting traffic and terrain. Any flight into conditions with less visibility than that, as in clouds, necessitates flying under Instrument Flight Rules (IFR). Under an IFR flight plan, FAA controllers assume the responsibility to assign headings and altitudes to keep you clear of terrain, obstacles, and other traffic. Constant radio communications beginning with the control tower and subsequent handoff to departure and enroute controllers is mandatory.

In our cockpit, there were no radios tuned to any departure control frequencies that I could tell. As we continued to climb toward the mountains completely engulfed in clouds, I queried the pilot over the intercom, "Are we on an IFR flight plan?" He responded, "No, I'm not IFR qualified. Are you?"

Well, this was a pickle. We were flying illegally in clouds in an aircraft I had just been introduced to minutes before, not talking to controllers, not squawking a discrete code assigned to all IFR flights, with a pilot who was not IFR rated, in a plane with ice accumulating on the wings!

My first concerns were our blind heading toward the mountains and that wing ice. Wings require smooth airflow over them to generate lift. When ice accumulates on the front edge of the wings, it can rapidly upset that airflow, leading to a stall and loss of aircraft control, resulting in a bad day for all concerned. It is the evil dragon all private pilots have nightmares over.

I looked over at the pilot in disbelief and quietly, but firmly, suggested that he make a slow but deliberate course reversal and descend to warmer outside air temperatures. He did so under my watchful eye, while I quickly tried to understand the controls, should I need to take over. We eventually descended to the point that we broke out of the clouds into clear air, and the wing ice gradually fell away. Now, however, we were too low to get across the mountain range.

Being more familiar with the area than I, he suggested that we could stay low and fly up the Columbia River Gorge to the east to get through the mountains under the cloud layer, but it would add twenty minutes to the flight. Dumbfounded that he had not suggested that in the first place, I stated that I thought that was an excellent idea. We eventually made it to Redmond, and I had a nice tour with the Lancair folks. By the next day the clouds had cleared. I had an impressive demo flight with the opportunity to get some good stick time and even perform a few takeoffs and landings. The Lancair IV flew like a dream, and I loved it.

Upon landing, I told the factory marketing people that I was sold, and asked where I could buy one.

That's when they dropped the hammer on me: "You can't buy one already made, you have to build it!"

"What on earth are you talking about?"

"This is a kit aircraft," they replied. "You purchase the kit, we ship it to you, and you can assemble it in about nine months."

I had built lots of model airplanes as a kid, but this was a whole new level to consider.

After returning to Jacksonville, I did some research on kit homebuilt aircraft. These airplanes fall under the FAA's Experimental Aircraft category. Homebuilts were nothing new and indeed had been put together in various forms in factories or even home garages for decades. Each builder assumed all the legal responsibility for his creation, so he didn't have to go through the millions of dollars of FAA-mandated flight testing required of commercial airplane manufacturers. Because the builder was also putting in all the sweat equity, the cost per plane was dramatically less than a "store bought" Cessna, Beechcraft, or Piper commercially produced aircraft with similar or fewer capabilities.

In many cases, the Experimental market was able to incorporate new technologies more rapidly than the commercial producers: once a commercially produced plane gained FAA approval after all the time and money spent in flight testing, any changes to that approved design required an almost herculean and expensive effort to generate the onerous paperwork and perform the requalification testing required for the change to be okayed by the FAA. Hence, updates to certificated aircraft were few and far between.

The Lancair IV incorporated amazing new composite technology, using carbon fiber as the strong but lightweight backbone of the aircraft structure. In the early 1990's, the only significant aviation use of carbon fiber was in the tail planes of the F-18 fighter and the flaps on Boing 757 and 767 jetliners—it was considered just too expensive to use elsewhere. Because of the carbon fiber and other technologies, the Lancair IV was in a class of its own, with speeds between that of a standard propeller aircraft and a jet, at a cost that was a fraction of the cost of a new prop plane. I broke out my checkbook and ordered the first of the three sub-kits needed to fabricate my airplane.

Two weeks later, a three-foot stack of building manuals arrived in the mail. By the third page, I was overwhelmed: I had none of the tools, compressors, and shop tables they were talking about. A call to the Lancair factory in Oregon was forthcoming, and a confession that I was in over my head was made. A sympathetic factory contact suggested a call to D.L. Simmons, a fellow in Tennessee with experience building experimental aircraft.

D.L. was a pilot who lived in an air-conditioned hangar at a small airport in central Tennessee. He had tons of composite experience building race cars and had every piece of shop equipment needed. Most importantly, he had already helped some other builders complete their kits. I took a Flying Club airplane to visit him and was impressed with the quality of his work; before I left, he had agreed to partner with me in the construction of my Lancair IV. I would build my plane in his shop, under his guidance, and commute back and forth several times a month to make it happen. Little did I realize that the factory's nine-month estimate to complete the building process would stretch into a five-year adventure.

CHAPTER 19

Adventure Down Under

Flying the Australian Outback

One tenet of our FROG group was that we should work hard but take time to play hard, too.
Perusing an aviation magazine one day in 1993, I read an article about "flying your own plane" around Australia with an adventure group called Australian Outback Flying Safaris. Visiting Australia had been a dream for Sue and me, so we contacted the expedition leader, a jovial character with infectious enthusiasm and a desire to show off his native land. Alan Miles was married to a United Airlines flight attendant and split his time between Australia and Minnesota.

After a thirty-minute phone conversation with Alan, I was ready to sign up for an adventure down under. Sue was onboard, too, so we started arranging logistics to realize our Australian exploit on the next scheduled Safari in April 1994. Alan had never had children on one of his trips but said he'd be glad to welcome ours. Danielle and Michael were in fourth and second grades at that time, so Sue talked to their teachers about granting a month-long absence. Initially resistant, the schoolteachers and administrators eventually granted permission with the understanding that the kids would continue to study basic subjects daily while abroad and would return to give a full report and presentation to their classmates. As a former teacher, Sue was glad to take on their educational supervision during the trip.

The Australian Civil Aviation Authority (CAA), their equivalent of our FAA, had a reciprocal agreement with the USA: with a valid US pilot license and medical certificate, Australia would grant a day VFR Australian license after a flight review and briefing by a CAA check pilot. Though flying a plane was no different there than here, the rules of the road and nomenclature down under were unique—the traffic pattern in Australia was called a circuit, and the altimeter setting was called the QNH, for example. Navigational aids called VOR's were a rarity in Australia, whereas they were comprehensively sited every fifty to one hundred miles apart in the USA. As a result, an older technique called VFR pilotage was universally used in Australia: using time, compass headings, and wind calculations to plot a course to a destination—a technique unchanged since before WWII.

After a long series of commercial flights island-hopping across the Pacific Ocean, we arrived in Brisbane, Australia—the only large city we would visit during our month-long stay. Upon arrival, we met fellow pilots and aircrew who would man the other four planes on our Safari. It was a fascinating and motley crew: in addition to Alan and his lovely wife who were to lead us in their Cessna-182, we had a female undertaker and her partner from Minnesota, a shrimp farmer from Ecuador, and a father/son team from Illinois.

After introductions, Alan laid out the routine we would adhere to for the ensuing three weeks. He also taught us local customs and practices unique to Australia (such as checking the bottom of your toilet seat each time before sitting to look for dangerous frogs) and warned us about all the poisonous native critters. I remember his sage advice to this day: "Now you might be wondering how you can tell if something is poisonous in Australia. It's simple: if it's moving, it's poisonous!"

Each evening before a flight, the pilots would gather for a detailed briefing including maps, weather forecasts, destination airport overview, anticipated winds aloft, times and waypoints, etc.

Chapter 19

All navigation was to be done by dead reckoning, as few navigational aids existed outside major cities. GPS navigation was in its infancy, and many of us had rented hand-held units before our arrival. Unlike modern GPS systems, these small units would clip onto the yoke and merely allow input of destination latitude and longitude; there were no moving map screens. Once aloft, an arrow would point to the desired course on a small screen, along with some markers to indicate if you were off track to the right or left of that course.

After breakfast each travel day, the pilots would pre-flight their planes while the passengers loaded baggage, water, and snacks. Just before a designated takeoff time, engines would be fired up and radio checks completed. Then, one by one, each plane would take the strip and lift off in turn. As we were the only Cessna-172 with four people aboard, we were the heaviest and slowest so would usually be last in line. I use the term "strip" loosely, for as it turned out, of the thirty plus landings and takeoffs we did over the ensuing weeks, only five or so were on pavement; the rest of our landing zones were on dirt roads, pastures, gravel deposits, etc.

Flights would normally take place during the mornings, when the weather was clear, smooth, and a bit cooler; by early afternoon we would alight at our destination, check in to our accommodations, and then tour the local area and meet the region's inhabitants. Occasionally we would spend two days at a spot, and doing laundry would be an option.

After Alan's overview at our initial arrival hotel in Brisbane, the pilots headed to nearby Redcliffe Airport the next morning to meet and fly with the CAA examiner. Once we had mastered the nomenclature and rules pertinent to Australian flying, and once he had reviewed our US documents and passed his flight check of our skills, we were awarded an Australian CAA Pilot's license. During the two days it took for everyone to complete this gauntlet, we had time to tour sights around Brisbane including a rain forest and Koala preserve—the latter a huge hit with Danielle and Mike.

On the third morning our adventure began as we flew north along the coast toward our first two overnights on Brampton and Great Keppel Islands. Alan's droll navigational advice for these first two days was succinct: "Okay, mates, we're heading north up the beach: keep the bloody blue side on your right, and the brown side on your left." (Figures 19-24)

After those island visits where we swam with emus, fed flocks of lorikeets, and gaped at nightly swarms of fruit bats, we launched westward into the arid interior of the country. VFR pilotage was critical, as hours would go by without any signs of human habitation: no buildings, no roads, and no powerlines.

After a refueling stop at Mt. Isa, we pressed on to ultimately land on a road at a remote cattle station for lunch. While there, we met the station owner and his young family. Our kids sat in on a school lesson with the rancher's children being conducted via the School of the Air: cattle stations were so remote that CB radios were used to conduct classes over the entire area, as in-person meetings were impractical. After the station owner treated us to a sumptuous lunch, we helped the family drive several hundred head of cattle to another part of their station several miles distant, using motorcycles instead of horses. Later we refueled the planes from 55-Gallon drums and departed through clouds of dust to continue westward.

At each stop throughout the outback of Australia, we found the locals to be friendly and engaging. They were as interested in us as we were in them and were proud to show off their rugged way of life. In some ways, the people of the outback reminded me of Americans in the 1950's—neighbors were there to support each other but were self-reliant, there was little crime (no one locked their car or home doors at night), and a can-do upbeat attitude permeated their existence.

During one overnight stop, a small group of shabbily clad aborigines stopped by to say hello. We asked them about life in the bush and their tribal ways, but they instead wanted to opine the geopolitical implications of the closure of the Clark Air base on the Philippine Islands and subsequent risk of Chinese expansion of influence in the region! I learned a lesson that evening about not judging someone by their appearance and not stereotyping a people based solely upon impressions from television. As it turns out, the aboriginal peoples get a free education in Australia, up through graduate degrees. Some stay in the cities pursuing a professional life, but a great many of them return to their roots in the bush after graduation. These humble people we met that night were smart and well-educated.

The aborigines took a shining to Danielle and Mike and volunteered to show them some tribal foraging techniques handed down over the generations. The next morning we shuttled out to a spot in the bush, and the aboriginal group appeared seemingly from nowhere at the appointed time. Then began an hour-long lesson on hunting for bush tomatoes and cooking up whitchetty grubs they had our kids dig up from the roots of nearby turpentine trees. The children said the roasted grubs tasted like peanut butter French fries and even asked for seconds! After the lesson, the aborigines bade us a hearty farewell and we returned to our camp. Our leader, Alan, stated that even though he was Australian, he had never heard of or seen these foraging techniques: our children had unlocked the doors of communication between two very different cultures.

The next few weeks were filled with amazing and wide-ranging adventures covering two thirds of the continent. We stayed at the Crocodile Dundee hotel, overflew the massive Kakadu National Park south of Darwin, toured the Royal Flying Doctor Service operations base in Alice Springs, rode camels, climbed Ayers Rock (now a forbidden practice, as this spiritual site was returned to the aborigines and renamed Uluru shortly after we left), slept in an underground hotel near Coober Pedy and its legendary opal mines, drove a houseboat upstream for two days on the Wentworth River, and raced across brackish lakes in a homemade speedboat near the Gold Coast. At every stop, we met amazing people living a rich and fulfilling life.

I learned a few aviation tricks from the outback bush pilots as well. Our Cessna's would tend to sink a few inches in the soft sandy earth overnight. To get them moving the next morning, those pilots taught me a technique of rocking the elevator up and down while applying some power to bounce the plane gradually out of the hole—it worked every time. Another tip involved safe fuel management in our aircraft while traversing rugged country. The Cessna's gravity-fed fuel system had a four-position indicator for which fuel tank was feeding the engine: "Off," "Left," "Right," or "Both." In the States, we almost always kept the fuel feed position on "Both." In the outback, however, bush pilots suggested we alternately switch from "Left" to "Right" and back again every thirty minutes. That way, if the engine started to sputter when one tank went dry, an immediate switch to the opposite tank relit the fire and gave you twenty minutes or so to find a spot to land. A good safety tip, indeed, for an area where landing strips were few and far between. I just wish they had shared that tip before a sphincter-puckering flight a few days later…

A third trick I learned while flying over the Great Simpson Desert in the Cessna was to ride thermals. Gliders routinely use thermal updrafts to stretch out their time aloft and glide distance, but it turns out you can do the same in a wee Cessna. One day we were once again "tail end Charlie," being the heaviest and slowest plane in the group (although we immediately took off one after the other every morning, within ten minutes or so everyone else was out of sight). It was a blazingly hot day over the desert as we flew south toward the remote Mt. Dare Station when I noticed that some large buzzards were using thermals to climb occasionally along our route, even though there wasn't a cloud in the sky. "Well, what have I got to lose," I remarked to Sue. "Let's see if we can use those thermals, too, to climb to a higher and cooler altitude." Sure enough, I went where the buzzards went, and soon we were in a thermal elevator lifting us one thousand feet per minute. I circled and rose several thousand feet before resuming our course south, gradually diving down to our original altitude and picking up speed in the descent. Soon enough, I spotted another buzzard group rising in a different thermal and followed suit. These cycles of rising in a thermal and speeding down to the next one were repeated several times over the next two hours.

We finally alit at our destination and to our surprise found that we had beaten most of the other aircraft!

Although the flying usually went off without a hitch, there was one day of misadventure late in the journey. We were scheduled to have our longest leg of the trip flying east from Wentworth in southern Australia, across the fertile farmlands of that area and over some low mountains as we headed toward Melbourne and the east coast. We had reviewed the route extensively at the pilot briefing the evening before the flight, and with the projected winds aloft thought we could make our refueling stop, over four hours away, with an adequate reserve if we managed our fuel carefully.

The plan sounded fine, but the reality didn't quite work out for two reasons: the headwinds were worse than projected, and two pilots were a bit sloppy when it came to leaning their mixture to save fuel. I should note that I was by far the least experienced pilot on the trip, with just over two hundred hours flight time, as opposed to the thousands of flight hours the other pilots described nightly over beverages at the bar. Perhaps because I was a nitpicker when it came to leaning my fuel mixture, as had so recently been drilled into me by my instructors, or the fact that I had my whole family aboard, I was ultra-cautious with fuel: I would rather be slower due to over-leaning, if it gave me a few miles extra range. Other pilots in the group were more concerned with speedy low-level joyriding over hills and dales, however, than they were with their range. Those activities burned fuel faster. Put another way, I was playing Volkswagen, and they were playing Ferrari…

All went well until about four hours into the flight when we heard "Mayday, Mayday" over the radio, as the undertaker duet called out that they had run out of fuel (although we couldn't see each other, the radio calls still connected the gaggle that had spaced out over forty miles or so by this time). Their engine had quit, and they were gliding down to make an emergency landing. The pilot reported back about ten minutes later that he had landed safely on the dirt track of a countryside horse-racing venue. Fifteen minutes later, our Ecuadorian shrimp farmer and copilot announced that they, too, were extremely low on fuel and were beginning an emergency descent. They called out GPS coordinates of their position every thirty seconds or so as they came down, which Sue diligently wrote down. The timber of the shrimper's voice raised an octave when his engine finally sputtered and died. As we were the last duckling in trail, we flew overhead a few minutes later and confirmed with them by radio that they had landed safely in a cow pasture.

We had about thirty miles and one final ridge to traverse before descending into our refueling stop. Sue and I were watching our fuel tank gauges bouncing off the "Empty" markings (yes, the fuel selector valve was on "Both," so when they both ran dry, that would be it). She looked me in the eye and said quietly, "You promised me we wouldn't run out of gas." It was one of my "Lord, get me out of this and I will never do that again" moments. With relief, we crossed the ridge and landed safely at the airport where I pulled up behind the two other aircraft in the group awaiting a turn at the fuel pump. After refueling, I determined that we had four liters of fuel left when we landed…

Our leader in his speedier plane had landed well before the rest of us. He was highly miffed after hearing of the plight of the two downed aircraft, and we heard some new Aussie vernacular that doesn't bear repeating. We were plotting how to rescue the downed crews and aircraft about forty-five minutes later, when across the ridge one of the missing Cessna-172's came roaring down to the strip. After shutting down, we gathered around as the pair exited their plane to hear their story. This was the plane that had landed on the dirt racetrack, and after climbing out of their fuel-starved bird, they realized no one was around to help them. One of the pair hopped the track fence and hiked a road to a gas station, where he purchased two fuel cans and about ten gallons of auto gas. He then hiked back with the fuel and fired up the engine after dumping it into one wing tank. They taxied completely around the track once or twice building up enough speed that they could perform a soft-field takeoff on the straightaway.

The other pair was not quite so creative. As we heard later, they had barely stopped before a fence after skidding across a slippery cow-flop filled pasture. Our leader unloaded his more powerful Cessna-182 except for a jerry can filled with aviation fuel and departed solo to find the errant pair. He managed to land in the field alongside them and dispense the few gallons he brought along. He also dispensed some crash-course knowledge on short field takeoffs over an obstacle. After transferring all their luggage into his plane to lighten their Cessna-172's load, he watched with bated breath as the shrimp farmer taxied back to the far side of the field, ran the engine to high power, released brakes, and made a run for the opposite field edge. At the last minute, as instructed, he popped full flaps which lifted the plane over the fence with about two feet of clearance. The lightened Cessna-172 climbed out and continued to the fuel stop, with Alan following closely behind in his plane.

Those two planes were a mess when they landed, with their bellies and sides completely covered in fetid sticky cow poop. Later that night, after finally arriving at our destination for the day, the two fuel-starved crews were assigned to clean up both birds. Upon finally returning after dark to our local watering hole, they also had to buy drinks for everyone. With classic Aussie wit and understatement that evening, Alan remarked, "Good lord, mates, you never call out that you're 'going down' or declare an emergency over the radio unless your wing just fell off—that'll cause too much paperwork with the CAA authorities if they catch wind. If you run out of petrol, on the radio you should rather just state that you're making a precautionary landing!"

The remaining flights were uneventful, and all the rented planes (two cleaner than the others) returned safely to Redcliffe.

Both Danielle and Mike had completed their assigned coursework in the evenings of the trip and handed it all in upon their return to Jacksonville. As promised, they also each gave a thirty-minute presentation to their entire grade at their elementary school with PowerPoint slides and a laser pointer, and even passed around cultural items they had returned with for the children to handle. It was a pretty impressive performance for second and fourth graders, and their teachers and school administrators were blown away.

To this day, both kids avow that the Australian adventure was the most memorable of their lives: they loved the places they went and people they met—they appreciated that the Aussies were from a different culture but had desires and hopes similar to Americans. Mike even returned years later to spend a college semester abroad at the University of Melbourne.

One of the best aspects of the trip is that it encouraged me to finally pull my brushes and canvases out of retirement to start painting again. I continued to paint scenes from our travels in the decades to come, many of which hang in our home today.

CHAPTER 20

Rekindled hope

NASA is hiring

I have always been fascinated by NASA's efforts to explore and understand the air in which we live as well as the heavens around us. Their efforts are not frivolous; rather, they are critical to the survival of humanity. The human species is doomed to extinction, as is demonstrated in the archeological record for virtually every complex species that has gone before us. Species rise, flourish, and after time are gone either due to pestilence, climate change, or a cataclysmic event. In our case, the most likely cause of humanity's demise will be collision with an asteroid or meteor—an event akin to that which decimated the dinosaurs. The only conceivable way to ensure our species' survival is to colonize another heavenly body, or as the adage goes to "not keep all our eggs in one basket."

With my researcher/investigator mindset, I had always wanted to be a part of that great undertaking but had had my hopes dashed—as a teenager I had been told by USAF physicians that my poor eyesight meant that I could never fly a military jet, much less a spacecraft. Things had evolved with NASA over time, however. Years after the last lunar trip by Apollo in 1972, the Space Shuttle Columbia lifted Americans back to space with the first Space Transportation System (STS) mission in April 1981. The loss of the Challenger Shuttle during STS-51 was a big setback in 1986, but by the 1990's the program was back in full swing. The knowledge of our universe was greatly expanding, in large part due to the efforts of the Shuttle-deployed Hubble Space Telescope and similar instruments. Exoplanets and other previously unknown objects were discovered.

In early 1995 I read an article describing the whole new generation of astronauts that embodied NASA's Space Shuttle era. As opposed to the heady days of Projects Mercury, Gemini, and Apollo with their strict test-pilot astronaut requirements, the new era included new types of astronauts known as Mission Specialists and Payload Specialists. The new categories of astronaut had a broad range of duties, mainly involving the care and feeding of myriad payload experiments carried in the shuttle bay, satellite deployment, and space walks done in preparation for building the anticipated International Space Station (ISS) in 1998. All types of scientists were being recruited to the astronaut corps, and the physical standards were not quite as rigid. Most surprisingly, the average age of an accepted astronaut then was forty-two, older than I was at the time. Perhaps it wasn't too late for me after all?

NASA called for a new class of astronaut candidates (ASCAN's) every two years or so, as needs arose, and the next class was to be selected in early 1996. I had a long discussion with Sue about my dormant desire to apply to become an astronaut, and we discussed the effects it might have on our family in the unlikely event that I was selected. To my delight, she was very supportive, stating, "If you don't at least try, you will always wonder."

Thousands of applicants submitted their hopes in writing prior to each cycle, and I threw my name into the hat as well. I sent off volumes of Civil Service paperwork, curriculum vitae, and letters of reference. One of my patients back at Travis AFB was Glennis Yeager (As in "Glamorous Glennis" adorning the starboard nose of the Bell X-1 in which her husband broke the sound barrier in 1947). I had a nice relationship with Chuck Yeager, and he agreed to submit a recommendation letter to NASA on my behalf. I was pleasantly surprised to hear from NASA a few months later: they were interested in me. NASA initiated my background security check and had me undergo a comprehensive examination by doctors in Jacksonville. I passed both.

Of those thousands of applicants in 1995, NASA called 120 "finalist" applicants to the Johnson Space Flight Center in Houston for a week of interviews and even more rigorous physical examinations, scans, and blood work; from that pool, thirty-seven eventually would be chosen as ASCAN's. In late October, I got a phone call from NASA—I was one of the 120 invited for the in-person interview. The Johnson Space Center Astronaut Office invited interviewees in groups of twenty to come down, and I entered those hallowed halls in November of 1995. We were welcomed by none other than astronaut John Young, one of the twelve men to walk on the moon during the Apollo days. He gave us his congratulations, and said that all of us in the room were people they wanted as astronauts, but who they selected during that cycle would be determined by NASA's anticipated needs over the next few years—sometimes they needed more Pilots, sometimes more Mission Specialists…

John Young said if we didn't get selected to keep applying, as they might need someone with our skill set at a future selection board. Indeed, at a famous astronaut hangout just outside the center later that evening, I found out that several of my group had already been there for interviews two or three times previously. Our group of twenty was made up of folks from all walks of life: we had a US Marine Corps Harrier test pilot, a volcanologist, several medical doctors, and engineers. One final quip from John Young before he turned us over to the schedulers informed us that in NASA's eyes, our specialties and talents that got us here were only relevant to a certain point. In reality, all those degrees and accomplishments meant was that we were trainable—astronauts had to become experts in all aspects of science as the needs of the mission dictated including engineering, geology, meteorology, medicine, physiology, etc.

After his briefing, we were sent off for labs. To this day I still see all of us lined up down a long hallway in old school chairs with our arms stretched out and shirt sleeves raised as lab techs drew fourteen tubes of blood from us—all at once. Two of the group passed out right then. "Thank God that wasn't me" was what the rest of us were thinking. After that we had myriad scans, tests, and probes of every orifice of the body imaginable over the ensuing days. Between these tests and facility tours were scattered extensive psychological batteries and grilling by teams of psychiatrists asking arcane things like, "Would you rather kill your mother or paint your desk green" and "Women don't like BLANK". Over a beer that night, one female of our group chuckled as she told us that she filled in the blank with "power tools." (Figures 25-26) If you ever saw the movie *The Right Stuff,* you saw the actual clinic we were in (it had been in use since the Mercury days) and can imagine the types of exams we underwent.

Every evening, we all met at that bar just off the Center property to discuss what we had endured that day so that others on a different schedule might know what to expect. Those were some humorous evenings, and we bonded instantly. I still chuckle as I recall the Marine pilot describing his experience with the colonoscopy (we received no anesthesia, so could watch the whole procedure on a television in front of us), using words like "jinking" and "dodging" with hand motions to characterize the movements of the scope.

In addition to all the testing, we were encouraged to interact with the astronauts: we had all-access badges to every nook and cranny of the Space Center, including the Astronaut Office floor complex. To a person, I found this group of amazingly accomplished professionals from diverse backgrounds to be kind, engaging, and truly excited about their work and mission. They always stopped what they were doing when I peered into their offices, invited me in and took pleasure in interacting with me and answering all the questions I posed. One fellow I chatted with for quite some time was Story Musgrave, a veteran physician astronaut who had recently returned from the Hubble repair mission. He would end up holding the record for the most shuttle missions of any astronaut (seven, if memory serves) and on his final re-entry years later did something never done before or since: he stood up on the flight deck out of his seat for the entire event (he had been slated to return seated on the windowless mid-deck, but really wanted to see out the flight deck windows during his last flight return).Story and I would cross paths a few times in the future, as well, as we were both members of the Flying Physicians Association.

Our group was also wined and dined by the astronauts at off-site functions that week: I even sat next to George Abbey, Director of Flight Operations at the Johnson Space Center, at a picnic table over a casual BBQ dinner one evening at a legendary astronaut hangout called The Outpost. The astronauts took us to their homes to meet family and relax, and the head of the astronaut office, Hoot Gibson, took me out to see his experimental homebuilt Cassutt aircraft that he had built for racing after learning that I was currently building a Lancair. We had tours of the training facilities and even mockups of the ISS, and were taken on a tour of Ellington Field, where the astronauts kept up their flying skills with a fleet of T-38 Talon supersonic trainers.

At the end of the week, each candidate had a debriefing with his assigned NASA flight surgeon to review the week's test results. Unfortunately, my right eye had tested slightly out of limits on a test called the Landolt C eye test. This was a distant vision test during which a progressively smaller version of the letter C was displayed, and the examinee was to say which way the opening of the letter was pointing. I could see it clearly if I squinted. The nurse had caught me and told me to "Stop that!" She asked what I would do if I was in orbit and not able to sort out the opening and wasn't too thrilled with my answer, "I'd squint." In addition to the eye, a cardiac echo showed that the septum (wall) between my two ventricles was wider than they liked to see. Both issues resulted in me being medically disqualified from consideration.

Though keeping a straight face, I was crushed internally by the news. The flight surgeon tried to console me by noting that the whole board had discussed my case, and that these medical issues were regrettable, because I was exactly the type of person they were looking for during this selection round, and I had been high on the board's list. I am sure he meant well, but this news only seemed to make it worse. I could perhaps have gotten a waiver with Lasik surgery for the eye (though Lasik was not yet approved by NASA) but couldn't do a thing about my heart.

I consoled myself that God needed me somewhere other than at NASA, so I headed home with the sad news. I sat my kids down after school that day to tell them what I had been up to that week, and to let them know that daddy was never going to be an astronaut. I tried to make a life lesson out of it though, saying that I was proud to at least have tried, and encouraged them to do the same in their own lives with their own dreams down the road.

Two of the twenty in our group were indeed selected that year: Don Pettit and Charlie "Scorch" Hobaugh. We had all made a pact while at the bar during that week in Houston that if anyone was selected, he or she would invite the others to their Shuttle launches down the road. Scorch was true to his word, and I was invited to one of his launches and landings a few years later. I also kept up with a few of the others for several years.

CHAPTER 21

Cancer strikes

At home, a bad lump appears

It wasn't long before I realized why God needed me back home with my family. Our world was rocked one day in the summer of 1996 when Sue announced, "I have a lump on my breast mammogram."

I had heard that statement from many women (and a few men) patients over the years but hearing it as a husband rather than as a clinician was an entirely different experience emotionally. The initial pit in my stomach upon hearing Sue's words only deepened when I examined her and confirmed the thickening. My colleagues went out of their way to ensure she had a rapid and thorough evaluation: a diagnostic mammogram, ultrasound, and core biopsy were all done within forty-eight hours, and breast cancer was confirmed.

I had a long history of cancer in my family; both my mother and grandmother had been diagnosed with breast cancer and an uncle had prostate cancer. Sue was aware of their struggles and initially had a hard time believing that it was happening to her as well. After all, she was only forty-two years old…

Our surgeon friend, Jack Crump, said he could fit her in to remove the lump within a few days, but Sue was hesitant. We had for months planned a trip to the former East Germany as part of a group tracking down a missing train bearing artifacts hidden by the Nazis in WWII, and she did not want to miss that. Still in denial about her diagnosis, Sue insisted that we make the trip as planned and said she would have the surgery once she returned. Days later in the remote forests of East Germany, however, she woke up stating, "What am I doing here, I need to take care of this!" After overcoming some logistical hurdles getting back west, I called Jack from the airport in Amsterdam to let him know we were winging our way back to the USA. Within twenty-four hours of our return, the breast lump was removed and sent to pathology.

The pathologist came back to us a day later with good news: the cancer was very early stage (so-called ductal carcinoma in situ, or DCIS). Sue elected to go the breast preservation route, so began a seven-week course of daily radiation treatments to the remaining breast tissue, as well as start a five-year program taking an oral medication called Tamoxifen. Other than sunburn on her treated skin at the end of the radiation course, she tolerated her treatment well and was cured. She continued all her mom duties and played tennis on a lady's tennis team throughout and after her treatments but never told many friends about her ordeal. Several years later, however, she opened up about her experience when she realized she could be a pillar of support for others undergoing diagnosis and treatment for this all-too-common malady.

Though we didn't realize it at the time, twenty years later the specter of cancer would raise its head again for Sue, in an unusual way. My mother had undergone a mastectomy for breast cancer back in the 1980's, been cured of that, and had moved to Jacksonville in 2006. Shortly after her arrival, she noticed a new lump in her remaining breast. That proved malignant, and she underwent a mastectomy. By this time there were genetic tests available that could assess the risk of developing breast and other cancers in families at high risk by looking for genetic rearrangements called BRCA1 and BRCA2. With my mother's strong family history of breast cancer, we were concerned about the subsequent risk not only for her to develop other cancers, but also the risks for Danielle and Mike, should one of those markers be present and passed down to them. My mother was hesitant to get the test done, however. Because of Sue's remote history of early breast cancer, she was technically eligible to get the genetic test done as well, though the chances of it being positive were remote. She made a deal with mother: if my mother got the test, she would, too. They both went in for the blood sample draw, and several weeks later, the results came back. My mother's genetic screening was negative, but Sue was unexpectedly positive for BRCA2!

After much thought and consultation, Sue elected to have bilateral mastectomies, as her ultimate risk of developing cancer in both breasts with that genetic rearrangement exceeded ninety percent. Fortunately, no cancer was detected on either side. BRCA2 patients also have a higher risk of uterine, ovarian, and (to a lesser degree) pancreatic cancer. Fortunately, she had undergone removal of her uterus and ovaries years previously for other reasons, so those were not a concern. Even now there is still no good screening test for pancreatic cancer, however, so we are not totally free of concern after all these years.

I was glad I could be at Sue's and my mother's sides during their ordeals. Seeing cancer care from a husband's viewpoint rather than just a clinician's viewpoint made me a better and more empathetic doctor. Truly, cancer does not affect just an individual: it affects the entire family.

CHAPTER 22

Expansion

FROG outgrows its lily pad

The new millennium arrived and the world didn't end, despite the predictions of many, but the medical private practice landscape changed dramatically. Turbulent waters and stormy seas arose with the new century as ill regulatory and fiscal winds gathered over the healthcare seascape.

At the federal level, CMMS (Medicare) was feeling pressure to restrain health care costs across the board, and insurance companies followed suit. Physician reimbursements for special procedures and sophisticated treatments were put on the chopping block, and payments to radiation therapy facilities were slashed.

Though we had made amazing technological advancements in the fight against many types of cancer between 1975 and 2005, it became harder to afford new equipment to take advantage of those advancements or to hire staff to operate the machines. In the retail world, if a product's cost rises, that cost is ultimately passed on to the consumer. In the regulated medical industry, however, costs could not be passed on to the medical consumer, CMMS, or the insurance companies.

FROG had been able to build and manage successful clinics in remote areas by purchasing gently used linacs for a few hundred thousand dollars in the late 1980's. When it came time to replace the aging equipment with newer machines incorporating advancements years later, however, used equipment was not available. New machines became prohibitively expensive, costing several million dollars each. More specialized dosimetrists and physicists were required to run this new equipment, and new computerized treatment planning systems were required as well. The equipment and staffing cost pressures arose at the same time reimbursements were shrinking. In addition, partner physicians who had paid to build these centers out of pocket by taking on large loans had finally paid the notes off and had no desire to sign on multi-million-dollar loans all over again.

FROG's situation was not unique: both private practice and hospital-owned radiation therapy centers throughout the country were facing similar challenges. Smaller rural centers were hit the hardest. FROG partners met with other regional center owners to see if an alliance might help us negotiate better prices from vendors for newer equipment through bulk orders of several linac systems at once. We also explored ways we might cut costs by sharing systems and personnel. The result was a collaboration formed in 2005 called the North Florida Radiation Oncology Group (NFROG) that included centers in northern and central sections of the state along with the historic FROG centers. As planned, the centers shared physics staff and equipment and tried (with modest success) to negotiate better rates from vendors. Within the network, NFROG provided widespread access to revolutionary pinpoint accuracy treatments via a dedicated Tomotherapy Unit in Tallahassee and Cyberknife centers in Jacksonville, Gainesville, and Sanford, Florida.

The NFROG collaboration also brought attention and interest from other private practices around the country, and in 2006, a new national umbrella corporation was established to link a broader network of private radiation oncology centers. Once again, we needed to come up with a name, and after the hat with suggestions was passed around between original co-founders, the one I had proposed was adopted: OnCURE Medical Corporation.

Largely through West Coast contacts that we had maintained since our Stanford days, we reached out to groups of a similar size with excellent reputations. The intent of creating OnCURE was to establish a critical mass of outstanding private radiation oncology centers across the country. This large group would have even better leverage in terms of bulk purchasing major equipment such as linacs and provide an effective lobbying voice to meet with industry and the insurance market. Another purpose was to allow cross-pollination of ideas between centers and encourage development of a set of "Best Practices." We were highly selective about who we solicited to join OnCURE, looking for well-established centers already dominant in their marketplaces and staffed by excellent physicians. Many groups and centers were interested, but few were chosen. As the appointed national Vice President of Medical Affairs for OnCURE, one of my tasks was to site visit potential partners to assess the "fit" of the groups. Over the next few years, OnCURE became the third largest private provider of radiation oncology services in the USA, with thirty-nine clinics based in Florida, California, and Indiana.

Centrally located in Englewood, Colorado, the OnCURE Medical Corporation provided an overall administrative umbrella for all the centers, including Human Resources, a Legal Department, Billing and Financial Services offices, and an acquisition team. We held national meetings for center physicians to provide continuing medical education credits, present best practices, and have equipment presentations by manufacturers. Although initial plans included facilitating a national OnCURE research effort, the logistics and local politics of IRB's precluded us from realizing that goal.

CHAPTER 23

Going National

The rise and fall of OnCURE

During the OnCURE years, CMMS attempted to create ways to pay for cancer treatment more efficiently. As part of a Political Action Committee (PAC) dedicated to helping CMMS with this quest, our team spent months developing a methodology for a proposed CMMS "single payment plan" that would include all the management costs for a particular cancer site in one global fee. The idea was to replace the hundreds of billing codes submitted to CMMS by a variety of practitioners and facilities for management of a cancer case with one revenue-neutral submission. Our initial test model for a "global billing" fee was prostate cancer: a single global fee would be paid by CMMS to a cancer center on behalf of a prostate cancer patient, and the center would bear the responsibility for further distribution of those funds, depending on what treatment the patient chose, be it surgery or radiation therapy. If the center was able to provide the care for less than the CMMS payment, it would profit. If it cost the center more, the center would take a loss. Efficiency of patient care and management was thus rewarded, and CMMS could better predict their yearly medical dollar outlays. I was one of a team of OnCURE and other private practice group representatives to travel to Washington, D.C., to personally brief the CMMS decision makers.

CMMS was intrigued by our proposal and asked us to work up similar cost figures for other cancer disease sites. Over the ensuing year we did so, but in the end, CMMS came back to our PAC stating that we were thinking too small—they wanted to do something similar but on a much larger scale for a host of medical conditions beyond just cancer management.

Ultimately, CMMS encouraged local healthcare systems to create new entities known as Accountable Care Organizations (ACO's) to do just that. For practical purposes, ACO's could only be created by a large hospital or group of hospitals in a particular region. Hospitals trying to create an ACO needed to have on board all the specialists potentially needed to accurately bid on care packages for different disease entities. To best identify and predict the costs of each element of a disease management package, hospitals deemed it best to have all their involved physicians salaried. This push to employ virtually all physician specialties was one major factor that ultimately led to the decline of private practice in America. Though some private practice groups such as OnCURE tried to compete by creating disease-specific management proposals, they were ultimately unable to satisfy the government's desire for a more broad-based population health care payment approach.

Beside the federal government push away from funding cancer-specific novel payment schemes, OnCURE later had additional market and fiscal pressures: although OnCURE clinics and practices were recognized as "the best in class" in each of their markets, hospitals and other groups nevertheless built new centers to compete with the old guard. In addition, as noted previously, the cost of new state-of-the-art equipment continued to dramatically rise in the early 2000's.

Although the OnCURE clinics across the country were still profitable and seeing a full load of daily patients, the tens of millions of dollars needed to replace old equipment every eight to ten years became prohibitive. Some savings through bulk purchasing had been realized, but those savings were not nearly enough to offset huge new equipment costs. To raise capital, the OnCURE Board of Directors (BOD) elected to bring on venture capitalists. As the Vice President of Medical Affairs at that time, I accompanied the OnCURE senior management to give presentations to various firms west of the Mississippi River while my partner Shyam Paryani did the same east of the Mississippi. We raised over $100 million dollars with that effort. When even this capital proved insufficient to meet the needs of updating thirty-nine clinics, the new BOD (including the venture capitalists now sitting on the Board, and in the driver's seat) made the decision to take out a large loan at a hefty interest rate, with a balloon payment due five years later. The venture capitalists planned to flip the company within three years and pay off the balloon payment well before it was due.

Unfortunately, extraordinarily bad timing led to OnCURE's demise: only a couple of years after taking on that debt, a recession hit the economy, and acquisitions in the marketplace dried up. No reasonable suitors came forward, and the balloon payment came due at the five-year point. Unable to make the payment, the company eventually declared bankruptcy in June 2013—despite the robust patient volumes being served at the impacted clinics. The venture capital investors elected to cut their losses, and OnCURE was sold to another national radiation oncology service provider for pennies on the dollar. In the ultimate of ironies, that buyer went bankrupt themselves for largely the same reasons only a few years later.

CHAPTER 24

ICON

A multi-specialty cancer group in stormy waters

Though the creation of NFROG and OnCURE were meant to address the ongoing livelihood of the brick and mortar clinics themselves, a parallel effort was made to counter the hospitals' thrust to buy up all the professional physician groups. Of note, hospital-employed practitioners were both covertly and overtly arm-twisted into referring only to other hospital employee specialists. Though the legality of this restraint of trade was a gray area, it certainly didn't stop hospital administrators: they wanted control of all groups of specialists in relevant fields, and if those groups refused to be assimilated, they were gradually pushed out of the hospital systems by replacements hired directly by those health facilities. One by one, the specialty groups caved in and became employed: the hospitalists were the first to fall, followed by pathologists, radiologists, primary care doctors, cardiologists, neurologists, neurosurgeons, etc.

The pressure was on the cancer specialty groups to be assimilated as well, including the radiation oncologists (FROG), groups of medical oncologists, and even urologists (prostate cancer accounted for a huge proportion of a urology group's workload). As a push back to the hospitals, and to better coordinate cancer management via close integration of referrals, shared ancillary services like laboratory and radiology procedures, research staff, and to provide unified billing, a new organization uniting these professional groups in the Jacksonville area was formed in 2011: the Integrated Community Oncology Network (ICON). Akin to our United States constitution, the overall governance of ICON was to be centralized with Board members from each division (like our Federal Government in the USA), but each division governed its own internal affairs (like our States' rights concept in the USA). Recognizing the history and legacy of each contributing group, each division of ICON kept its historical name. Thus, to all outward appearances, FROG remained FROG, North Florida Cancer Specialists (our medical oncology partners) kept their name, and the historic McIver Clinic (our urology division) kept its name as well.

ICON largely achieved the goals it had set: patients were seen by both medical and radiation oncologists in a timely fashion, often within twenty-four hours of each other, so that treatment plans could be generated quickly and efficiently. Not infrequently these patients were seen on the same visit by all the involved clinical specialists. Lab and PET/CT results were available to all these ICON clinicians, and as a result, duplicate tests were largely eliminated. The research department also noted an increase in patient referrals and registrations, as teams across specialties became aware of each other's trial offerings.

Insurance companies did not like having to negotiate professional fee global contracts that included multiple specialties, but we had some success there as well. The hospitals were not amused, however, and whisperings of excluding ICON clinicians from hospital staff began. We were considered a threat, as ICON was providing stellar cancer care and ancillary services including lab tests and PET/CT scans at a fraction of the price hospitals were charging for similar services—largely because ICON was not burdened by bloated hospital administrative staff levels and expensive facility operational expenses. The situation was almost reminiscent of the historic 1588 battle of the Spanish Armada in the English Channel, in which the smaller, nimbler English fleet was pitted against the larger but less responsive ships of the Spanish Armada. The English fleet could outmaneuver the Spanish galleons in the shallow waters and won the day. ICON was the equivalent of the nimble English fleet, able to pivot and respond by updating equipment, techniques, and procedures to meet the changing needs of cancer patients and staff more quickly than any hospital system could.

Though ICON won those early battles, it eventually lost the war for a variety of reasons. Pressure by hospital systems to restrict referrals (or threaten to) from employed hospital doctors to non-employee physicians and insurance companies balking at multispecialty contracts drove wedges between different ICON divisions.

Internally, the fact that ICON doctors staffed multiple competing hospital systems complicated things further in this new environment. Some ICON division doctors had staff privileges at some hospitals that other ICON division doctors did not. A case in point was St. Vincent's Hospital in Jacksonville: clinicians in our ICON medical oncology division had longstanding relationships and busy clinics on the St. Vincent's hospital campus, but St. Vincent's also had a longstanding exclusive relationship with a competing radiation oncology group (a so-called "closed staff" model). The hospital did not want to open the staff to ICON radiation oncologists. ICON even explored a merger with the competing radiation oncology group to eliminate the conflict, but that group had no desire to upset the status quo.

Finally, bickering arose between physician partners in different divisions over perceived disparities of income between divisions—some specialties were paid more than others, and those that were paid less by insurers wanted a piece of what the higher earners were making. In most cases this was an "apples vs. oranges" comparison, but strife voiced by a vocal minority served to undermine the cohesiveness of the ICON group at large. This strife and ill will only worsened when the insurers also dramatically slashed reimbursement for various lab and radiology procedures: those services that had once provided extra income for the physician members now required those same members to forfeit income to service the debts on MRI and PET/CT operations. Though radiation oncologists were used to the ups and downs of a capital-intensive practice (with all the linacs, computers, clinics, and other equipment that needed constant upkeep and replacement), these vagaries were a rude awakening for doctors within less capital-intensive divisions.

Ultimately, after less than five years, the dream of sustaining a private multi-specialty cancer management practice faded, and ICON was eventually disbanded. As that happened, another wrinkle in the regional cancer care landscape arose with BMC's decision to court the MD Anderson Cancer Center.

CHAPTER 25

Paths diverge

The pond dries up in 2014 and fractures FROG

By 2010, the Jacksonville medical arena was becoming more crowded and competitive. The Mayo Clinic, historically based in Rochester, Minnesota, opted to build a satellite Clinic based in Jacksonville in 1986 to better serve its South American and Southeastern USA clientele. St. Vincent's hospital set up a staff-sharing model with the Mayo Clinic for some specialties, acquired the old Mayo-owned St. Luke's hospital, and built a third facility just north of St. Augustine. The University of Florida acquired the old University Hospital on the north side of town and set about upgrading the facility and even installing a Proton Center for cancer treatment. Baptist Health System had built or acquired a series of regional hospitals under its umbrella, including the main Baptist Downtown (BMC) facility, Baptist Beaches, Baptist Nassau, and Baptist South hospitals, with Baptist North and Baptist Clay hospitals added not long after. Finally, the for-profit HCA Health System chain bought Memorial Medical Center as well as nearby Orange Park Medical Center.

The BMC radiation therapy service, staffed by the FROG group exclusively since the 1960's, maintained the most advanced radiation therapy treatment staff, equipment, and program in the region. The premier department had a storied and impressive history.

Dr. Walter P. Scott, along with Dr. B.T. Paryani, oversaw the creation of the Edna & Charles Williams Cancer Center at BMC in Jacksonville in the early 1970's. The Williams Center later served as a key division of the newly built Baptist Cancer Institute adjacent to BMC. The Williams Cancer Center provided a broad range of services including consultation and radiation treatment planning, external-beam therapy, brachytherapy, stereotactic radiotherapy, therapeutic radioisotope administration, research protocol administration, and ongoing care and follow-up for adult and pediatric patients with a variety of malignant and non-malignant conditions.

The Williams Center had a long history of excellence on the First Coast: the first high energy linear accelerator in Florida was installed here in 1978, and it later was the home of the first High Dose Rate (HDR) implant program, hyperthermia program, and the first intraoperative brain tumor and head & neck tumor radioactive implant programs in the region. FROG physicians began performing prostate seed implants in the 1970's and instituted a world-leading real-time intraoperative dosimetry program to improve the accuracy and safety of those implants in the mid 1990's. The Center was the first in the region to offer frameless stereotactic radiotherapy/radiosurgery for brain lesions and was home to the first Gamma Knife Center between Orlando and Atlanta. The Center was also a referral hub for total skin electron therapy for a rare lymphoma type known as mycosis fungoides. For decades, the FROG team at Baptist performed nearly all the pediatric radiation therapy in the region and was an approved site for Total Body Irradiation (TBI) for both pediatric and adult patients undergoing bone marrow transplants. FROG pioneered the use of intravenous radioactive medicines to hunt down cancers via the bloodstream, as well.

The Williams Cancer Center and Baptist Cancer Institute provided opportunities for patients to participate in a tremendous variety of cancer research trials sponsored by the National Cancer Institute and numerous other leading institutions and organizations. As a result of our research commitment, our Center was the first in the region to incorporate the use of radioprotectors during radiation treatment to shield normal tissues. FROG physicians were involved in the investigation of intravascular irradiation to help prevent repeat "clogging" of arteries at risk in the heart and legs, and in dialysis shunts. In addition, a few of us even invented devices used for the treatment of cancer patients.

One would think that Baptist administration would have been very happy with that record, and indeed they were—mostly. The admin team was not overly thrilled that FROG doctors served and staffed several radiation therapy centers throughout the region in addition to those owned by Baptist. Not only did they have to "share" our expertise with competing health systems, but not having us as employees thwarted their efforts to create an ACO. As a highly successful private enterprise, the FROG team in turn had no particular interest in becoming employed staff of any single hospital system.

Baptist's displeasure at sharing FROG with other facilities over the years had initially been offset by the fact that FROG brought most of our patients from out-lying clinics to the Williams Center for treatment planning and simulation services: Baptist was reaping the financial benefits of those technical charges that added to the Williams Center's bottom line. In addition, we leased many of our clinic staff from Baptist and they were making a percentage profit on that contract. In a perfect storm of calamities beyond FROG's control, both of those revenue streams for the Baptist Health Care system dried up.

First, insurance companies started playing hardball with different hospital systems and would flip flop every year or two on who they allowed in their panel, and who they excluded, to squeeze every dollar from their negotiated payment rates. Year after year, some of the hospitals we served were in-network, and some not. It became fiscally impossible to have patients simulated and planned at Baptist if BMC was not in their insurance network. This insurance company whammy hit hard, as Baptist lost a big chunk of revenue. To make matters worse, OnCURE then had to step in and foot the bill to set up new simulation and treatment planning facilities independent of the Baptist system.

Second, a new administrative legal team at Baptist reviewed all employee leasing program arrangements (ours was but one group they had contracted with) and decided to get out of the leasing business entirely over fears of liability in centers that they had no administrative control over. For the Baptist bean counters, another revenue stream disappeared because of that decision, and yet another win-win tie to FROG disappeared. Once again, OnCURE had to dramatically expand its HR resources to cover the hiring of replacement nurses, radiation therapy technologists (RTTs), dosimetrists, and physicists.

A much bigger issue for Baptist administration, however, was the medical oncology side of the equation. There were several competing medical oncology groups throughout the city that served many hospitals and were not identified with any one hospital. Many of these groups had no allegiance to Baptist, and in a desire to cut the expenses for their patients under treatment they began developing their own labs and private imaging centers. The hospital coveted those ancillary fees, which they used to offset heavy losses incurred by providing indigent care for uninsured patients in the Emergency Room and elsewhere, and the hospital was upset that the fees were evaporating.

Baptist had historically maintained an "open staff" policy, meaning that if you were qualified you could practice at a Baptist hospital based on your merits rather than your allegiance. In addition, once hospital credentials were granted to any particular physician, those privileges were hard to legally revoke barring any malfeasance by the clinician. Thus, it was hard for Baptist to "clean house" of cancer doctors they did not consider team players. How could they trim the staff to a manageable and obedient size?

Enter the MD Anderson Cancer Center in Houston: MD Anderson had and continues to have a stellar reputation for cancer care and is one of the leading cancer treatment centers in the USA. Indeed, our "Stanford East" doctors knew several MD Anderson senior physicians, as they had also trained at Stanford before joining the MD Anderson faculty or were colleagues on national research trial groups. MD Anderson had seen the lucrative Florida market as a potential place to spread their reach, but their initial foray into Florida by way of acquiring a hospital in the Orlando area had not gone well; despite over twenty years together, they decided to part ways in 2013. Jacksonville represented a second chance to enter the Florida arena.

For its part, the Baptist Health System was concerned with the rise of all the surrounding healthcare competition and was looking for a way to truly brand themselves as cancer leaders in the marketplace. Could an affiliation with MD Anderson Cancer Center be to both parties' interests in that regard? Baptist would get stellar name recognition and MD Anderson Cancer Center Houston would get a potential referral source in north Florida for difficult cases. Both of their missions to serve the cancer community would be enhanced. Complex and protracted negotiations between Baptist and MD Anderson eventually resulted in an agreement to partner on a large outpatient cancer center.

The proposed center's new name, Baptist MD Anderson Cancer Center, would be emblazoned prominently on the building façade adjacent to busy interstate I-95. All relevant cancer treatment specialists would be employed by the new organization, so Baptist could finally legally "close" the medical staff and insist that all doctors wanting to use the Baptist MD Anderson facility be employees. The new organization would have tremendous visibility and cache in the region, helping solidify Baptist's position in the community, and its ability to control costs and salaries would help them prepare ACO contracts.

As the recent Past-President of the Baptist Medical Staff, I had been privy to many executive conversations about the potential MD Anderson affiliation. I understood the concerns of the administrative leaders but also was concerned they might unintentionally "throw out the baby with the bathwater," losing some stellar physicians along the way as well as the flexibility of private groups to respond quickly to new advances in cancer management without all the bureaucracy inherent in a large system. I also voiced concerns about the massive debt the organization would be incurring both in terms of infrastructure and annual fees paid to MD Anderson Houston for the right to use their name. Finally, I was concerned that the speedy and efficient care of our cancer population would be crippled by the need to run every decision through Houston before acting, as well as by the slower work process inherent in an institutionalized process and the stifling of creativity and ingenuity. As one local physician put it, "If you want a standardized "Toyota" treatment, go to MD Anderson or Mayo Clinic; if you need creative "Ferrari" ideas for a difficult and unique condition, however, you'd be better served by a stellar independent group with sharp brains and the latest technology." Little did I realize how prophetic those words would be.

Mine was but a small voice in a large crowd, however. The deal was consummated, and a large new facility began to rise from the ground. Baptist leadership approached me in late 2013 to ask if I would bring my Baptist FROG doctors in to become the Radiation Oncology Division of the new Baptist MD Anderson organization. They stated that they were pleased with the service FROG physicians had provided Baptist facilities over the preceding decades and would prefer to have us on board as employees, but they had no interest in the rest of our FROG partners who were staffing non-Baptist facilities. Furthermore, if we opted not to accept their offer, they were prepared to recruit new physicians to replace us. The proposal was difficult to swallow for many reasons. Ethically, FROG had functioned as a cohesive unit in the region for decades and had hired physicians with the understanding that they would be a part of our entire team. The BMC operation was our "mother ship" facility, and cutting the others out would have left them without access to some cutting-edge therapies. At the same time, FROG was legally bound to staff our OnCURE-owned facilities, and several of us still had leadership and equity positions in that company. Although OnCURE was on the auction block by that time, we couldn't abandon that ship while negotiations were underway, and we were not allowed to discuss the impending bankruptcy with Baptist.

During my twenty-four years in the USAF, I witnessed first-hand the compromises and lethargic pace of change inherent in any large bureaucracy. Though I cherished my "employed" time serving my country in the USAF, I was not interested in becoming an employee in the civilian world—I had borne witness to the overwhelming benefits inherent in a free-market private practice system over the years and did not want to take a step backwards.

My feelings aside, we had to consider the fate of the other partner and associate FROG physicians. Although non-compete agreements were in place with all the FROGs, our remaining FROG leadership (Drs. Shyam Paryani, Sonja Schoeppel, Anand Kuruvilla, Mark Augspurger, Dwelvin Simmons, Abhijit Deshkumh, and I) elected not to enforce those. We had extensive discussions with the FROG members and ultimately spun off all those doctors serving in Baptist centers, offering them three choices: they could 1) leave FROG and become employed Baptist MD Anderson staff, 2) leave FROG and leave the area, or 3) stay as FROGs and be reassigned to other clinics. With all the turmoil ongoing with the OnCURE facilities, most of those given this choice elected to switch over to the Baptist MD Anderson staff model, with our blessing. For all intents and purposes, by mid-2014 FROG as we had known it was finished.

I am proud to say that the new core of the radiation oncology department at Baptist MD Anderson was in excellent hands under the leadership of Dr. Michael Olson, along with Drs. Sonja Schoeppel, Cynthia Anderson, and Mark Augspurger—all former FROG partners. Under their care, the department has continued to grow and flourish, and I could not be prouder of them all.

There were some initial bumps along the way for the new department, however, when the MD Anderson Houston physics department demanded that Baptist take down and mothball about one million dollars worth of sophisticated leading-edge external beam and radiosurgery treatment planning equipment that we had installed. Houston did not yet have that advanced equipment, and since they wanted to review in detail everything Jacksonville was doing, they insisted the Jacksonville department essentially "dumb down" its equipment to a level that Houston could interpret. On the Baptist MD Anderson side of the equation, this was the equivalent of removing the resolution and accuracy of an existing HDTV and reverting to the fuzziness of an old standard TV set.

In addition, because Houston insisted on reviewing all Jacksonville plans and dosimetry as well as each cancer case at their weekly tumor boards, prolonged delays in getting patients underway were incurred—often taking two weeks or more to initiate a treatment that we had previously gotten underway in three days. Cancer treatment delays were aggravated even further by the rise of egregious preauthorization requirements imposed by insurance companies. Opportunities for patients to participate on many national leading-edge treatment trials were eliminated as well, as new research trials at Baptist were shelved pending a slow reconstitution of capabilities over the ensuing several years under Houston's control.

My decision to not accept chairmanship of the department was the right one for me, as I would have chaffed under the remote yoke imposed by Houston. Nevertheless, I agreed to backfill and work in the clinic on a part-time basis over the ensuing five years until new full-time staff came on board.

Outside the Baptist MD Anderson Cancer Center, other global issues were increasingly a source of nationwide frustration for all clinicians and hospital staff: HIPAA and the rise of EHRs.

CHAPTER 26

ONE CHEER FOR HIPAA

"The road to hell is paved with good intentions."
—St. Bernard of Clairvaux

In the summer of 1996, the Olympic Games were held in Atlanta, the DVD player was invented, and President Bill Clinton signed into law the Health Insurance Portability and Accountability Act (HIPAA). HIPAA was passed with dual goals of making health care delivery more efficient and increasing the number of Americans with health insurance coverage. These objectives were pursued through three main provisions of the Act: 1) the portability provisions, 2) the tax provisions, and 3) the administrative simplification provisions (Ref8).

The portability provisions supposedly ensured that a patient's health care information could be transferred safely from one health care provider to another should the patient relocate or transfer to another health care team. This, in turn, was intended to reassure workers that they needn't fear losing health care continuity should they switch employers or physicians.

The intended simplification provisions were meant to codify proper transfer of medical records from one entity to another. This provision was later modified several times with a final HIPAA Privacy Rule becoming enforceable by April 2004. Rather than relying on a physician's or hospital's discretion to release a patient's information to another physician, family member, hospital, or even emergency room, the new law instead imposed complex, unrealistic, and impractical standardized procedures with no room for a clinician's judgement. Potential severe penalties were imposed for violations of the rules, which ultimately turned the intention of the law on its head—instead of easing the transfer of information (so-called portability) it made transfer of any information ponderous and difficult, often delaying or preventing information transfer completely.

From an average physician's standpoint, unwieldy forms needed to be signed, witnessed, and shared with multiple entities before any data could be sent regarding a particular patient, even if the patient had verbally requested it. This was especially ponderous if the patient was calling from a distant location asking for their records to be forwarded, as they were not physically present to sign the releases needed. Even if the forms had been properly completed at one time, they expired after a time and needed to be re-signed annually. The forms required the patient to specify in advance just who they wanted the information released to, even if they themselves didn't know yet who that was to be after a move. All the additional time required to complete these forms necessitated hiring more administrative staff by offices throughout the nation, increasing costs for practices and delaying timely clinical information transfer. Despite all the time and expense incurred to comply with these onerous new regulations, there were no federal funds allotted to reimburse offices for these costs: they were "unfunded mandates." Physicians, hospitals, and patients alike became frustrated with all the paperwork and transfer hurdles.

Unintended consequences included potentially adverse clinical outcomes due to delays in critical information exchange. In addition, increased inconvenience and cost to the US medical system at large was also evident: it was often just easier for a doctor to re-order new tests at his facility than go through the hassle of getting perfectly good prior testing results from another site.

Incident to all the HIPAA regulations was the requirement for a transition to an Electronic Health Record (EHR) over time. At first blush, the EHR held out the potential to solve many problems with written charts in a clinician's office or hospital record: the error-prone need to decipher the hieroglyphics of a doctor's handwriting would be eliminated, medication orders could be organized and checked for interactions and proper delivery, lab and radiographic study results could be displayed, etc. What the laws requiring these systems failed to do, however, was reimburse medical facilities or providers for the cost of the systems and the huge time requirement for computer training and data entry: yet another huge federal unfunded mandate was born.

The extra time it took—and continues to take twenty-eight plus years later—to complete EHR daily data entry made patient care more inefficient: a hospital nurse's eight-hour shift easily became a nine and a half-hour shift to allow time for all the charting data entry, for instance. To further refine costs paid to providers, CMMS (and the other insurers shortly thereafter) began to reimburse based on the complexity of a physician/patient interaction. The lengthier the written write-up of an interaction with more details included, the higher the insurance reimbursement. The practical result was that even formerly succinct daily treatment notes became bloated multi-page tomes to try to glean higher insurance reimbursements. Instead of a succinct two-page admission history and physical summary, multipage documents containing largely useless and irrelevant information became standard—a blatant waste of effort, as only the last two or three sentences of the document routinely contained any clinically relevant information. And yes, all the extra personnel hired to assess the length and complexity of these notes for proper insurance claim coding and submission resulted in yet another unfunded mandate.

The federal government demanded the creation of these EHR's but left it to private vendors to develop competing computer programs to market to providers. Unlike development of the internet, where the government laid out an operating standard that all internet program developers used to create software, there was no standard "information backbone" that all EHRs needed to adhere to. The result was a "wild, wild west" of programs flooding the marketplace, none of which talked to one another. It was essentially impossible to transfer data electronically from one physician's office to another who used a competing software program, and most could not transfer to any of the larger EHR software programs used by the hospitals. Even worse, once a provider and his clinic chose and used a system for a few years, he was often trapped and tied to that original system because it could not communicate or transfer patient records to any newer improved system.

Thus, in the early- to mid-2000's, these HIPAA and EHR requirements brought the concept of information portability to its knees: it had been far easier and more efficient to transfer data before HIPAA was ever enacted.

All these frustrations were exacerbated in the radiation oncology clinics across the nation, as most had already been using one or two unique computerized systems for treatment planning or treatment delivery (in BMC's case, we already had three: Varian, Electa, and BrainLab systems; all were necessary for patient treatment planning, and none talked to each other, so data often had to be repeatedly entered by hand three times to update each system). The addition of another EHR on top of all these systems created a huge time drain daily. We had previously been able to treat all our patients and complete all our tasks during a 7:30 a.m. – 4:30 p.m. shift daily before the HIPAA and EHR mandates. After the mandates, the average day blossomed to a 7 a.m. – 7:30 p.m. workday—all to serve the same number of patients.

Later, I was asked to temporarily staff a radiation oncology center in rural eastern Kentucky. Prior to the HIPAA and EHR mandates, the center had been successfully serving and treating patients in a small community from 8 a.m. – 5 p.m. daily. After the mandates, patient treatment hours were cut in half to allow for several hours of newly required charting in the mornings. The clinic lost fifty percent of its functionality overnight, revenues plummeted, patient treatments were delayed, and the clinic closed in bankruptcy within six months.

These frustrations were all coming to a head in 2014, at the same time as the turmoil in the Jacksonville radiation oncology marketplace.

CHAPTER 27

SNIFFING OUT CANCER

Medical life after FROG: the NaNose

By early 2014 only two of the original four FROG partners remained: Walter Scott had taken a well-deserved retirement a few years before and was enjoying life in Central America, and John Wells had retired in 2013. In addition, the physician administrative guru and leader of FROG, who had stopped treating patients years before, redirected his sights, financial merger and acquisition interests, and time to arenas well beyond the FROG marketplace, without all his FROG colleagues' knowledge or participation. As a result, he had lost the confidence of ICON and FROG physicians alike. Whether or not malfeasance occurred was irrelevant: in the military, leaders were sacked over the mere appearance of impropriety. In military jargon, this sacking was couched as a removal from the position due to a "loss of confidence in a person's ability to lead." Unfortunately, there was no mechanism within the bylaws of the FROG partnership agreements to sack our administrative partner. Considering the turmoil ongoing within FROG and the upheaval underway at Baptist, I elected to resign from the FROG group in April 2014, to devote my full attention to an important research project involving lung cancer detection.

Through my decades treating cancer patients, tremendous strides had been made in the management of most cancers; indeed, by 2014 our radiation oncology clinics were not just offering palliative treatment to improve symptoms but instead were curing over eighty percent of the patients we saw. Nevertheless, we had not made much progress against stubborn cancers such as rare glioblastoma brain tumors, slightly more common pancreatic cancers, and extremely common lung cancers: the five-year survival rates for each of those diseases remained dismal. Despite better surgery, chemotherapy, and radiation treatments, those cancers were usually fatal because they were too advanced or had spread by the time they were diagnosed.

Lung cancer remains by far the leading cause of cancer death worldwide, largely due to smoking and environmental exposures to asbestos and other agents. In 2012, lung cancer was the third most common cancer in the USA behind prostate and breast cancers but accounted for more deaths annually than the other top four cancers combined (prostate, breast, lymphoma, and colorectal cancers) (Ref9). The five-year survival for lung cancer in 1980 was a poor fifteen percent. Thirty years later, despite all our technical progress, it had barely risen to seventeen percent.

In the radiation oncology arena, development of a new branch of treatment called radiosurgery offered a promising new curative treatment for lung cancer if the tumor could be found when it was still small and isolated (less than the size of a quarter). Because lung cancers that small were asymptomatic, they were rarely discovered at that early stage. If they were detected and operable, surgical cure rates approaching sixty percent or more were seen. Unfortunately, many heavy smokers had damaged their lungs (a condition known as chronic obstructive pulmonary disease, or COPD) to the extent that even if a cancer was detected early, they could not medically withstand such a surgery. Radiosurgery, however, did not require any open surgery or incisions, so most patients even with severe COPD could be treated with this new technique; early reports suggested cure rates similar to surgery for these early cases, with five-year cancer-free rates in the sixty-seventy percent range. Now that an effective radiosurgical treatment program was available in many parts of the USA, the key to raising lung cancer cure rates was, and remains, early detection.

The FROG team was an early adopter of radiosurgery in Florida, having the region's first Cyberknife, Gamma Knife, and Novalis-TX radiosurgery machines. By 2009 we had successfully treated scores of lung cancer patients, but we wanted to help expand the use of this exciting modality even further.

In 2010, my partner, John Wells, investigated the whole problem of lung cancer early detection. Why was it not a national priority? Two main reasons emerged. First, no reliable early detection modalities existed: clinical trials demonstrated that simple yearly chest x-rays, even in heavy smokers, were not effective in picking up lung cancers when they were still small enough to be treated, and standard computerized tomography (CT) scans were just too expensive to use as a screening tool. Second, there was a stigma attached to lung cancer, with a perception that "smokers brought this cancer on themselves, so why should we invest in curing it." Screening funding for lung cancer was simply not as sexy or appealing as funding for breast or pediatric cancers.

John discovered that Duval County in northern Florida had the highest per capita incidence of lung cancer in the country and realized that early detection efforts here might significantly and positively impact our patient population. His Orange Park colleague, pulmonologist Stuart Millstone, M.D., had recently attended a national lung cancer meeting and met a pioneering Israeli oncologist and pulmonologist: Nir Peled M.D. Nir was conducting clinical research at the Sheba Medical Center in Tel Aviv, partnering with research scientist Dr. Hossam Haick and his team at the Technion in Haifa (the equivalent of MIT in the USA). Hossam and Nir were exploring the use of exhaled breath for early lung cancer detection using a panel of nanosensors. The initial work they had done looked promising, but they needed more patients to verify their findings.

Drs. Millstone and Wells were intrigued with the Israeli work and set up a retreat near Dr. Millstone's ranch in remote Westcliffe, Colorado, attended by radiation oncologists, medical oncologists, pulmonologists, and Dr. Peled in 2011 to explore possible collaborations. At that meeting, Nir presented his data on the exhaled breath system that he and Hossam had dubbed the "NaNose." (Figure 27) They envisioned a proprietary panel of nanosensors detecting certain volatile organic compounds that could be fit onto a wafer about the size of a piece of chewing gum. That wafer, in turn, could theoretically be inserted into a device smaller than a cigarette pack (how ironic) with an opening for a patient to blow into. The strip could then be analyzed and if a certain array of compounds was detected, the presence of lung cancer would be highly likely. Their first thirty patients in Israel that had used the nanosensor panel suggested an accuracy for the technique of greater than ninety percent. The Westcliffe group brainstormed for two days over ways to further this research.

As a result of our meeting, the group agreed to enroll patients from our large Florida at-risk population in a study to further explore the NaNose concept. I was tasked with writing a protocol for submission to the IRB in Jacksonville and was to become the Principal Investigator for the United States in the research effort.

In addition to medical brainstorming, my artist's itch also got scratched during that conference: during an afternoon recess from those intense sessions, several participants escaped for an afternoon of plein air painting in the valley looking westward toward the beautiful Sangre de Cristo Mountains. (Figure 28)

Upon our return to Jacksonville, I got to work. Rather than just test the screening effectiveness of NaNose breath analysis, we decided to include other nascent promising technologies in the trial including OncImmune's blood auto-antibody test called Early-CDT; specialized sputum analysis from a Seattle based company, VisionGate, with a test they called LuCED 3D, utilizing optical projection tomographic microscopy; and PET/CT scanning. The first of three planned studies was written, submitted to the IRB, and approved; enrollment at different centers in northern Florida began. Called locally the ISRUSAL01 trial, its official title as registered in the national clinical trials database was *"Non-Invasive Biomarkers for Early Detection of Lung Cancers: Element 1: Non-Randomized Phase II Evaluation and Validation in Newly Diagnosed Lung Cancer Patients."*

For this trial, we enrolled fifty patients who had recently been diagnosed with lung cancer. A PET/CT was performed on each, and samples of blood, sputum, and breath were collected and sent to the respective test providers for analysis. The samples sent to Israel were used not just for our trial but also added to the large international database of samples being tested around the world.

Of all the tests done, getting the samples of breath to the Technion in Haifa for mass spectral analysis was the most complex and costly. Each sample vial of breath had to be kept cold with dry ice and shipped off via a specialized air freight service at a cost of over $1000 per shipment. We had a small grant from the Williams Foundation locally to help defray some of the costs, but the bulk of them were paid directly by our FROG doctors out of pocket. No investigator ever received a penny for the time and effort they or their staff expended on the trial—they contributed willingly to a cause they felt strongly about.

We only had one potentially disastrous development in the trial, when our first batch of shipped breath samples did not arrive as expected at the Technion on the scheduled arrival date. Frantic calls by our research assistant to the air shipping company finally discovered what had happened: the aircraft had made an unscheduled stop in Russia due to mechanical difficulties and was awaiting a replacement part. Fortunately, our samples were fed with fresh dry ice daily by a crew member during the delay, so that they eventually arrived safely in Israel. I am sure a package landing from Russia stamped all over with Biohazard markings raised some eyebrows at the Israeli customs port, but after reassuring calls from the Technion, the samples were finally allowed in and delivered safely, weeks late.

As a personal bonus, John Wells and I traveled to Israel to meet with our collaborators in Jerusalem and Haifa and spent a few extra days taking in the rich history of that storied land.

This final research effort consumed years of my time and attention and resulted in several published papers, but the one I am most proud of turned out to be the most read article in the international journal ACS Nano in 2017, entitled *"Diagnosis and Classification of 17 Diseases from 1404 Individuals via Pattern Analysis of Exhaled Molecules"* (Ref7). As of 2024, that landmark paper has been cited in over 450 subsequent publications.

Though this research activity and my retirement from FROG largely took me out of the clinic, for the next five years I still saw patients on week-long stints performing locum tenens work (the medical equivalent of a "substitute teacher") at the Baptist MD Anderson Cancer Center, the Mayo Clinic Waycross Cancer Center, at CSNF centers in and around Jacksonville, and occasionally in Kentucky and even Idaho. These weeks presented wonderful opportunities to connect with patients—one of my favorite aspects of medicine—and helped me pay for some of the study research expenses.

I treasure the nearly forty years of opportunity I had to provide care for my patients and their families. Curing their aliments or helping ease their struggles has given immeasurable meaning to my life. In the end, I hope in some small way I kept my promise long ago to my ailing grandmother, Amy Rosborough.

CHAPTER 28

Taking Wing

Birth of Lancair IV-P N654DM

One of the best stress relievers for me outside the office was flying, and at long last my Lancair IV-P was ready to stretch its wings. After nearly five years of building my plane in Tennessee, approvals from my FAA-sanctioned DAR (Designated Airworthiness Representative) were obtained in late April 1997.

Building an aircraft, albeit from a kit, was a character-building process. Though I had been flying for over a decade, it amazes me in retrospect how little I knew about the intricacies of these birds we fly. The experimental aircraft movement encouraged creativity based upon solid scientific foundations. The aeronautical creativity evident thousands of years ago with the legends of Icarus and later illustrated musings of Leonardo da Vinci were replaced by solid scientific strides in the nineteenth century by Sir George Cayley in England and Karl Wilhelm Otto Lilienthal in Germany: both were expanding aeronautical science with successful glider construction and flights. Who made the first powered flight is generally credited to Wilbur and Orville Wright in 1903, but that claim might be contested by advocates of *Clément Ader*, Gustave Whitehead, Samuel Pierpont Langley, or Alberto Santos-Dumont.

Regardless of who was first to accomplish successful powered flight, there is no doubt that the field of aeronautics developed astronomically during the twentieth century. From the Wright Flyer's short 1903 hop over the sand dunes of Kitty Hawk, North Carolina, to the first supersonic flight of the experimental Bell X-1 Glamorous Glennis in 1947, only forty-three years had elapsed; twenty-two years later, we were standing on the moon. The variety of experimental aircraft developed between and after those milestones is breathtaking: aircraft have been created in all shapes and sizes, meant to explore and fill unique niches in the world of flight. Some popular and well-known lines have also been commercial successes, produced by Cessna and Piper (both started in 1927), Beechcraft (started in 1932) and Mooney (started in 1948).

Over the last decades of the twentieth century, production costs for those companies rose precipitously, largely due to 1) the increasingly strict and expensive FAA-mandated testing for any new or modified commercially produced design, 2) the rise of expensive and often egregious litigation over aircraft accidents (manufacturers were often sued after an accident even if they didn't have parts installed on the downed plane), and 3) by the 1960's, the number of pilots wanting to purchase and fly aircraft began to slowly ebb as WWII pilot veterans aged out of the aviation arena, resulting in fewer sold planes over which to distribute research, development, litigation, and production costs. These factors resulted in stagnation at the general aviation production companies. Improvements to an extant design were slow to come as any changes might suggest to a litigant that prior models were not as safe! Perhaps this is why a Cessna-172 produced in 2024 looks largely unchanged since its debut in 1956, sixty-eight years previously.

By the 1950's, aeronautical engineers and craftsmen with a mechanical bent began returning to the grass roots of aviation by creating new designs with modern techniques and materials. These designs could be purchased as plans or kits and assembled by builders privately. Once built and passing inspection, they would be registered under the Amateur-Built Experimental category by the FAA. As each builder would in essence be his own manufacturer, these designers didn't need to worry about expensive litigation, and they were also free to tweak and improve designs over time. All manner of aircraft began to appear, from simple gliders and powered parachutes to amphibious aircraft that could land on water or pavement, taildraggers at home on remote dirt strips, fast turbo-charged high and fast flyers, and even micro jets. Some experimental aircraft were still made of tube and fabric, others of wood or metal, and yet others of space-age composite materials. Today, there is an experimental airplane for every mission and for every budget.

To encourage the sharing of ideas in this new arena, the Experimental Aircraft Association (EAA) was founded in 1953 by Paul H. Poberezny. The EAA's first meeting took place in a corner of the Milwaukee Wisconsin Air Pageant that September and from those humble beginnings the EAA has opened chapters and membership worldwide. The EAA hosts the world's largest exposition and airshow each July: AirVenture at Oshkosh, Wisconsin. From a few original die-hards, the EAA membership has grown to over 300,000 enthusiasts.

Currently, somewhere between ten and twenty-five percent of all piston-powered aircraft in the USA are registered in an Experimental category. These amateur-built aircraft can be completed for a fraction of the cost of a commercially available plane, can be maintained by their builders, and have demonstrated an established safety record comparable to those built in commercial factories. As things like avionics change and are improved, they can be incorporated into the amateur-built planes without having to go through an expensive FAA recertification process.

I chose the Lancair-IVP because my mission was to get across the country quickly and safely, and because I needed four seats to accommodate my wife and two children. The plane was built of lightweight but strong carbon-fiber composites that would not rust in my humid Florida home base, but it used a standard aviation-certified Continental TSIO-550B2B 350-horsepower engine.

During the Lancair's fabrication, D.L. Simmons and his son Brad were invaluable teachers of the mechanics of the build process and interpreting sometimes arcane kit instructions. D.L. was especially rigorous, down to nuances like telling me never to turn a bolt once it's put through a hole—only turn the nut "so you don't wallow out the bolt hole." I learned a lot... I also read voraciously on such things as materials science, electronics, electromagnetic interference (how close can you install a kilohertz communications antenna to a megahertz GPS antenna, for instance), engine theory and maintenance, airframe safe construction practices and finishing, and flight-testing procedures. At the end of it all I sometimes wondered if I shouldn't have received an honorary engineering degree...

The first twenty-five flight hours were to be flown within a one hundred nautical mile radius of the airport using a flight test syllabus I had acquired from the EAA. The syllabus contained a series of test cards that I completed during each flight to progressively demonstrate the safety of the aircraft and gradually expand its flight envelope. Initial taxi tests at progressively higher speeds were followed by short flights to test the controls and equipment, and later to expand the flight envelope, conducting various high-angle attitudes, stalls in different configurations, speed tests, measuring the effectiveness of the speed brakes, and formulation of lift over drag charts, etc. Tests included some limited aerobatics including steep turns and aileron rolls. After each flight, we would review the list of squawks I had documented and correct those before the next flight. Fortunately, there were few issues.

After a bone-head final test flight error I caused, the bird required some additional cosmetic work, but eventually I ferried it back to northern Florida. Once there, a craftsman from central Florida completed interior finishes (seat covers, headliner, etc.) and the plane was ready for final weight and balance calculations and some high-altitude flight testing. My plane was not only pressurized, but its engine featured dual turbochargers. The turbochargers enhanced its performance up high and were the reason that the Lancair IV type earned the distinction of being the world's fastest piston-powered four-passenger aircraft in 1992. It maintains that unbroken record as of 2024.

After completing the Lancair, I opted to enter it in several EAA

Chapter 28

airshows for judging over the ensuing year. In 1998 we entered five shows and were lucky enough to win five awards: Best Workmanship at the Sun 'n Fun airshow in Lakeland, Florida, a bronze Lindy at AirVenture in Wisconsin (the Lindy in EAA circles is the equivalent to an Oscar in Hollywood), and Best Homebuilt in three smaller shows. The judges were impressed with not only the aesthetics of the plane, but also the extra safety features I had incorporated into the airframe such as the use of depleted uranium as a counterweight in the rudder. Use of that high-density element required less volume than conventional lead and made it impossible to get the plane into an unsafe aft center of gravity condition if one stayed within the weight limitations of passengers, fuel, and baggage. I had also installed several redundancies in the avionics suite to add to my safety margins when flying in foul weather. My favorite accolade, however, came in 2009, when the National Air & Space Museum asked to display my Lancair during the annual *Become a Pilot Family Day Aircraft Display* at the Udvar-Hazy facility near Dulles Airport. (Figure 29)

The original reason I had built the Lancair was to fly it to Travis AFB in California for my reserve duty. In the end, the one and only time I got to do that was in 1999, my last year of USAF service. I made the trip from Florida in 9.5 flight hours, stopping overnight in Albuquerque, New Mexico, to visit friends, and at the Southern California Logistics Airport (formerly George AFB) for fuel, where twenty-seven years previously I had spent my senior year of high school. Many controllers in 1999 had never seen or dealt with a Lancair, and due to the high speed displayed on their radars, I was often queried as to just what type of jet it was!

Weekly relaxing forays aloft in the Lancair were abruptly interrupted just two years later. All normal flying activities in the USA came to a grinding halt on September 11, 2001, after a group of radical Islamic terrorists commandeered commercial airliners that they then crashed into a field in Pennsylvania, the Pentagon in Virginia, and the World Trade Center towers in New York City. We waited with bated breath to see if any other atrocities were in store as world tensions rose. Non-military flights in US airspace were suspended for weeks by the FAA, until the skies gradually reopened to commercial and private aircraft as tensions eased.

Over the ensuing decades, I traveled to all corners of the USA in my Lancair and still fly it weekly. Almost every journey has left some lasting memory, but a few stand out.

A few years back, while travelling over the wilds of western Wyoming enroute to visit in-laws in Logan, Utah, I was mesmerized by the barren geology and absence of civilization below me. I could make out remnants of an old wagon trail settlers had used when migrating to new lives out west in the 1800's, as well as evidence of the forts that had been built and manned by the US Army back in those days to protect them. Imagine my surprise during these musings as I soared overhead at 22,000 feet when the Center controller announced over the radio, "N654DM, radar contact lost." "What do you mean, lost," I quickly replied, "I'm right here at FL220!" He chuckled as he explained that there were still a few remote spots in the USA that did not have radar coverage, even at my high altitude. I had just entered one of those dead zones. I felt truly alone and was happy to hear him report thirty long minutes later that he had re-acquired my radar return as I emerged on the far side of the hole.

On another adventure, Sue and I once landed the Lancair on remote Mackinac Island, a popular tourist destination just off the northern coast of Michigan. As I unloaded our luggage, a horse and buggy pulled up beside the plane. The juxtaposition of the sleek composite airframe next to a tired horse and ancient wagon was a bit jarring. The driver explained that no motorized vehicles were allowed on the island, so off we clip-clopped on the mile-long trek to our hotel.

One of the most amusing Lancair trips I took, however, was to a summer family wedding in Poughkeepsie, New York. I had called the FBO (Fixed Base Operator, like a gas station for aircraft) at the local airport a week in advance to reserve hangar space for my plane, as I prefer to keep it inside at night. The gentleman answering the phone asked what my arrival time would be. "I don't know, maybe two or three," I responded. A week later, I flew north non-stop from Florida on a beautiful cloudless day, with some nice tailwinds.

I arrived in the Poughkeepsie area a bit earlier than expected, with plenty of fuel, so asked New York Center if they'd mind if I flew up and down the Hudson River for a while to take in the scenery. They approved my request, so I had a leisurely aerial tour of West Point and other quaint sites nearby. Eventually, I told Center that I was done sightseeing, so they vectored me in for a landing at Poughkeepsie airport. To my pleasant surprise, there was a "FOLLOW ME" truck idling at the end of the runway. I followed the truck to a remote area of the field next to some hangars.

As I hopped out of the plane after shutting down the engine, the FBO truck driver jumped out yelling, "That was AMAZING, just AMAZING!"

"What do you mean?" I asked.

"I was the person you spoke to on the phone last week. When I asked you what your landing time was, I thought you were pulling my leg when you said, 2:03; but sure enough, at precisely 2:03 I heard the chirp-chirp of your wheels as they touched down on our runway! I couldn't believe your precision!"

I didn't have the heart to tell him that he'd misheard me: I'd said I would land between two and three, not AT 2:03. My landing at 2:03 p.m. was completely accidental! Nevertheless, he thought I was an amazingly precise aviator, and who was I to disabuse him of that! I received the best service and handling that weekend that I've ever had, before or since.

My favorite use of the plane over the years, though, has been for those flights that combined my passions for flight and medicine as I flew to and from innumerable Flying Physicians Association (FPA) meetings around the country.

CHAPTER 29

THE FLYING PHYSICIANS ASSOCIATION

A chance to blend two passions, aviation and medicine, came to light almost by accident in 1998 when I was asked to give a lecture in New Mexico to an organization called the Flying Physicians Association (FPA). The origins of the FPA were intriguing.

In the early 1950s, doctors who were also pilots had a terrible safety record. It was sometimes said that doctors had more money to buy fancy planes than skill to fly them. To reverse that trend, the FPA was formed in 1955 based upon three foundational mission concepts: Education, Charity, and Fraternity. Six geographical chapters were organized: Northeast, Dixie, Great Lakes, Southwestern, Western, and International. Remarkably, nearly 800 physician pilots joined the organization that first year, and within a few years membership had swelled to several thousand.

Each chapter held spring and fall meetings over a long weekend at some interesting locale off the beaten path that members would fly their aircraft to. As the pilots often were accompanied by spouses and families, social networks emerged. In addition to the regional meetings, a week-long annual conference would be held every summer at a spot selected by the current President of the FPA.

Meetings were set up to provide continuing medical education (CME) lectures as well as aviation safety talks, and often a purely recreational "fly-out" after the meeting was set up as well. The CME was very popular for a variety of reasons. Because the pilots were attending a recognized medical education activity, their flight expenses were tax-deductible. In addition, the CME offered member physicians of all backgrounds and specialties a chance to hear the latest updates in specialties they had not followed since graduation from medical school, often decades before. Historically, specialists become so focused on their area of expertise that they might be oblivious to current practice in other fields: this was certainly true for me.

After I joined the FPA in 1998, though, I always learned one or two "cocktail party" nuggets totally unrelated to my field that I could amaze my colleagues with back home in the ensuing months; for instance, what latest concepts in contraception were being practiced, why an anterior approach hip replacement might be better than the old posterior approach, what irreversible MRI changes occur in the brains of kids watching television and video games that impair their school learning, how and why you can use intestinal parasitic worms to treat ulcerative colitis and Crohn's disease, etc. In turn, I would lecture to the rest about the latest results and techniques from my own specialty, including treating prostate cancer with radioactive seeds, the use of radiosurgery, and even our NaNose research.

Aviation lectures included a variety of topics such as proper ways to maintain one's aircraft, proper instrument flying techniques, how to handle in-flight and ground emergencies, medical aspects of flight, and many others. Invited aviation-related speakers would also lecture about a broad spectrum of more general topics: everything from record-setting flights around the world to a recap of space flight activities from current or former astronauts. We once even had a fascinating though arcane lecture (including videos) describing the adverse medical effects of nude skydiving!

Before or after these lectures, fun activities showcased the unique features and attractions of the locale we were visiting. We might all head out together on river, fishing, or hiking expeditions, take museum or art gallery tours, or even enjoy operas or theater performances.

The ultimate impact on physician pilot safety was outstanding and exceeded expectations: FPA meeting attendees developed a shared safety culture and had an accident rate well below that of average general aviation pilots in the USA. This format for the FPA meetings has continued over the last sixty-nine years, and the excellent safety record of FPA members persists to this day.

The mission of charity in the FPA is also worth mentioning. Many physician pilots fly their planes to and from charitable missions, either alone or in groups as the case might warrant, and many are volunteer pilots for Angel Flight and similar organizations that carry patients and families to medical centers for specialized treatment not available in their home communities. One doctor in the Carolinas flies to an isolated community on a barrier island off the coast to hold regular medical clinics for the local population—and he has done so for years.

After the massive earthquake near Haiti in 2010, much of that country's infrastructure was devastated, including its medical facilities. Relief aid was stacking up on the tarmac in Port au Prince, as there was no way to transport the aid to the hospitals. Sadly, looting gangs stole a large portion of that aid. One hospital outside the main city of Port au Prince was desperate for medical supplies and reached out to a sister hospital in Boston. Word of the hospital's needs reached the FPA, and a mission was organized. FPA members solicited and obtained what the Haitian hospital had requested and doubled it. Members willing and able to make the flight to Hispaniola were networked, and all met at a designated airport in south Florida on a specified date, their aircraft filled with the needed supplies.

On the evening prior to our long over-water flight, a briefing was conducted by Mr. Jim Parker, a specialist in flying through the Caribbean. Jim owned a company called *Caribbean Flying Adventures*, and before that had been a Diplomat and Deputy Administrator for the USDA

Foreign Agricultural Service (FAS): Jim had an extensive knowledge of the area and a prodigious contact list. He was the backbone of our FPA effort to deliver supplies to the needed hospital.

The next morning, twenty-one FPA aircraft and crews departed Florida heading southeast. After overflying the Bahamas, or in some cases stopping there for fuel, all aircraft safely penetrated stormy weather to land at an airport outside Santo Domingo, the capitol of the Dominican Republic. Landing there avoided the lawlessness of Haiti just over the mountain range to the west. We arrived with much fanfare by the Dominicans, who welcomed us warmly with a band, reporters, and cold beer! After we all unloaded our supplies (Figure 30), an enormous white Russian-built United Nations helicopter swooped in, we quickly packed our supplies into its belly, and just minutes later it lifted off again, heading westward toward Haiti. We heard late in the day that it had landed directly on the lawn of the hospital to deliver our goods. Mission accomplished! A day later, one of our pilots made a daring landing on a road south of Port au Prince in foul weather to perform an emergency evacuation of some stranded aid workers. Upon his safe return with the bedraggled workers, we were feted with a party in Santo Domingo. In the spirit of the FPA post-meeting "fun fly outs" we spent a couple of days touring the Dominican Republic before heading back to Florida.

In March 2016 I flew the Lancair solo for another charity mission, this time to the Texas border. A Christian mission group had called FPA headquarters in Houston asking for medical assistance during a three-day mission trip to the Mexican city of Ciudad Acuña, sister city of Del Rio, just across the Rio Grande River. Favorable winds allowed me to make the trip from Jacksonville to Del Rio non-stop, where I met up with another couple that had flown in. We stayed in a motel on the USA side of the border at night, but for the next few days took a van across the Rio Grande to a clinic set up in the city, carrying bulk supplies and medicines that had been warehoused in Texas by the mission group. After unloading those, we saw a variety of patients in this free clinic.

Cancer patients were sent my way, and I witnessed some heartbreaking cases in both adults and children. We were able to make some referrals to larger centers, but probably not enough to meet the needs of the citizens there. Nevertheless, they were appreciative of our efforts and insisted on serving us a huge daily lunch of local foods they had prepared. During my long flight home after the event, I pondered just how lucky we were to have good medical care in the USA, and just how close we were to a people that didn't have such access.

A few years later we received a call for help in the panhandle of Florida after a hurricane left a large swath of the state without power, shelter, or drinkable water. To make matters worse, treefalls and flooding limited access for relief efforts to reach a big rural population. I answered the call, flew to a staging area outside Tallahassee, and from there flew a load of drinking water and tarps to a small airport in the panhandle. Many FPA doctor pilots flew similar missions through the years and still fly them today.

Fraternity is the third leg of the FPA, and perhaps one of its greatest attributes. That first talk I gave to the FPA during their 1998 Annual meeting in Santa Fe, New Mexico, was entitled *"Homebuilding an aircraft for the physician—should you or shouldn't you…"* The talk was well attended with several hundred in the audience. My first comment posed to the audience was, "Raise your hand if you routinely wash your own car." A few folks raised their hands. "Those of you who raised your hands are candidates to build a plane. The rest of you? Forget about it! If you don't even wash your car, the chances you'll successfully build a flying machine are slim to none." There were chuckles in the audience, some nodding of heads, and the ice was broken.

My talk was well received, and the pilots and their families were welcoming to me, Sue, and our children. After each day, we joined in fun activities: I had a great time fly fishing with my son, Michael, and we had an interesting tour of the Los Alamos Laboratory facility and museum (Sue still wears "Fat Man" and "Little Boy" bomb earrings from there).

Chapter 29

We felt an instant bond with this whole group, and have attended yearly meetings ever since, expanding my medical and aviation knowledge base and visiting places we would have never seen. The meetings were opportunities to bond with like-minded folks: members tended to be accomplished yet humble, and all had interesting stories to tell. In a real sense, they became extended family members, and the meetings became reunions as much as medical events.

Over time, I was honored to be asked to enter the FPA leadership track, a challenge that I gladly accepted. After serving in progressively bigger roles, I was eventually elected to the Presidency of the FPA in 2015. Sue and I enjoyed traveling to the various regional meetings during my tenure and were responsible for site selection for our national and winter Board of Directors (BOD) meetings.

After canvassing several cities over eighteen months in 2014 and 2015, we selected Minneapolis for our 2016 National Meeting, and extensive planning got underway. Prior to that, in January 2016 we hosted our winter BOD meeting in St. Augustine, Florida. The weather that week was atrocious, requiring multiple aircraft to deviate and land elsewhere to avoid massive thunderstorms and driving rain. Once safely on the ground, many participants were forced to proceed to St. Augustine in rental cars. I was amazed and pleasantly surprised that everyone who had registered eventually arrived, one way or the other. These were truly "can do" people. The weather gods smiled on us more favorably in July: the Minneapolis weather was spectacular over that Independence Day week, the lectures were outstanding, and the social events we arranged (a lot of them directly the result of Sue's outstanding initiative) got rave reviews. After handing the gavel off to the next President that year, I assumed another round of duties as the Past-President for another year.

Since then, I have also served in the most work-intensive role an FPA member can assume, that of the Program Chairman for a national meeting. The Program Chairman is responsible for locating and locking in a group of twelve-sixteen speakers from around the country for the following year's National Meeting, setting up their schedule and getting their PowerPoint presentations far enough in advance that they can be reviewed and approved by the CME Committee. Once screened, the talks had to be submitted to a CME national credentialing body for approval—only such sanctioned credits could be used by attending members to help maintain their state licensure. I met the challenge in 2021, despite the fact that the Covid-19 pandemic put a year-long hold on our meeting plans until effective vaccines rolled out. Fortunately, my scheduled speakers kept their commitments even after that year delay.

The real hero in preparing successful meetings, though, was Executive Vice President Alice Henderson, FPA's sole paid staff member, who provided expert guidance. Alice kept the organization together through both fat and thin years until her untimely passing in March 2023. She not only handled all the finances of the FPA but also maintained our "corporate memory" including past magazine articles, award histories, and memorabilia. A detail-oriented organizer, she made sure our "T's" were crossed and "I's" dotted for both the organization and the Internal Revenue Service. Alice even oversaw publication of our national magazine entitled *The Flying Physician* twice yearly and our quarterly *Bulletins*.

Though I saw a lot of our country during moves as a USAF dependent, probably the bulk of my memories of traveling the highways, byways, and airways of our great land are related to all the FPA adventures Sue and I have had over the last few decades. Indeed, of my more than 3000 hours as a pilot, a large chunk of them have been traveling to and from FPA meeting destinations.

Sadly, the FPA, like many other organizations, is feeling the changes in our society, and like those other organizations, our membership is falling. This drop is not because there are fewer physician pilots: a cross-referencing of the FAA and AOPA (Aircraft Owner and Pilot Association) database we did several years ago determined that there are still several thousand of us out there. Other reasons must account for waning membership.

The increased cost of flying at a time of diminishing physician reimbursement is one reason for dwindling membership and the rise of two-wage-earner families is another: coordinating two vacation schedules is more challenging than one. The pervasive rise of the multimedia culture is yet a third distraction from in-person journeys: with limitless travel entertainment videos currently available at the mere push of a button, the wanderlust we knew in the past can largely be satisfied by convenient television programming. To some, couch-surfing has sadly become preferable to actual travel.

A bigger difficulty for physician pilots has little to do with flying but rather their recent change in employment status. In the 1960-80's, most physicians were in private practices; If they wanted to take two weeks off to attend a FPA meeting and fly-out, they merely arranged coverage or rescheduled their patients and closed their doors for that time. By 2020, however, the situation flipped, with more than seventy percent being employed by a hospital, large multi-specialty group, or government organization. Employed doctors have limited control over their schedules. They have limited time off, must schedule it far in advance, and are often restricted from taking more than a few days off in a row. Administrators have veto power and can rescind scheduled vacations on a whim.

Other organizations are facing similar downhill membership spirals: the average Joe/Jane just isn't a "joiner" anymore: he/she isn't joining charitable societies like Rotary International or the Elks, or churches, or the military, or garden clubs, or even local homeowners' associations. The American concept of "community" is fading in favor of focus on "self."

During a famous speech in January 1961, President John F. Kennedy said, "Ask not what your country can do for you; ask what you can do for your country." No truer words were ever spoken and never were they timelier than now. Sadly, I fear we are becoming a "me" society rather than a "lets grow together" society. Unless or until a great awakening reverses this course, we will continue down a lonely road of isolationism: as a nation, as a community, and as an individual.

Organizations like the FPA must find ways to become more relevant and indispensable to constituent members in this era—no easy task. I ardently hope they are successful. Barring that, multitudes of physician pilots going forward will never know the tremendous spirit and sense of fulfillment the FPA has to offer.

CHAPTER 30

NESTS AFAR

Homes away from home

I loved my profession as a radiation oncologist and looked forward to tackling new challenges every day of my life. Hearing the occasional gripes of other less enraptured colleagues in other fields, I appreciated even more just how lucky I was.

With that said, the management of complex pediatric and adult cancer patients and their families could be highly stressful, both at work and home. Like the extensive preflight briefings we would review prior to any aeronautical mission, I would mentally review each sequence of events and movement of my hands in my head the night before a big medical or surgical procedure. The pressure to perform perfectly and mentally review the many risks, benefits, and options involved in the use of potent radiation treatments was sometimes nearly overwhelming; my treatments would hopefully cure my patients but also had the rare chance of killing them. Whether to treat or not wasn't always cut and dry, and I would spend hours fleshing out many gray areas to help patients decide. Often, they would just say, "What would YOU do, doc?" and leave the decision to me.

To maintain my sanity and recharge my mental batteries, I occasionally needed to get away. Far away…

In the early 1990's, a FROG partner had bought a vacation condominium on the island of Grand Cayman. Sue and I were invited to visit, and we both fell in love with the neighborhood and the island itself. Grand Cayman was clean, crime-free, beautiful, and only an hour's flight from Miami. Restaurants were plentiful and watersports abounded. The condo we visited was on the grounds of a Hyatt Hotel, adjacent to the island's Arnold Palmer-designed 18-hole golf course and abutting a canal that emptied into the large North Sound Bay, home to reefs, fish, and stingrays. Before departing Cayman a few days later, we had purchased the condo next door.

For the next thirteen years the Cayman retreat was our home away from home. We hosted many family gatherings there over time and the four of us completed our open-water scuba diving training there as well. My partner and I even hosted a long weekend retreat for all the FROG doctors, including their spouses and children. For that event, I set a new personal record for the largest one-time charge ever on my American Express card, as I chartered a Boing 737 to fly us all after work on Friday night directly from Jacksonville international Airport (JIA) to Grand Cayman—only a ninety-minute flight. We were on the island in time for cocktails and dinner! After two days of fun, we reversed course on a late afternoon and were back home in time for the kids' normal "school night" bedtimes. We cleared Customs and Immigration at JIA, an event so unusual in Jacksonville that the Immigration folks asked if we would mind going through the procedure twice so they could train two different teams of staff. We happily obliged. A day later I was even happier when the FROG group reimbursed me for that flight so I could pay off the huge pending credit card bill.

When we were not enjoying the condo ourselves, the Hyatt Hotel would rent it out throughout the year. These rentals covered our expenses, so the situation was a win-win for Hyatt and for us.

All good things must come to an end, it is said, and the Cayman condo situation was no exception: in September 2004 a category-five storm named Hurricane Ivan tore through the Caribbean. It swept over

Grand Cayman with sustained winds of over 200 miles per hour. The island was decimated by the winds and water as the entire west end of the island (including the airport and the location of our condo) was underwater for over six hours. Communication with the outside world was cut off and power was out for weeks, so mold in buildings grew rampant. Shortly thereafter, all the local vegetation and trees died due to saltwater exposure and intrusion—our island paradise had become hell on earth. The condo complex was a sturdily-built concrete construction three floors high. The homes of all the first-floor residents were decimated by flooding, and those on the third floor suffered a similar watery fate as winds ripped off their roofs. Ours was on the second floor and relatively protected by the units above and below: we only had three windows break and a few minor electrical issues.

Because so many people had lost their homes on the island, the few remaining intact domiciles were used to house displaced residents. By the time communication was reestablished with the island, our condo had been commandeered as a refugee haven for multiple families and their pets: it remained a haven for the next nine months. Although most refugees were respectful of our property, the wear and tear after their travails was considerable, and a full refurbishment a year after the storm was necessary. Even worse, the Hyatt Hotel property was destroyed beyond repair. Hyatt left the island, and the hotel property owner entered a years-long lawsuit with his insurance company over damage compensation.

Tourism in the Cayman Islands evaporated for quite some time following the storm. It became evident after a few years that our ability to defray expenses by renting our unit wasn't going to return in the foreseeable future, so we sold it at a huge loss. We made a mental note not to buy something so far away ever again, and our accountant "reassured" us that we had enough long-term capital losses to cover the next 120 years of tax returns!

On an entirely different tack and far away from hurricanes, we looked at and ultimately purchased a vacation home at a fly-in community in the Appalachian Mountains.

Fly-in communities offer unique attractions to pilots and physicians. Indeed, pilots and physicians have nearly identical psychological profiles and usually get along well together. Akin to boating communities near water, pilot communities have sprung up beside runways around the country, where like-minded people can congregate, socialize, assist each other, and, well, tell stories.

One such community high in the mountains north of Ashville, North Carolina, was called Mountain Air. This gorgeous mountaintop property hosted a beautiful clubhouse and restaurant overlooking the highest runway and golf course east of the Mississippi River at an elevation of 4700 feet. Our compact pedestal home had a panoramic view into three states. Mountain Air was pleasantly cool at that elevation, even in the heat of summer, and a great escape from the humidity of Florida, but after a time we realized it had some limitations. The runway was short—less than 3000 feet. The mountain top was often obscured by clouds necessitating a landing over forty miles away at the airport in Asheville. There were no hangars on the mountain, so planes had to sit out in foul weather, and there was no fuel available up there either. Even a trip for groceries involved a thirty minute drive to reach the nearest grocery store.

Two family issues put an even bigger damper on our visits to our Mountain Air refuge. First, our children were budding teenagers who much preferred spending weekend time with their friends in Jacksonville to sitting on a remote mountain top. Second, Sue was diagnosed at the young age of forty-two with breast cancer. The idea of facing the unknown in terms of required treatment and even her survival put trips to the mountain on the back burner. To simplify our complex life at that point, we elected to sell our unit less than two years after joining the community.

Five years later, life was settling down: Sue had no evidence of cancer recurrence, and the kids were heading off to college soon. The allure of the mountains began to resurface, so we looked again in Mountain Air for a small home. Much to our chagrin, prices had skyrocketed since we had left (after all, in the aviation world a home in a fly-in community is akin to a home on beachfront property—there's a limited supply) to the point that a home at the bottom of the mountain now cost more than what we had paid previously for a stunning property atop the mountain a few years previously.

Undeterred, I hunted for something similar, and by 2002 found another newer community that fit our needs and desires even better: Heavens Landing Airpark located in the mountains of extreme northeastern Georgia. The Heavens Landing development was another private fly-in community with a runway situated in a small valley between two hills with home sites atop those hills, being built by developer and race car driver Mike Ciochetti and a small group of aviation aficionado investors. The runway was 5000 feet long, longer than my home airport in Jacksonville. Its runway was also situated at a lower elevation than Mountain Air—2700 feet—so not shrouded in clouds nearly as often. The developer was to build hangars on the field, install a fuel farm to gas up the planes, and even have runway lights and an instrument approach into the field. The nearby town of Clayton was only seven miles away and there was a nearby alternate airport in the lower piedmont, should the weather preclude a landing in the mountain community. We literally got in on the ground level of Heavens Landing and ultimately built a small but comfortable mountain bungalow and a nice hangar for the Lancair.

The best part of Heavens Landing, though, eclipsing even the spectacular surrounding scenery, was the group of people we met and befriended over the ensuing years. I have never met such an array of accomplished yet friendly people, all wanting the peace of idyllic natural surroundings and the camaraderie of similar folks. We befriended residents from all walks of life: current and retired military, corporate and airline pilots, a US Navy Blue Angel pilot whose flying skills graced the *Top Gun Maverick* movie, a retired SR-71 Blackbird back seater, a retired Navy ship captain, a retired USAF General (himself an F-4, F-16, and B-1 bomber pilot), an entrepreneur who owned one of the last remaining brass forge companies in the USA, an outstanding female warbird and airline pilot and leader who served several times as the President of the Warbirds of America, a New York City real estate tycoon, an insurance executive philanthropist, and even a retired astronaut. The list goes on… I was humbled to be allowed into the fold, and we made friendships that will last a lifetime. We will always cherish those times around the campfire, sharing meals at each other's homes or hangars, the movie nights, the walks along the runways and taxiways, and the shared flights together.

Connie Bowlin, our Warbird friend, even arranged a spectacular grand opening event for the Heavens Landing community, entitled "A Gathering of Eagles," in which she brought five WWII aces to Heavens Landing and Clayton to speak and mingle with us, including Chuck Yeager (first man to break the sound barrier), triple aces Bud Anderson, Robin Olds, and Tex Hill (a leader in the famed Flying Tigers in China), and German ace Gunther Rall (the third highest scoring German ace pilot of all time with 275 aerial victories, despite being shot down eight times himself). I was in awe of this group of legendary pilots, who were just witty "regular guys" amongst other aviators, and will long remember my conversations with them that weekend.

CHAPTER 31

Flying misadventures

Rough times aloft

I am sometimes asked if my flying has always been routine or if any emergencies ever arose. Truthfully, if any pilot has been flying long enough some incidents and times of "pucker factor" will have arisen, and I am no exception. Though my thousands of hours aloft have largely been uneventful, a few flights were anything but.

During initial pilot training, one rite of passage for a solo student pilot is a long cross-country flight: the pilot must plan and fly a large triangular course far away from his home base and land at two distant airports. At each of those, he must shut down the plane, walk to the FBO, and have his logbook signed to bear witness to his arrival. During my1980 long cross-country in a tiny Cessna-152, I had chosen to fly from the San Francisco Bay area east into the California central valley to land at a small but tower-controlled airport situated amid endless fields of crops. At that time of year, a weather phenomenon called Thule fog often obscured the ground in the central valley until about midday. I had been aware of this and timed my long slow flight to arrive after the Thule fog had dissipated. Back then, there was no GPS to guide you—VFR pilotage was used. Prior to the flight, a weather briefing included predicted winds at the altitude I was to be flying. Based upon the distance to different checkpoints, the speed and direction I was to be travelling, and those winds, I calculated the proper heading and predicted times for each leg of the flight.

Nearing arrival at my first destination, I noticed that the fog had not yet completely dissipated; I could see the ground immediately below me, but looking toward any horizon just showed monotonous haziness. Reassuringly, I had picked up the tower communications from my intended destination airport and was cleared to approach and land on runway eighteen. I still couldn't see the airport out in front of me, but as my predicted time remaining for the leg wound down, I dipped a wing and saw a runway right below me, marked clearly with eighteen at the end. I spiraled down and landed without incident, then asked for parking directions over the radio.

The tower controller responded, "Where are you?"

I told him I had just pulled off the runway onto the taxiway. "I still don't see you," was his reply.

About that time, I realized I didn't see a tower on the airfield anywhere, either. I had landed at the wrong airport. As it happens, there was another even smaller airport just west of my intended field with identical runway markings to the one I was aiming for. Realizing my mistake after looking at my sectional map, I told him something clever like, "Oh sorry, I'll be with you in a minute." I took off from that small (and fortunately deserted) field and hopped two minutes east to the proper airport. Ugh. I am sure my face was crimson as I asked the FBO attendant to sign my logbook before lifting back into the skies. The fog had completely disappeared by then, and the rest of the flight was routine.

Fifteen years later, I was routinely flying a 1960's era vintage twin-engine US Army T-42 Cochise (known in the civilian world as a Beechcraft Baron B-55, and still in its original faded and chipped US Army green paint scheme) from NAS Jacksonville to work on the Lancair project in Tennessee. This plane had been used for Army pilot instrument training for decades and was later handed down from the active US Army through the reserves and National Guard to finally end up at the NAS Jacksonville Flying Club—its last stop before the boneyard. I had three "adventures" in this aircraft over the two years I flew it.

On a beautiful day flying north over the hills of eastern Alabama I lost both engines—and it was my fault. New to the plane, I had recently been delighted to discover buried in the baggage compartment the original 1966 US Army operations manual for the bird. In the manual, the "best practice" procedure for extending the range of the T-42 was described in step-by-step Army detail. The T-42 was equipped with four fuel tanks: an outboard and inboard tank on each wing. Between the pilot and co-pilot seats was a rat's nest of fuel transfer valves and handles to shunt fuel to the engine from one tank or another, or even across the plane to the opposite wing's engine, as needed.

To relieve the boredom of the long flight, I decided to try out the extended range procedure: Step one involved feeding both engines initially from fuel in the outboard tanks. At the first sign of a sputter due to fuel starvation on one side, the pilot was to switch to the inboard tank on that side to resume fuel flow. The pilot would then perform the same procedure on the other side when that engine started to sputter sometime later. I set the fuel switches accordingly and sure enough, a while later, the left engine sputtered, and mere moments later completely quit! Not five seconds later, while reaching down into the rat's nest to find the proper valve handle to switch tanks, the right engine also died! Silence in the cockpit was interrupted only by the wind whistling past and my curses while hunting for the right valves to turn. The odds of both fuel tanks draining to empty simultaneously were infinitesimal, but it had happened. My hand flew between all the transfer switches until, after what seemed like minutes but was actually only several seconds, the engines coughed back to life. After wiping the sweat from my brow, I shut that ancient procedure manual tightly, and after landing stowed it back deep in the baggage compartment where I had found it.

Months later, while flying back home alone at night from Tennessee in clouds and turbulence in the T-42, I had another rare simultaneous failure. This time it wasn't related to the engines but rather the electrical system, and this time I was not to blame. The main instrument gauges in the T-42 were electrically powered and on this particular aircraft the electricity was not provided by a modern alternator, but rather by a vintage generator. For safety, the plane had a backup generator powered by the opposite engine feeding a backup set of instruments. In the soup, at altitude and in the clouds at night, generator #1 gave up the ghost, and my main directional and attitude indicators began to unwind and give false readings. Recognizing a problem, I immediately switched my instrument scan to my backup indicators. Minutes later, my alternate generator #2 also unexpectedly failed, and with it my backup instruments. To make matters worse, all the cockpit lighting began to dim as the aircraft battery charge faded away.

The only way to keep oriented in the clouds was to alternately point my flashlight between my wet compass, the altimeter, and the airspeed indicator (the thought being that if I kept the compass heading the same my course would be straight, and if I kept the altimeter and airspeed the same, I would be level). This was getting nerve-wracking after a bit, and I said a silent prayer asking for divine intervention to get me out of that fix. Moments later, I popped out of the wall of the giant frontal cloud bank into a clear night sky—I could see stars above and the lights of cities below. Upon landing, I kissed the ground.

My final incident flying the T-42 was in 1995, while flying the plane all the way to Oshkosh, Wisconsin, for display in the Warbird area at AirVenture (they had never had a T-42 on display and asked that I bring it up). Along with me were my close friend Brad Mottier and his father, Charlie (both pilots). Our plan was to fly halfway to make a refueling stop and then continue to Rockford, Illinois, for an overnight rest. The next morning we would make the last short hop from there to Oshkosh.

We departed on a sunny Florida afternoon, climbed to 8500 feet, and began navigating northwest to our first destination using VOR equipment onboard. Just 100 miles north of Jacksonville, however, both VOR radios died within a few minutes of each other—yet another rare twin failure I had never experienced. We decided to push on, using the

Chapter 31

basic wet compass and maps to carry on to our refueling stop. Ten minutes later the compass face glass burst open and all the compass fluid drained to the floor. The compass head fell over on its side, and we had no working navigational instruments in the panel at all. Now over the mountains and committed, we carried on using maps, VFR pilotage, and the theory that if I kept the sun over my left shoulder, we would be heading northwest! After a bit, I heard some rustling in the back seat. Charlie had purchased a new handheld gizmo called a GPS device just before leaving and was opening the box (GPS was a new thing to all of us back in those days). He put some batteries in the unit and fired it up, simultaneously reading the directions on how to use it. He entered our destination waypoint, and we proceeded there with Charlie periodically calling out course heading changes from the back seat. Upon landing to refuel, we placed an order for one hundred gallons of avgas for the plane and four AA batteries for the little GPS unit! The remainder of the trip was relatively uneventful, and the T-42's display on the Warbird line was a popular spot during the airshow. (Figure 31)

Back in Jacksonville after the trip, I heard "the rest of the story" about that wet compass. The Club chief mechanic was so proud that one of his planes was going to be on display at the world-famous airshow that he decided to give the T-42 a good sprucing up the day before my departure. For some reason he decided to take a broom into the cockpit to sweep things out, and in that cramped space had hit the face of the compass with the broom handle. He saw the cracked face, but as the compass was not leaking, he opted to leave it alone. As we climbed high the next day, however, the cabin air pressure decreased to the point that the compass face burst open to release all the lubricating fluid due to the pressure differential. That is the first and last time I have ever heard of or witnessed such a failure.

My most embarrassing, humiliating, and self-inflicted misadventure occurred on the final day of flight-testing my beautiful new Lancair in May 1997, as I was returning to land at the remote home base airport in central Tennessee. On that fateful day I forgot to deploy my landing gear.

Two prior flights that day had gone smoothly. I had always flown the test program flights alone for safety's sake and to ensure my attention was completely focused on the tasks at hand for each test flight. I had always gone through the proper checklist for each phase of flight. Except on that last flight…

The final day's initial test flight entailed "swinging the compass," a procedure to make sure that the wet compass in the cockpit accurately indicated the direction in which the plane was pointing. Electromagnetic currents could "pull" the compass pointer in different directions with different aircraft orientations and electrical loads, and those needed to be measured and compensated for by carefully adjusting some magnetic ferrules inside the compass itself. To do this calibration a compass rose painted on the tarmac was required, as well as a person outside the cockpit to make sure the pilot had the plane sitting over the compass rose in a particular direction before making any adjustments to the cockpit compass.

The airport at which we built the aircraft did not have a compass rose, so Brad Simmons and I flew to a different field about twenty minutes away to perform the calibrations. All went well and with my flight test program complete, we headed to a second airport to pick up a case of oil. The third and last flight of the day found us discussing all that remained to do before I flew the bird to Jacksonville the following morning. We discussed objects to pack, the oil change we were going to do right after landing, and even where we were going to have a celebratory dinner that evening. I was both tired and distracted. I didn't follow the checklist.

A smooth final approach in the warm golden glow of the setting sun and still air that late afternoon ended in earsplitting screeching and grinding of my beautiful Lancair as it came to an unnaturally quick stop on the concrete—on the centerline but three feet lower than it should have been—because I had forgotten to deploy the landing gear. The bottom of the plane suffered some cosmetic damage, but my spirit was completely crushed. How could this be? I was a cautious pilot, wasn't I?

Chapter 31

Forgetting to put down that handle was such a stupid omission: I always thought that it would happen to the "other guy." Now, I was that other guy. In aviation circles, there is an aphorism regarding pilots who fly retractable gear aircraft: "There are those that have, and those that will" forget to deploy their gear at some point.

After lifting the plane onto a trailer and towing it to our shop, I made the call to a sympathetic FAA inspector who listened to my tale of woe. At the end of it, he asked if there were any injuries to me or others, or any damage to other property. I said, "No." He then quietly said he thought I would punish myself enough and that no other action was needed, nor any paperwork: he didn't think it was worthy of filing an official report.

My co-workers at the airport dismounted the engine, sent it for a tear-down inspection, and later reinstalled it upon its return (a teardown is mandatory after any sudden engine stop to reveal possible internal damage). The propeller was toast with all three blades bent and required replacing as well. The skin damage beneath the aircraft was repaired and repainted per instructions from the Lancair factory; fortunately, the brunt of the landing skid was absorbed by the two exhaust pipes sticking out below the fuselage.

After a three-month delay, I finally brought my Lancair home to Jacksonville for the first time, both excited but also humbled and ashamed of my faux pas. In addition to committing to never omit a checklist again, I instituted a rule of "sterile cockpit" during take-off and landing: no one was to talk to or otherwise distract the pilot (me) during those phases of flight. When I upgraded the instrument panel with new digital equipment twenty years later (Figure 32), I installed a "gear warning" alert to remind me to lower the gear any time the airspeed was below a certain limit. In 2024, with over 2400 flight hours in that cockpit since the last flight test, I still bring out the checklist every time.

Several years after the T-42 broom-in-the-cockpit issue, another maintenance snafu led to a declared emergency, this time in my Lancair.

Returning from an FPA meeting in Nashville, I was cruising along at FL190 (19,000 feet) about thirty miles north of Atlanta, when I suddenly felt a massive jolt as I was thrust forward against my shoulder harness. Simultaneously, the cabin air turned to a white fog, the engine quit, and red warning lights were popping up all over the instrument panel. It was as if the plane had smacked into an invisible wall high in the sky. A fast check of my cabin altimeter confirmed that I had lost cabin pressurization, and I quickly donned my oxygen mask while opening the oxygen bottle valve. A scan around the cockpit and wings showed that all my "parts" were still there, and I wasn't trailing any smoke. I declared an emergency and began an emergency descent into the Atlanta airspace. Controllers began vectoring me to a nearby airport and Delta pilots landing at the huge Hartsfield International Airport were wishing me luck over the radio.

At about 10,000 feet, I noticed that the engine was starting to make some power again. I deduced that somehow the conduits forcing ram air from the turbochargers to the engine cylinders had popped open, resulting in an overly rich fuel to air mixture ratio. In standard aircraft piston engines, the fuel to air mixture ratio is carefully controlled to yield the optimal combination to produce power in the cylinders (the so-called stoichiometric ratio). Turbocharged engines essentially think they are at sea level even when flying high because of all the extra air being rammed into the cylinders with each stroke. Those engines also inject commensurately large quantities of fuel to ignite in the cylinders. Without the proper rammed airflow into the cylinders, however, the fuel would not ignite. I leaned the fuel flow back significantly, and the cylinders relit once the proper ratio of fuel to air ratio was reached. Upon safely landing, I de-cowled the aircraft and sure enough, one of the air hoses from the turbocharger to the engine had popped off. Why did this happen? Just prior to my flight to Nashville, the Lancair had come out of its annual engine inspection at a local maintenance facility. To check spark plug condition, some air hoses had been loosened and moved to give a junior mechanic access to the spark plugs. After the plug testing, he had replaced the hoses but forgotten to tighten down the clamps. Unfortunately, the supervising senior mechanic had not checked the torque on those hose clamps either. Things held together on the way north but finally popped apart on the return trip.

This episode brought home a saying by legendary engine maintenance guru Mike Busch, who always claimed that "the most dangerous time to fly a plane is right after it comes out of maintenance." To check one item, another might accidentally be compromised. Mike has the metadata to prove his point, and I am one of his believers. On a side note, Mike is also enamored with the FPA's safety culture, frequently presents at our meetings, and is an honorary FPA member.

The only other two emergencies I have declared over forty-four years of flying were both related to landing gear problems. In the first instance back in the early 1990's, I was flying a Beechcraft Bonanza F33 to Cedar Key on the west coast of Florida. Entering the pattern to land, I did not get the usual "barber-shop pole" indications confirming my main gear was down and locked. I flew back across the state and up and down the St. Johns River to reduce my fuel load and try different maneuvers to get the main gear down. Ultimately, I cranked the gear down manually using the emergency deploy handle under the copilot seat and landed safely back at NAS Jacksonville. It was later determined that the electric gear motor worm drive that retracted and deployed the main gear had burned out—a known issue in the older Bonanzas. The last event involved the nose gear in my Lancair. After departing from an airshow display near Lakeland, Florida, I climbed to 13,500 feet for a relaxed return flight to Jacksonville. After liftoff I hit the gear up switch but quickly noticed that the nose gear light remained green, indicating that it was still deployed. I slowed down, put all the gear back down, and flew it back home that way. After passing by the tower for the controller to confirm that I indeed had three wheels down, I went around the pattern and landed without incident. Inspection of the nose gear showed that the tubing of a major U-shaped metal fork on that gear had fractured, and the resulting two pieces had jammed together like a nasty broken femur injury. The fatigue failure of the tube was later attributed to a metallurgy production defect when it was fabricated two decades before. Luckily for me the pieces jammed in the down position. After an extended countrywide search, I found a replacement fork in Texas and was soon back in the air.

Once back on terra firma I reflected on each of these in-flight situations and emergencies. What could I have done sooner to either avoid or contain the situation? Thorough aircraft and systems knowledge had helped me keep a calm head to work through the issues, and I owed that knowledge to both voracious reading and my instructors' repetitive drilling me on procedures. Their oft-quoted aviation mantra still rings in my head during stressful flights: "aviate, navigate, and then communicate," in that order. Ironically, I also credited my grueling medical internship for letting me know how I would behave when "the chips are down and the pressure is on." After all, it's not the emergency that makes or breaks a pilot, but rather how he responds that reflects his true character and determines the emergency's outcome. That lesson transcends aviation and has guided me throughout my life.

CHAPTER 32

GLOBETROTTING

One of the strongest bonds Sue and I share beyond our family is the love of travel and the experiences gained through interacting with people in their native environments around the world.

From our first honeymoon visit to Jamaica, we decided to travel and experience the world and its cultures whenever possible. Even before having children, we had experienced living in the United Kingdom (two cultures separated by a common language) and had explored the game reserves of Kenya, seeing strange and wonderful animals and meeting native tribes in their villages of dung-coated huts.

Growing our family didn't slow us down, either. Our first big family adventure combined flying and cultural exposures all over Australia for a month in 1994. The love of travel and cultural exchange eventually passed on to our children as they too expanded their horizons through travel as young adults: Danielle to Spain and Italy and Mike to parts of Europe, Asia, and back to Australia.

Mountain biking trips with a group of intrepid fellow travelers also scratched our travel itch over many years, as we were introduced by fellow cancer researcher Neil Abramson to Chuck and Judy Nichols, a wonderful couple who ran Nichols Expeditions out of their Poison

Spider Bicycle Shop in Moab, Utah. Neil and a group of athletic bikers from Jacksonville had traveled with Chuck and Judy on many biking exploits, and we were adopted into the group.

Our first bike trip was a several day adventure into the remote wilderness of Canyonlands National Park in southern Utah. After ferrying us to a remote dirt strip in small planes, we biked up, down, and around some breathtaking arid scenery and got to know our fellow travelers well. In the group was another newbie, Mr. John Wilbanks, who was then a junior administrator at BMC. John would later rise through the ranks to become Chief Operating Officer of the entire Baptist Health System, but I still remember him as just another smiling member of our unwashed pack bonding along the difficult and dusty trails.

After that first Utah bike trip, we enjoyed several more Nichols Expeditions tours in North, Central, and South America, as well as Europe. Just south of our US border, we traveled by train from the Gulf of California east into the mountains to bike the high country of north central Mexico. There, we met reclusive Tarahumara Indians and an expatriate American gold miner as we followed the rim of the massive Copper Canyon (like our Grand Canyon, but green with foliage) and biked to a secluded village nestled along a stream at the bottom.

Two years later we explored parts of Alaska as we biked along the earthquake trail in Anchorage (dodging the occasional moose), hiked a glacier in Wrangler St. Elias National Park, and flew float planes both to remote fishing camps and to a bear sanctuary on the Katmai peninsula to gaze upon grizzlies feasting on wild salmon snatched from raging streams.

On one European trip while biking through Slovenia, we witnessed amazingly pristine scenery and met wonderful local farmers and villagers. On one springtime afternoon during that adventure, our local guide became lost in the countryside. While pedaling down a remote rural lane that day, we happened upon a wedding reception. They were as surprised to see us as we were them, but a few minutes later the bride and groom graciously invited us in and we partied the day away with the whole group—they in their finery, and we in our bicycle clothing—all singing, dancing, and trading food (they shared their wedding cake, and we shared our Skittles and trail mix) though we couldn't understand a word being said to each other. Joy is infectious in any language!

Another year found us biking through the cool arid highlands of Peru along the Valley of the Kings near Cuzco down to the warm and humid lost city of Machu Picchu, perched atop a narrow river gorge. (Figure 33) Once again we met local farmers, attended colorful marketplaces in remote villages, and even stopped to watch an enterprising family hand-make roof tiles in molds by the hundreds. As we rode slowly at an elevation of 13,000 feet, we peered even higher to see ancient terraced hillsides sculpted by industrious Incan farmers centuries before.

Danielle and Michael joined us on another bike trip to South America, this time to beautiful Patagonia in southern Chile. In fertile valleys surrounded by snow-capped rugged volcanic peaks, our sense that we might be in Bavaria rather than a land below the equator was reinforced when we distinctly heard German being spoken by farmers in their fields as we rode by. Our guide later explained that there had been a huge influx of German immigrants in the late 1800's fleeing famine in Europe, and those hardy souls had brought their culture with them. Indeed, most of the homes nestled in the fertile valleys along our route resembled typical Swiss Alpine chalets. We got drenched in a few driving cold November rains, but tried to reassure the kids that their hardships would instill warm memories. Those reassurances were met with sidelong glances and derisive eye rolls by our teenagers, so the jury might still be out on that…

An older neighbor had once suggested we take our kids skiing as youngsters, as it was one thing that they would still willingly do with us old folks in their teenage years. We took that advice to heart, and at least once a year would rendezvous with my old medical school classmate, Bob Silverman, and his family at different ski resorts throughout the western USA and Canada. Our kids grew up together in that way, and we enjoyed memorable family moments during those brief vacations in the snow.

Hiking trips largely replaced biking tours for Sue and me in later years, most of them with Bob and Anne in such varied locales as the Azores (my favorite), Croatia, Montenegro, Iceland, the Swiss Alps, and eastern Quebec.

We even got my parents in the cultural travel spirit when they joined all four of us for a memorable trip through Scandinavia one summer to celebrate their fiftieth wedding anniversary. The weeklong journey was a whirlwind of ferries, trains, and vans taking us all around Denmark, Sweden, and Norway. The people, scenery, and food were great, and memories of the experiences we shared lasted the remainder of my parents' lives. My father's roots were pure Swedish, but he had never visited there. I had been to Stockholm for business twice before and had met several relatives; my hope was to have my father meet them as well. Unfortunately, everyone who can apparently leaves Sweden in August to enjoy sunny beaches along the Mediterranean—my dad's relatives included. He missed seeing them by three days.

As I love all things mechanical and enjoy a good challenge, I was delighted when my T-42 co-pilot friend, Brad Mottier, invited me to participate with him in a British auto rally sponsored by the Historic Endurance Rally Organization (HERO) called *The Scottish Malts* in 2003. (Figure 34) One of many rallies sponsored by HERO for vintage cars, the *Malts* saw us racing from one Scottish distillery to another all around the country for a week. At each distillery we performed various automotive skill tests and were rewarded with a tiny airline-sized bottle of their local product for later display in a personal trophy case.

Between distilleries, time and navigational challenges abounded, and no modern conveniences like maps, GPS devices, or mobile phones were allowed while on the road—instead, dense books containing a series of obtuse directions (Figure 35) were our only directional guides. Things would be fine until you were caught on a back country road behind a slow tractor or stopped completely by a herd of sheep. Miss a turnoff, and you were lost. At random points along the route, time trial stations were set up and your time noted as you passed. At the end of the event, prizes were awarded to those completing the entire course closest to the ideal time, and the winners were separated by just seconds after the week. The prize for Team Mottier/Johnson? We won something like "nicest car" for our 1974 Datsun 240Z. Leaving the awards gala, Brad quipped, "I think we just won the equivalent of Miss Congeniality!"

Another HERO event piqued my interest in 2005: the *London to Lisbon Rally*. Brad was unable to go but offered me the use of his Datsun that he kept in Cambridge, England. I thought this would be another wonderful bonding and travel experience for Sue and me to do together, as she loves to drive (I've often suspected that in a prior life Sue was a semi-truck driver). She agreed, and off we went to start the rally on the grounds of the famous Greenwich Observatory near London.

The rally plan was to begin our time trials as we headed southwest from the Observatory through the English countryside to Portsmouth. All the vehicles would then be placed on an overnight ferry to Bilbao, Spain, where we would resume rallying westward through the Pyrenees Mountains of the Iberian Peninsula, turn south to rally through the interior of Portugal, and finish on the Grand Plaza of Lisbon.

My British author friend, Chris Davey, and his wife Liz were there to cheer us on as the race kicked off in London. Unfortunately, trouble began as soon as we left the Observatory: the car was running rough and would stall at low idle speed, totally unlike the smooth-running engine of a few years back during the *Malts*. We limped along to Portsmouth. Once safely aboard the ferry, I called Brad and the Cambridge mechanics for advice. Brad said his crew had been modifying the engine to set it up in the configuration used when an identical Datsun had run the *Paris to Dakar Rally* decades before. That setup required removing the standard Datsun factory fuel injectors and replacing them with Weber carburetors. The mechanics admitted they hadn't had time to get the proper fuel nozzles for the carburetors, so had substituted something else.

Departing the city of Bilbao two days later to continue the rally, I had to keep the engine at or above 3000 rpm to keep it running;

that meant completing the entire rally in first or second gear most of the time, with the engine loudly protesting and flames (caused by the improper air/fuel mixture ratio) belching from the tailpipe with every downshift. One irate vintage MG roadster driver closely following me around tight mountain curves wanted to bill me for repainting his damaged "bonnet" due to all the flames and smoke hitting the front of his car. I flew the auto mechanics from England to a small town in the Spanish mountains for help, but their efforts at tuning the improper equipment were doomed to failure.

Between the car's woes and the fact that much of northern Portugal that year was ablaze with raging wildfires along our path, my hopes for a romantic relaxing journey and finding a new shared interest with Sue were dashed. At one point, high in the mountains above the tree line, I tried to distract her from the car's woes by pointing out interesting scenery. "Look at that pretty orange bush up ahead," I yelled over the noise of the engine. As we approached, I realized that it wasn't a bush; it was an overturned car that had run off the embankment in foul weather the day before. "No, don't look at the bush, look at that big gray rock on the other side of the road," I lamely called out, but it was too late—she had already spotted the wrecked car, which only intensified her distrust of the whole event.

Sue's only favorable memory of the trip was loading the car on the trailer in Lisbon at the end of the trip and then walking the city for two days before returning home. *London to Lisbon* was our one and only rally together.

Another avid globetrotter in our FROG group was Dr. John Wells. Before attending medical school, John had been an F-4 Phantom pilot in the US Marine Corps, stationed for a time in Japan. John and his wife Shari loved to travel. As they were a bit older than Sue and me, they hit major life milestones years before us. For his sixty-fifth birthday, John and Shari decided to celebrate by going on a spectacular month-long National Geographic Expedition: *Around the world by Private Jet*. He asked whether two of his FROG compatriots and their spouses (the

Johnsons and Paryanis) would accompany him and his wife. Though Sue and I initially balked at the steep price of the journey, we ultimately signed on, as the trip checked off many places on our bucket list. In the end it was the best travel decision we ever made, and a trip that still comes up regularly in conversation fifteen years later.

National Geographic has been deeply involved with cultures across the world for well over a century, and the Society has the cachet and contacts to gain entry to sites only dreamed of by other organizations. The night before our journey was to begin from Washington, D.C., the Society Director presented us with our official Expedition flag. He related that this was indeed an official National Geographic expedition that had taken over a year of planning by hundreds of individuals across the globe. Our chartered private Boeing 757 jet was outfitted with eighty first-class seats and crewed by three pilots, two flight engineers, a dozen flight attendants, a doctor, and a cook. The plane carried enough spare parts and supplies to carry us around the world (this preplanning was justified weeks later, as the crew replaced a main gear tire on a remote airport in Tanzania). Our mission was to meet, learn about, and embrace cultural exchange with several groups as we girded the planet, crossing the equator seven times on the trip. Flight days were packed with onboard lectures about upcoming stops, and each night we slept in fantastic local lodgings.

The adventures of this trip alone could fill a small book, but a few images will suffice to give one a flavor of the journey: watching reed boat fishermen breaking the surf along the coast of northern Peru as they paddled out with their nets; hiking beneath the Moai statues of Easter Island (Rapa Nui) while listening to a Chilean archeologist outline theories about the rise and fall of the native population generations ago; visiting the home and final resting place of *Treasure Island* author Robert Louis Stevenson on Samoa; scuba diving on the Great Barrier Reef with an ex-Navy Seal as my buddy; visiting the temples of Angkor Wat and Ta Prohm in Cambodia, serenaded by musicians sadly crippled and maimed by the Khmer Rouge communists during their genocide of the late 1970's; witnessing a panoramic and festive indigenous people's performance in a massive outdoor amphitheater in the foothills of the Himalayas near the town of Lijiang, China; slipping in via the private side gate of the Taj Mahal to marvel at the beauty of the "temple built for love" in Agra, India, and that night celebrating the spontaneous wedding of a couple in our group; a private tour of Olduvai Gorge in Tanzania for Sue and me hosted by Louise Leakey, granddaughter of renowned paleoanthropologist Mary Leakey who discovered our human ancestor Zinjanthropus in that remote site years before; being feted at night under torchlight in Karnak's temple in Luxor, Egypt; given a private lecture and tour of the pyramids by world-famous archeologist Zahi Hawass, Minister of Tourism and Antiquities of Egypt; and exploring the grand bazaar in Marrakech, Morocco, before returning to the USA via the Azores.

In late 2015, relations between the USA and Cuba briefly thawed, allowing Americans to freely travel there for the first time since 1959. A fellow FPA pilot, Dr. Felix Tormes, and I traveled with Jim Parker and a small group of aviators in our private aircraft to Varadero, about two hours east of Havana, for an eye-opening visit to this beautiful but cash-strapped country. The rooms in our upscale "resort" were clean but the linens threadbare, the sinks had no stoppers, and the toilets had no seats. The local food was delicious, though, and we found the people to be friendly, gregarious, and gracious. As I have noted throughout the world, people often survive and thrive despite their government, rather than because of it.

An organized tour by one of the two federally sanctioned (i.e., military-controlled) tour companies insisted on taking us to the southern side of the island to visit a museum dedicated to the successful repulse of the "imperialist American invader pigs" who had aided an anti-Castro coup attempt by 1,400 Cuban exiles in 1961. We were bemused by the obvious propaganda, but an unexpected opportunity arose when we stopped for refreshments afterward next to the Bay of Pigs: a roadside hut advertised scuba diving for a small fee. We convinced the reluctant tour guide to extend our stop by an hour, and five of us took the opportunity to dive on the beautiful unspoiled and colorful reefs of the Bay. During our journey, we interacted with people harvesting sugar cane plantations, making cigars in factories in old Havana, and producing fine Cuban rum. Artisans abounded and displayed works for sale in warehouses near the Havana harbor.

During our week there, we were enchanted by the beauty of Cuba and its people but saddened by their obvious oppression. Felix and I were greatly relieved as we safely flew from the beaches of the Cuban north coast toward Key West, Florida, when Havana Control finally ordered us to switch to Miami Center.

In mid-2024, Sue and I traveled to England and France to celebrate the 80th anniversary of the June 6th D-Day invasion of Europe during WWII. The visit to Omaha Beach and the American Cemetery was a moving reminder of our history and those that sacrificed all to preserve democracy. The visit had been on our bucket list for years, and while in England the week before, I had arranged to fly a 1944 WWII vintage Supermarine Spitfire Mark IX. A dream of flying behind the throaty roar of a Merlin engine was fulfilled as I logged "hands-on" stick time in my flight logbook. (Figure 36) Being nestled within a machine that had fought and survived battles in the South Pacific decades before was humbling, to say the least.

Throughout our travels, we especially sought out local art museums and artisans, as we had found that artwork best encapsulates and amplifies the hopes, dreams, and fears of a society. We often bought small works when abroad, and many of those adorn our home to this day. On other occasions, I commemorated a place or time in my own painting. (Figures 37-45) Indeed, creating art would soon consume much of my life…

CHAPTER 33

MY CANCER

My prostate done me wrong; or, rough air below…

While I was still active in the clinic, patients would often ask me what I would do were I in their situation. In 2021 I would have the opportunity to answer that question in a very personal way.

Throughout my medical career, I was involved with and witnessed the gradual and dramatic improvement in early detection and curative treatment of prostate cancer in the USA. The most important detection advance in the latter decades of the twentieth century was the prostate specific antigen (PSA) blood test. Before that test, the only way prostate cancer could be detected was with the old "finger wave" digital rectal examination that looked for lumps or nodules in the gland. By the time a clinician felt an abnormality, the prostate cancer was often spread beyond the gland, making curative treatment less likely. The PSA, however, usually detected the cancer when it was still confined to the gland, and amenable to curative treatment. Despite this advance, it took many years before PSA screening was to become routine during annual physical exams.

Nowhere was this reversal of clinical fortune more evident than in my radiation oncology cancer clinic: before PSA, two-thirds of all the men with prostate cancer under my care were there for management of symptoms related to metastatic incurable cancer having already spread to the bones, causing pain, and impacting lifestyle. After PSA, the situation was reversed as over two-thirds of all my prostate patients were being treated for cure.

By the time my own rising PSA was detected, the whole process of detection and treatment was customized to each man, and many options could be tailored to each presentation. My PSA had not risen much: it was still below what previously had been considered an "upper normal" of four. We knew by then that more important than the absolute level was the rate of rise: in my case, my PSA had been measured annually over many years at about 2.5, but the most recent reading had jumped to 3.5. A repeat test after a course of antibiotics confirmed that rise. I could have waited another six months to check it again but elected to have an extensive set of template biopsies done. Much to my surprise, of the thirty-one core biopsies of the prostate done, twenty-nine were involved with a nasty Gleason 4+3=7 adenocarcinoma, involving all parts of the gland. Genetic tests on the material indicated an aggressive tumor as well. Scans suggested the tumor was still confined to the area of the prostate, but with the high-risk features the cancer would likely have spread to other distant areas had I not pursued the biopsies and discovered it early.

Many years ago, surgery might have been recommended for this disease, but studies in more recent years with up to fifteen-year follow up suggested that an alternative approach using hormones and radiation therapy not only avoided many of the risks of bleeding, infection, and incontinence seen with surgery, but also offered improved disease-free survival over surgery (Ref6). In addition, rather than a prolonged post-surgical healing course requiring months away from the cockpit, one could be back in the saddle within just a few weeks by avoiding surgery.

I had always insisted that my patients see both a urologist and a radiation oncologist to hear all options before deciding on what treatment was best for them. I did the same for myself. In the end, I did exactly what I had recommended for patients in my situation over the years: I embarked on a series of monthly anti-androgen hormonal shots followed by a Pd-103 seed implant, and finally by five weeks of external-beam radiation treatment. I followed my own advice…

During my years wearing the white coat, one sacred duty when leaving the radiation therapy vault just prior to turning on the beam was to make sure I was the "last man out" and no staff member was inadvertently left inside before we closed the massive lead-clad door and turned on the beam. It was a strange feeling laying atop that treatment table as technologists left the room and the door closed. I had to bite my tongue to stop from calling out, "Hey, I'm still in here!"

Four weeks after the seed implant, I was back flying, and now over three years later my PSA is essentially 0: mission accomplished, thus far! I will continue to be checked every six months for at least the next ten years.

CHAPTER 34

AN ARTISTIC JOURNEY

Art is a universal form of human communication. It transcends time, borders, language barriers, culture, and even religion. Whether viewing the 17,000-year-old cave pictograms on the walls at Lascaux, France, or modern works in museums worldwide, nearly all humans respond to the emotions and memories evoked by art.

Artwork has always intrigued me, ever since I was stirred by the pastoral painting my parents acquired in Spain in 1960. (Figure 4) What was the shepherd thinking, while standing there with his flock? Were the sheep bleating and walking away or happy just standing quietly and chewing the roadside grass? There were just so many interpretations.

I loved the fact that the artist might have one thing in mind and could certainly set the stage with light angles, atmospherics, and content, but meaning was ultimately up to the viewer and could vary from one viewer to another. A piece of artwork could embody a place, a mood, a time in history, or any combination of the three.

Early on I knew that I wanted artistic creation to be a part of my life, but I wasn't quite sure how it would fit in.

I had no formal art training and in later years regretted that. Unlike many artist friends, I never learned the names of the old masters or the accepted dogma and meaning attributed to classic and iconic pieces of art. In light of that, my interpretations were purely subjective and mostly without academic merit. When viewing a piece of artwork, I knew what I felt about it, but not necessarily why I felt that way.

Like most other youngsters, I began doodling on scrap paper, usually at inappropriate times: during the sermon in church on Sundays or during a boring class in grade school. As my interests evolved around aviation, my early drawings depicted balloons, dirigibles, warplanes, satellites, and space capsule landings. I later drew fanciful depictions of spacecraft I envisioned including rudimentary engineering cutaways. When I dreamt up a new model rocket design in high school to enter in the Estes national design competition, I brought those rudimentary drafting skills to bear for my submission.

Needing something to cover the walls of my first apartment at Virginia Tech, I wanted to paint landscapes. To sort out how to do that, I tackled the problem as I had all other obstacles throughout my early life—I scoured the library. I read books on composition, color mixing, materials needed, and other basics. I even bought a few "how to" books from the local hobby store and, of course, watched a few episodes of Bob Ross's show "*The Joy of Painting*" on public television. How hard could it be?

After what I thought was endless preparation, I sat down with paint laid out, a canvas taped to an old textbook, and a brush in hand. And waited... After a bit, I finally just slapped some paint down, and eventually got it to look a bit like a mountain with some trees, but it wasn't quite the masterpiece I was hoping for.

Early attempts improved with repetition. Once more comfortable with the brush, I painted scenes and memories of places I'd lived or visited. Compositionally, I would often compose fictitious but meaningful scenes describing an entire trip in a single image: a mountain from here, a building from there, and a river from another place. All were real elements from disparate areas but placed together into an image that was only real in my head.

The creativity inherent in generating art also helped me in my medical pursuits, as I formulated cohesive radiation treatment plans to target a cancer and avoid normal tissues by creating complex and elegant blocks to shape the beams; during my time at Stanford, fellow residents claimed that they could always tell which were my patients' films by the curvaceous lines seen on x-ray view boxes across the room.

Initially an oil painter, I switched to more convenient acrylics for a time after being told by my new bride that my "studio" (the kitchen table) had to be cleared off by dinnertime! When our children came on the scene, they took top priority for several years; my art equipment consisting of a cheap collapsible easel and a fishing tackle box filled with my supplies was relegated to the bottom of a closet for a decade.

As the children grew up and became more independent, our travels resumed. I wanted to capture those trips for our walls once again, so my art supplies resurfaced, and some pieces were created. I wasn't happy with my progress, though. I had gained some insight into the mechanics of painting over the years but seemed to have plateaued: I wasn't getting better fast enough. I liked many of the paintings I had completed but wanted to learn more. I tried changing my media to mix things up, but my paintings still seemed rigid and tight, without any "soul." In 2006 we remodeled our Jacksonville home and included a dedicated art studio for Sue and me to share, so I couldn't blame my stagnation on a lack of space or materials. I once again realized that I "just didn't know what I didn't know." As my clinical medical career slowed after 2014, the desire to climb above my current artistic plateau grew.

A fellow FROG's wife, Nadine Johnson Terk, was an accomplished artist in her own right and asked if I'd like to attend a figure drawing class near Jacksonville Beach one night. Having no idea what figure drawing meant (I naively thought perhaps we were going to draw some boxes or designs) I showed up as instructed with my #2 pencil and a sketch pad. We were asked minutes after arrival to choose an easel and get ready for a three minute drawing; imagine my shock when the young lady next to me dropped all her clothes and posed on a chair. She was, of course, a model, and "figure drawing" meant drawing the human form.

Duh! Heck, I was a physician and certainly no prude, but this revelation left me momentarily speechless. I dropped my pad and pencil on the floor twice, and when the timer went off three minutes later my drawing of her most resembled an Idaho potato. As did my second attempt. And my third. I wanted to crawl into a hole.

My life's kaleidoscope twisted yet again, as I realized I needed a mentor. Just as in aviation there is a huge difference between book learning and actual "hands on the flight controls" instruction, so, too, it finally dawned on me that I needed a "flight instructor" for learning my art craft: someone to teach me the nuances not captured in a book or even on a television program (sorry, Bob Ross). How could I make that happen? I wasn't really a beginner, but was by no means an accomplished artist either, so wasn't sure where or what instruction to sign up for.

In 2017, the CoRK Art District studios (a cooperative group of artist studios within a group of old warehouses in Jacksonville) held its annual open house, a weekend event during which the public was invited in to peruse the studios of the professional artists. Sue and I wandered through the spaces, and as we neared the end of one building, I stopped in my tracks. Before me on the wall were landscape and figure drawings done with a looser and more expressive style, wonderful composition, and clever color schemes. They spoke to my soul. I commented quietly to Sue, "Boy, that's what I'd like to paint like." Little did I know that standing right behind us at that moment was the artist himself—Paul Ladnier. Paul was not only a master professional artist and member of the coveted Salmagundi Society in New York but was a professor emeritus of the University of North Florida.

Paul must have heard my comment, as he invited Sue and me into his studio for a personal tour. The more he said, the more I realized we had a lot more in common than just art. He was clearly a passionate teacher who lived and breathed art but also had a broad range of other interests outside the studio. I explained my dilemma and artistic plateau: to my relief, he didn't laugh. We chatted a bit further, but before we left, he asked if he could stop by my home and studio to look at my work (he had clients only a few streets away, so came to my neighborhood on a regular basis anyway).

Within a week, Paul was in my home and got a tour of the "Johnson Gallery—containing the world's largest collection of Johnson originals," as Sue used to describe it. In retrospect, I suspect this must have been a screening process, and he saw enough merit in my work to invite me to join a small cadre of students he was providing weekly instruction to in his studio. Thus began a long and fruitful mentorship and friendship, as Paul guided me on my artistic journey and helped me climb beyond my original plateau. I also returned almost exclusively to oil paints, as they allowed greater flexibility, blending abilities, and slower drying times than the acrylics I had been using. Looking back, I now realize that there is not just one plateau in the artist's journey, but rather an endless stream of them, hopefully spiraling higher and higher as skill improves.

In addition to honing my skills and compositions, Paul helped my figures move beyond those original potato drawings done years previously. My medical anatomy background helped immensely, and a new way of thinking helped my human forms take shape: to get a realistic pose, I had to think about painting a human from the inside out. I started with accurate skeletal constructs and then added muscles, ligaments, and skin. When proper lighting/shadowing, clothing, and perspective were thrown in, the results were a dramatic improvement for me. (Figure 46) I was certainly no John Singer Sargent, but at least my figures looked human.

Noting my interest in painting landscapes, Paul also encouraged me to explore the world of painting outdoors: so-called plein air painting. I had tried it once during the research retreat in Colorado previously, but getting my own equipment and meeting a like-minded group of artists really opened my eyes to a whole new way of painting.

Studio painters have the luxury of setting up their painting environment to their own desires: arranged lighting, comfortable indoor temperatures, a room full of painting materials and resources, large monitors or computers on which to place static images they want to replicate, refreshments and bathrooms just steps away, soothing music or quiet solitude at their option, and an infinite amount of time to complete a painting. Studio master Leonardo da Vinci, for example, was still tweaking his *Mona Lisa* masterpiece on his deathbed, years after he had begun the work.

The plein air movement, on the other hand, is more like the "Olympics" of painting: one really must be on his game to successfully create in the outdoors. The plein air artist must distill a huge vista in front of him to a smaller confined subject in just a few thoughtful minutes. He must be a confident and fast painter as well: Shadows and light elements and the relationships between them need to be locked down in the first fifteen-twenty minutes, as they quickly change with the sun's movement across the sky; the remainder must be largely completed within ninety minutes or so, as the changing sun angles also change the warmth and mood of the outdoor subject. Ambient conditions can also be challenging, with intrusive insects, wildlife, noisy city streets, glaring sun, freezing cold, blustery winds, and unexpected rainfall or cloudiness all competing to disrupt the artist's concentration. (Figure 47-48) Balanced against that, though, is the atmosphere surrounding the artist: the bad odors or fragrant aromas, the calls of birds or chattering of wildlife, the rustle of leaves or crash of pounding surf. A less appreciated benefit is that of interacting with interested bystanders, as they come up to comment on the work, their interest in art, their background and why they are there at that moment in time, etc. All these factors can be wrapped into the soul of a successful plein air painting and explain why plein air is my favorite and most challenging artistic pursuit.

On trips now, I try, at a minimum, to carry along drawing pads and tools. On one special journey to Spain in 2022, Paul and I packed our oils and materials in backpacks. Over two weeks, we became artistic gypsies, wandering the central plains and coasts of Spain in a rental car and stopping to capture plein air scenes along the way. (Figure 49-50) Our canvas panels were covered with scenes from Barcelona to Gibraltar, and many points between. We searched in vain for my old family dwelling in Zaragoza from the late 1950's but instead discovered an excellent museum dedicated to long-time resident Francisco de Goya, one of the greatest artists of the eighteenth and nineteenth centuries. The museum featured wonderful works by his mentors, Goya himself, and his students.

Prior to my formal instruction at the CoRK studios, I had painted exclusively for my own benefit, and largely to fill blank spaces on my home walls with memories. Rarely had anyone other than family seen my work. Paul encouraged me to get beyond that. In his view, showing one's work in different venues provides any artist an opportunity to become less timid and rise to new challenges. Also, an artist can have few higher accolades than recognition by his peers. Just as an occasional great shot keeps a golfer returning to the course week after week, an occasional art show award ensures an artist will return to his easel emboldened to continue his efforts to improve. For both good golfers and good artists trying to excel, the true competition is with themselves, not others.

In 2018, I began to show my works in local and regional shows and launched my art website: www.DWJohnsonFineArt.com. In time, accolades in juried and judged shows began popping up. Some show attendees started to comment that "they could always recognize my work" from across the room. I wasn't always sure if they meant that as a compliment, but in any event, they took notice! Since then, patrons have acquired my paintings for display on their own walls: I now have works in private collections from California to New York and from North Dakota to Florida (and abroad in Paris and London). Galleries in Florida and Georgia have represented and sold my work over the years and I have been fortunate enough to be invited to some select plein air events. There have been a few newspaper and magazine articles written about my art journey and I was even featured on a Podcast in 2023 (Ref10). In that same year, I was one of only two artists offered membership in the prestigious Florida Artists Guild (FLAG), an exclusive society of art professionals in Florida.

Ironically, as the mists have cleared somewhat on my artistic journey over the last few years, yet higher plateaus above me have appeared as well: the journey to improve is endless. The more an artist knows, the more he realizes just how much more there is to know. Paul often quips, "In the art world, you're only as good as your last painting." As my medical career and perhaps even my days as an aviator ebb, I hope to continue climbing this artistic mountain for years to come.

CHAPTER 35

A PAINTING IS LIFE

Why paint? What is the connection between visual artistic endeavors, the art of medicine, and the exploration of humanity? In so many ways, a painting reflects and embodies the twists and turns of life itself:

- As pigment is laid on a blank canvas, a painting takes on a life of its own, often heading in a direction the artist did not originally plan.
- In the beginning, painted forms are indistinct, blurry passages of light and dark.
- Over time, those areas of light and dark determine the values of the composition; Isn't it the same way in life? Our values shape our life in myriad ways.
- As the painting progresses, blurry masses become more distinct and relatable, just as do our desires, needs, and goals.
- Interesting paintings, like interesting people, are composed of varying and contrasting elements, rather than uniform bland characteristics.
- Like a person, no painting is perfect. Gross imperfections must be corrected early on, but more subtle flaws may only

become apparent after living with a painting for a while. Those problems too may be addressed but often require slow and deliberate corrections to effect gradual improvements.
- As a person hopefully finds direction and meaning in his life, so hopefully a painting "comes together" to become something more than a sum of its individual elements, and more valuable because of that.
- A good painting can affect many viewers, just as a person's life impacts those around him. A great painting, like a great person, can have long-lasting impact beyond the artist's own life.
- For a good painting to last, a good foundation must be laid with quality materials and thoughtful purpose. So it is in creating a meaningful life.
- A painting, like a person, doesn't appeal to everyone.
- A good painting stands on its own merits, not relying solely on the opinion of others.

These points might sound like flippant responses to a question posed by those NASA psychiatrists long ago, asking, "How is a painting like a life? Explain." In truth, they all have real and palpable meaning to me.

CHAPTER 36

COMMENTS ON LEADERSHIP

It was never a life goal to be a leader. I always remembered, however, my father's advice to "*try to leave the world a better place than you found it.*" In practice, trying to accomplish that thrust me into leadership roles, whether intended or not.

To make a favorable mark on the world, I first had to learn to do something that the world might value. Early on, that growth involved gleaning all I could from the treasure trove of knowledge contained in books: hence all those library visits in my youth, and later studying specialized textbooks and references in college, medical school, and residency. Even following residency, I continued to read the literature in my radiation oncology specialty to keep pace with the latest advances in the field. Later, I added to that published database with research contributions of my own.

Preserving the dignity and humanity of my patients was always paramount, and the opportunity to share in their lives and educate them about their disease and their treatments was a highlight of my career—something I was recognized for in a book entitled *Glimpses of Heaven* (Ref11). Hoping to further hone the ability to care for my incurable patients, I also attained board-certification in Hospice and Palliative

Care Medicine in 2012, complementing the Radiation Oncology Board-certification I had earned back in 1983.

In the art world, it was the same: I originally had little formal knowledge of the art world, but through reading, studying with Paul Ladnier and other professionals, and participating in many art leagues, I gained an appreciation for and a modicum of knowledge about the field. That knowledge has allowed me to create works that have been attractive and meaningful to others. Now, I try to encourage and pass forward my knowledge to new students whenever asked.

Once comfortable in my own knowledge, I sought out ways to help my patients and my colleagues, either through treatment, instruction, or smoothing their path along the way. I rejoice in the accomplishments of those I had a chance to influence either by word or deed at one point or another.

My father instilled in me a sense of humility: he always cautioned, "Doug, just remember that no matter how good you are at something, there is always someone out there in this big world better at it than you are." An expert in the realm of personnel activities and management during his long USAF career, he said the best way to lead people is to first stop and listen to what they are saying before coming to conclusions or taking any action. Every wall has two sides, and how a person views life depends on which side he is viewing. A leader can see both sides of that wall.

Another great rule of life was passed on to me by both my father and my Uncle Jon, who advised me not to take myself too seriously. A bright smile, affable personality, and real desire to know those who rely on you are valuable keys to success. In turn, those around you who sense your humanity and your desire to do the right thing and appreciate that you are in their corner when the chips are down, will willingly follow.

There is another saying in USAF circles: "The longer a pilot stays in the service, the more likely he will fly a desk." The USAF and all great organizations grow leaders through experience. It was no different for me in my medical, aviation, and artistic avocations.

As years passed during my medical career, I assumed greater hospital leadership roles, beginning with various committee memberships and chairmanships, followed later by promotion to Department Chair, and ultimately to serve as President of the BMC Medical Staff. In my parallel military career, I had the challenging but rewarding opportunity to serve as an IMA Wing Commander at the USAF David Grant Medical Center—the equivalent of a medical center Chief Executive Officer in civilian parlance. In other medical arenas, I was honored to be tapped as the Vice President for Programs for the local American Cancer Society and the Vice President for Medical Affairs for the national OnCURE Medical Corporation.

In my aviation life, my brief skydiving career led to election as the President of the Virginia Tech Skydiving Club early on. With my interest in experimental aircraft, I later found myself leading Chapter 193 of the Experimental Aircraft Association (EAA) in north Florida for several years. Finally, my passion for both flying and medical education resulted in my election to serve as President of the national Flying Physicians Association.

Leadership positions have followed me into my artistic pursuits as well: I have served as the President of the Jacksonville Coalition for the Visual Arts (the oldest and longest currently extant art guild in northern Florida) and am also on the BOD of the Jacksonville Artist's Guild and First Coast Plein Air Painters groups.

With a firm belief that no one has the right to complain about something without first being willing to be a part of the solution, I even threw my name into the hat and was elected for a time to our neighborhood Homeowner's Association BOD—probably the toughest of all my volunteer roles, requiring an open ear and a tough hide…

Good leaders begin as good followers, and I had many excellent examples to follow in my early career. I make no claim to being the greatest of leaders, or even close to that, by any measure. My efforts do reflect, though, the aphorism that leaders are made, not born. With perseverance and desire to improve the lot of themselves, others, and the organizations they belong to, most people can become effective leaders.

CHAPTER 37

Pearls

My advice to youngsters who don't know exactly which path to choose in life is this: Don't worry about it. There are many paths each of us will traverse over a lifetime and ample opportunities for those paths to crisscross. People get too focused on a single career focus; in reality, they will have time in life to excel in two or three different areas. Every individual's mountain (or set of mountains) may be different, but in the end successfully navigating the meandering path upward is just as important and satisfying as the view from the top. Once on top, try to smooth the path for others to follow you.

I am by no means perfect in any arena nor have ever presumed to be so. What I have tried to do, however, is counter my imperfections with humility, determination, and hard work. I have been blessed with an ability to learn many things, but that doesn't mean that they came to me easily. A strong work ethic, honesty, and integrity are underlying tenets to a satisfying and accomplished life. Being respectful of others along that journey earns you their respect in turn.

Some pearls of wisdom have proven valuable to me, and are worth passing along:

Chapter 37

- You can only do your best; if you've done that, hold your head high and don't sweat not achieving every goal. If you didn't try your best, sweat it.
- Be a ditch-digger if you want, but if you do, aim to be the best ditch-digger out there.
- Take care of your employees and subordinates, and they will take care of you.
- Under-promise and over-deliver.
- Value people for their skills, regardless of rank, status, appearance, or creed.
- Make your bed every day—literally. You will start your day by accomplishing something, and no matter how bad your day has been, you'll always have a clean and safe place waiting for you that evening (Ref12).
- Be careful how you make your bed, as you must also lie in it. You alone can create an atmosphere around you that breeds success.
- Others might open doors of opportunity for you, but it is up to you to walk through them.
- Never leave something until tomorrow that you can do today.
- Your word is your honor. Only you can lose your honor; no one can take it from you. Mind it carefully, for if lost, it is nearly impossible to regain.
- Like honor, education is something no one can take from you. Strive to learn as much as you can—it is your secret treasure.
- Learn a new "think" every day. Ask yourself each evening what new thing you know.
- Said another way, live to learn, and love to live.
- Own up to mistakes and correct or atone for them. Despite our best efforts, we all make mistakes. Others will judge us less by the mistakes themselves but rather by how we handle them.

- Don't take yourself too seriously; give yourself and others a break now and then.
- A smile and gentle humor are the best ambassadors; they might make a big difference to someone having a bad day.
- Be open to trying new things and set new challenges once old ones are met.
- Be prepared and believe in yourself.
- Some religion is good for everyone, but too much religion is bad for everyone. Religious values help define good mores, ethics, and standards, and are a boon to earthly and spiritual health. Overzealous religious practices, however, have brought down civilizations.
- Lead by example. People will remember your actions far longer than your words.
- Love your country and serve. "Service above self" is an ideal we should all aspire to, and serving your country, be it in the Armed Forces, Peace Corps, Civil Service, or your neighborhood will heighten the sense of patriotism and community around you. Our nation's existence rests not on the shoulders of only others: it rests squarely on yours.

CHAPTER 38

My kaleidoscope life

As Scottish author Sir Walter Scott once said, *"Oh what a tangled web we weave…"* How true that has been for me.

My lifelong quest to explore the heavens as an astronaut has led me along tortuous trails up life's craggy mountains. Sometimes steep and arduous sections paved with difficult stretches of struggles and setbacks have been balanced by pleasant stretches of achievements: successes in military and medical careers, cavorting in the skies, and capturing feelings and moments on canvas. I never attained that astronaut pinnacle, but not for lack of trying. I reached some amazing and unexpected hilltops along the way, though, and am thankful for the opportunities realized once there. In the end, my thwarted hope to explore the heavens as an astronaut was satisfied instead by a decades-long quest to explore another equally challenging task back on earth: the quest to eliminate cancer.

With each movement of a kaleidoscope, unique patterns emerge. As in life, the view over time changes though the scope's basic elements remain the same. As short- and long-term goals evolve, elements we value weave intricate and related patterns, each affecting the other, striking a beautiful balance through discipline and enthusiasm. Thus, creating harmony in a painting becomes intertwined with medically sorting out malignant disharmony in the human body. The discipline of precise radiosurgical planning and checklist use in the operating room is mirrored by the discipline needed in the airplane cockpit, and the beauty witnessed when flying through colorful ever-changing skies and over pristine landscapes allows the artist in me to better understand and capture these moments on canvas.

Passions for aviation, cancer treatment, and painting at first seem unrelated, but all share a common theme in my life: the need to see things creatively in three or four dimensions. An aviator must plan his route around, above, or beneath obstacles. A radiation oncologist must target cancerous tissues while avoiding constantly moving vital organs. Likewise, an artist must thoughtfully plan and deftly execute painting strokes to depict a three-dimensional world on a two-dimensional surface.

Similarly, passions for medicine and cultural exchange share an overlapping characteristic: a need to creatively think "outside the box" to solve complex problems. Just as hands-on medical experience hones a physician's ability to detect intricate nuances in medical diagnosis, so extensive travel across the world informs a thinker about the "other side of the wall" culturally and helps generate a basis of understanding between diverse groups.

I often hear from today's parents the quip about their children, "Thirty is the new twenty-two." That's nonsense. I would encourage today's youth to resist becoming paralyzed by the overwhelming career options and pressures incessantly presented by modern social media in our electronically connected world. Embrace action over inaction: a less-than perfect choice beats not making any choice. Choosing one focus does not preclude pursuing another along the way; indeed, an individual can (and should) embark on multiple paths through life as interests become clear. Sometimes those interests will run in parallel, and other times intersect and blend. Interactions in time, space, and understanding will constantly change and evolve, just like one's view through the lens of a kaleidoscope…

Chapter 38

People often asked me as I grew up if it was hard being constantly uprooted with all the frequent moves. Reflecting back, my itinerant childhood and subsequent military journey was a blessing, not a curse. I enjoyed the opportunity to live in amazing places, found that almost every corner of the planet held beauty, and that the people I encountered across the world were much more alike than they were different.

My hope is that I have left the world a bit better, following my father's advice so long ago. I hope that flying missions to provide medicines and supplies to the needy had a positive impact on them in hard times. I hope that long after I am gone, one of my paintings might bring a smile or warm thoughts to someone. Finally, I am blessed to have participated in groundbreaking cancer research that has improved the lot of countless patients and am comforted knowing that through God's grace, I have had an impact on many lives afflicted with pain and suffering. I am heartened when a patient I treated as a child returns years later to introduce me to his or her own children, or when I receive an unexpected call thanking me for my care in the distant past. A piece of me lives on in them, and for that I am forever honored and grateful.

My life's kaleidoscope still spins, creating colorful new connections and relationships, and I cannot wait to see what it will show me tomorrow.

BIBLIOGRAPHY

1. *The Daily Mirror Magazine*, NY, NY, Nov 5, 1933, pg. 13-14
2. "The logic of the "Cold War" demands complete integration of Negroes in all defense forces" *Our World*, June 1950, pg. 35
3. Johnson, D.W. Euthanasia--A Sociological Overview. *Contributions: A Journal of Student Papers in Sociology.* Virginia Tech, Blacksburg, VA Vol. 1, No. 1, 1975, pg. 25-34
4. Browne, D., Weiss, J.F., MacVittie, T.J., Pillai, M.V. (eds.). *Treatment of Radiation Injuries.* Plenum Press, New York 1989, pg. 237 ISBN 0-306-43729-5
5. Paryani, P., Scott, W., Wells, J., Johnson, D., Chobe, R., et.al. Management of Pterygium with Surgery and Radiation. The North Florida Pterygium Study Group. Int. J. Rad. Oncol. Biol. Phys., 28:101-103, 1994. PMID: 8270429
6. Amar U. Kishan; Ryan R. Cook; Jay P. Ciezki; et. al. Radical Prostatectomy, External Beam Radiotherapy, or External Beam Radiotherapy with Brachytherapy Boost and Disease Progression and Mortality in Patients with Gleason Score 9-10 Prostate Cancer. JAMA. 2018; 319(9):896-905. doi:10.1001/jama.2018.0587
7. Morad K. Nakhleh; Haitham Amal; Raneen Jeries; Douglas W. Johnson; Nir Peled; Hossam Haick; et.al.. Diagnosis and Classification of 17 Diseases from 1404 Individuals via Pattern Analysis of Exhaled Molecules. ACS Nano, 2017, 11, 1, pg. 112–125 doi 10.1021/acsnano.6b04930 *https://pubs.acs.org/doi/10.1021/acsnano.6b04930*

8. Institute of Medicine. 2009. *Beyond the HIPAA Privacy Rule: Enhancing Privacy, Improving Health Through Research*. Washington, DC: The National Academies Press. *https://doi.org/10.17226/12458* ISBN 978-0-309-14137-6
9. Cancer Facts & Figures 2012. Atlanta: American Cancer Society, Inc. 2012 *https://www.cancer.org/research/cancer-facts-statistics/all-cancer-facts-figures/cancer-facts-figures-2012.html*
10. *Hump Day Calls: Conversations with Creators*, 1 Nov 2023. *https://www.youtube.com/watch?v=dOJqPL4uBYE*
11. Harris, Trudy. *Glimpses of Heaven*. Revell (division of Baker Publishing Group), 2008, pg. 135 ISBN 978-0-8007-3251-6
12. Paraphrased from the 2014 University of Texas at Austin commencement address delivered by Admiral William H. McRaven, USN. *https://news.utexas.edu/2014/05/16/mcraven-urges-graduates-to-find-courage-to-change-the-world/*

ACRONYMS

3D: Three Dimensional
4D: Four Dimensional (3D plus time)
ACO: Accountable Care Organization
ACR: American College of Radiology
ACRIN: American College of Radiology Imaging Network
AFB: Air Force Base
AFRRI: Armed Forces Radiobiology Research Institute
AIDS: Acquired Immunodeficiency Syndrome
APO: Army Post Office
ASCAN: Astronaut Candidate
ASTRO: American Society for Therapeutic Radiation and Oncology
BMC: Baptist Medical Center Downtown
BMT: Bone Marrow Transplant
BOD: Board of Directors
BRCA: Breast Cancer Receptor Antigen
CAA: Civil Aviation Authority (Australian)
CB: Citizen's Band
CLL: Chronic Lymphocytic Leukemia
CME: Continuing Medical Education
CMMS: Centers for Medicare and Medicaid Services
COG: Children's Oncology Group
COPD: Chronic Obstructive Pulmonary Disease
CRA: Clinical Research Associate
CT: Computerized Tomography
DAR: Designated Airworthiness Representative
DMV: Department of Motor Vehicles

DNA: Deoxyribonucleic Acid
DOD: Department of Defense
EAA: Experimental Aircraft Association
ECOG: Eastern Cooperative Oncology Group
EHR: Electronic Health Record
ENT: Ears, Nose and Throat
FAA: Federal Aviation Administration
FBO: Fixed Base Operator
FDA: Food and Drug Administration
FDG: Fleuro-Deoxy-Glucose
FPA: Flying Physicians Association
FROG: Florida Radiation Oncology Group
G: Gravity
HDR: High Dose Rate
HDTV: High-Definition Television
HERO: Historic Endurance Rally Organization
HIPAA: Health Insurance Portability and Accountability Act
HPSP: Health Professions Scholarship Program
ICEC: International Cancer Expert Corps
ICON: Integrated Community Oncology Network
IFR: Instrument Flight Rules
IMA: Independent Mobilization Augmentee
IQ: Intelligence Quotient
IRB: Institutional Review Board
IRC: Institutional Review Committee
IVP: Intravenous Pyelogram
JABB: Johnson Adjustable Breast Bridge
JIA: Jacksonville International Airport
LEM: Lunar Excursion Module
LINAC: Linear Accelerator
LTC: Lieutenant Colonel
MAC: Military Airlift Command
MBA: Master of Business Administration

MCV: Medical College of Virginia
MENSA: A high IQ society for the top two percent
MP: Military Police
MRI: Magnetic Resonance Imaging
NAS: Naval Air Station
NASA: National Aeronautics and Space Administration
NCI: National Cancer Institute
NCO: Non-Commissioned Officer
NCOG: Northern California Oncology Group
NFA: Newburgh Free Academy
NFROG: North Florida Radiation Oncology Group
NMSS: Office of Nuclear Material Safely and Safeguards
NRC: Nuclear Regulatory Commission
NSA: National Security Agency
NSABP: National Surgical Adjuvant Breast and Bowel Project
OCS: Officer Candidate School
PET/CT: Positron-Emission-Tomography/Computed Tomography
PLF: Parachute Landing Fall
POG: Pediatric Oncology Group
PSA: Prostate Specific Antigen
RAF: Royal Air Force
ROTC: Reserve Officer Training Corps
RTOG: Radiation Therapy Oncology Group
RPI: Rensselaer Polytechnic Institute
SALT: Strategic Arms Limitation Talks
STS: Space Transportation System
TBI: Total Body Irradiation
TDY: Temporary Duty
TSA: Transportation Security Administration
TV: Television
US: United States
USA: United States of America
USAF: United States Air Force

USDA: United States Department of Agriculture
USGS: United States Geological Survey
USMA: United States Military Academy at West Point
USN: United States Navy
USSR: Union of Soviet Socialist Republics
VAH: Veterans Administration Hospital
VFR: Visual Flight Rules
VOQ: Visiting Officer's Quarters
VSD: Ventricular-Septal Defect
VT: Virginia Tech, Virginia Polytechnic Institute
VVHS: Victor Valley High School
WSI: Water Safety Instructor (Red Cross certification)
WWI: World War I
WWII: World War II

NAME INDEX

A

Abhijit Deshkumh 227
Alan Miles 192
Alberto Santos-Dumont 240
Alice Henderson 253
Amy Florence Henderson 11
Amy Rosborough 9, 45, 74, 239
Anand Kuruvilla 227
Andrew L. Johnson 1, 5, 6, 7, 15, 76, 142, 147
Anne Silverman 80
Anthony Howes 104, 148
Arthur C. Johnson 5, 7

B

Barbara Joan Rosborough 9
Bill Clinton 229
Bob Silverman 80, 274
Brad Mottier 161, 265, 275, 276
Brad Simmons 267
Bud Anderson 261

C

Charlie "Scorch" Hobaugh 207
Chris Davey i, 276
Christopher Kraft 58
Chuck Nichols 272, 273
Chuck Yeager 53, 203, 261

Clément Ader 240
C. Norman Coleman 102, 148
Connie Bowlin 261
Cynthia Anderson 227

D

Daniel Friedman 71
Danielle Annette Johnson 118
Dan Ludwig 32, 75
David Schreiber 148
David Roberts 26
Debbie Roberts 26
"Digger" Van Dyke 182
D.L. Simmons 191, 242
Don Pettit 207
Don R. Goffinet 101
Doug Johnson i, 62, 151
Douglas MacArthur 11
Dwelvin Simmons 227
Dwight Ludwig 26

E

Ed Henderson 28, 45
Ed White 37
Elsie Henderson 45

F

Felix Tormes 279
Fidel Castro 19
Francine Halberg 148
Francisco Goya 21

G

George Abbey 206
George Washington 46

Glennis Yeager 203
Gunther Rall 261
Gus Grissom 37
Gustave Whitehead 240

H

Harvey Wolkov 110, 148
Hazel (Henderson) Roe 45
Henry Fowler 11
Henry S. Kaplan 100, 148
Hoot Gibson 206
Hossam Haick 139, 236, 303

J

Jack Crump 208
Jamie Cesaretti 137
Jan Peer 131
Jim Parker 249, 279
Joel Buffington 26
Joel Cardon 8
John Wells 110, 122, 234, 236, 238, 277
John Wilbanks 273
John Young 204
Jon Rosborough 44
Juan Carlos I 23
Judy Nichols 272

K

Karol Sikora 104
Kenneth Russell 148

L

Lance Neibauer 188
Leonard Randolph 177
Linda Chak 148

Louise Leakey 279

M
Malcolm Bagshaw 101, 148
Marc Crnkovich 148
Mark Augspurger 227
Mark Schray 110, 148
Mary Austin-Seymour 110, 148
Mary Leakey 279
Michael Andrew Johnson 119
Michael Olson 227
Mike Busch 270
Mike Ciochetti 260
Mitchell Terk 137
Mottier 161, 265, 275, 276, 311

N
Nadine Johnson Terk 286
Nancy Roberts 26, 312
Neil Abramson 126, 272
Nir Peled 139, 236, 303

O
Orville Wright 240

P
Paul H. Poberezny 242
Paul Ladnier 287, 295
Peter Fessenden 148
Poison Spider Bicycle Shop 272

R
Rashmi Chobe 125, 303
Richard Hoppe 101, 148
Robert Louis Stevenson 278
Robin Olds 261

S

Samuel Pierpont Langley 240
Sarah Donaldson 102, 148
Saul Rosenberg 100
Shah of Iran 87, 312
Sheri Nolan 58
Shyam Paryani 110, 122, 125, 216, 227
Sonja Schoeppel i, 227
Stewart "Stew" Roosa 49
Stuart Millstone 236

T

Tex Hill 261
Thomas Kent 67
Thomas Pedrick 148

W

Walter P. Scott 124, 222
Wilbur Wright 240
William Morrison 148

Z

Zahi Hawass 279

ABOUT THE AUTHOR

Dr. Douglas W. Johnson is a renowned Radiation Oncologist, published cancer researcher, lecturer, and retired United States Air Force officer, having served 24 years as a cancer specialist, flight surgeon, nuclear safety consultant, and hospital administrator. He is also an award-winning artist represented in collections across the USA, and an avid pilot with over 3000hrs in 70 aircraft types, including his award-winning Lancair IV-P he built three decades ago—often performing international humanitarian missions. He hopes to reassure people of all ages by his example that there is more than one path to joy and success, as we each traverse our own kaleidoscopic life.

www.ingramcontent.com/pod-product-compliance
Lightning Source LLC
Chambersburg PA
CBHW050900240426
43673CB00050B/1945